Pragmatic ADO.NET

Microsoft .NET Development Series

John Montgomery, *Series Advisor*
Don Box, *Series Advisor*
Martin Heller, *Series Editor*

"This Microsoft .NET series is a great resource for .NET developers. Coupling the .NET architects at Microsoft with the training skills of DevelopMentor means that all the technical bases, from reference to 'how-to,' will be covered."
—JOHN MONTGOMERY, Group Product Manager
for the .NET platform, Microsoft Corporation

"The Microsoft .NET series has the unique advantage of an author pool that combines some of the most insightful authors in the industry with the actual architects and developers of the .NET platform."
—DON BOX, Architect, Microsoft Corporation

Titles in the Series

Keith Ballinger, *.NET Web Services: Architecture and Implementation with .NET*, 0-321-11359-4

Don Box with Chris Sells, *Essential .NET Volume 1: The Common Language Runtime*, 0-201-73411-7

Microsoft Common Language Runtime Team, *The Common Language Runtime Annotated Reference and Specification*, 0-321-15493-2

Microsoft .NET Framework Class Libraries Team, *The .NET Framework CLI Standard Class Library Annotated Reference*, 0-321-15489-4

Microsoft Visual C# Development Team, *The C# Annotated Reference and Specification*, 0-321-15491-6

Damien Watkins, Mark Hammond, Brad Abrams, *Programming in the .NET Environment*, 0-201-77018-0

Shawn Wildermuth, *Pragmatic ADO.NET: Data Access for the Internet World*, 0-201-74568-2

http://www.awprofessional.com/msdotnetseries/

Pragmatic ADO.NET

Data Access for the Internet World

■ Shawn Wildermuth

▼▼ Addison-Wesley

Boston • San Francisco • New York • Toronto • Montreal

London • Munich • Paris • Madrid

Capetown • Sydney • Tokyo • Singapore • Mexico City

The publisher offers discounts on this book
when ordered in quantity for bulk purchases
and special sales. For more information,
please contact:

U.S. Corporate and Government Sales
(800) 382-3419
corpsales@pearsontechgroup.com

For sales outside of the U.S., please contact:

International Sales
(317) 581-3793
international@pearsontechgroup.com

Visit Addison-Wesley on the Web:
www.awprofessional.com

Pearson Education, Inc.
Rights and Contracts Department
75 Arlington Street, Suite 300
Boston, MA 02116
Fax: (617) 848-7047

ISBN 0-201-74568-2
Text printed on recycled paper
1 2 3 4 5 6 7 8 9 10—CRS—0605040302
First printing, October 2002

Wildermuth, Shawn.
    Pragmatic ADO.NET : data access for the
Internet world / Shawn Wildermuth.
        p.   cm.
    ISBN 0-201-74568-2 (alk. paper)
    1. Database design.   2. Object-oriented
    programming (Computer science).   3. Web
    databases.   4. ActiveX   5. Microsoft .NET.
    I. Title.

    QA76.9.D26 W55 2002
    005.75'8—dc21

                        2002026088

To my dear Tricia,
without her patience and trust
this book would have never happened.

Contents

Foreword

I FIRST MET Shawn via email a number of years ago. He hung out at the same mailing lists that I did and had interesting things to say, so, when I needed some help on a project, he was on my list of potentials. I remember sending out an email late one evening, expecting a response sometime the next day. Forty-five minutes later as I was checking email one last time before going to bed, I already had a response from Shawn, who was three time zones later than I was. Not only was he willing, he was enthusiastic about the project and brimming with experience and ideas. That was the beginning of a relationship that brought us together daily for the next three years, and it's been fruitful for me ever since.

During the tail end of our project together, Shawn got another request for help on a project, this time from the Microsoft database community as a whole. The request was to fill a much-needed gap in the knowledge of Microsoft's latest database technology: ADO.NET. And once again, not only was Shawn willing, he was enthusiastic, setting up his own ADO.NET forum on the Web and jumping into DevelopMentor's new .NET mailing list, answering most of the deluge of database questions off the top of his head. The growing base of knowledge that Shawn was gathering about the importance of ADO.NET in a fully networked world, and the corresponding details that you need to make it actually work, eventually caused him to ask me whether he should write a book. I told him that if he could think of anything else to do in his free time, he should do that instead. Writing a good book (which I knew was what he was after) is too hard. The only way to make it through is if you've got a burning story in your heart that you can't not tell.

Thankfully for the rest of us, Shawn's story has burned its way onto the pages of the book you now hold in your hand. Whether Shawn has already helped you with your database problems online or whether this is your first exposure to his work, I'm quite confident that it will be, like mine, a very fruitful relationship indeed.

Chris Sells
www.sellsbrothers.com

Preface

ADO.NET IS NOT ADO. This is the most important fact that this book tries to convey. Understanding ADO.NET is not just about how to get database data or how to update the database—it requires an understanding of why it was built. ADO.NET takes a completely different approach in accessing databases than older Microsoft data access strategies. This is not your father's ADO.

This book intends to be neither a reference nor an "internals" book of how ADO.NET works. It is geared toward helping day-to-day developers get their jobs done. This book intends to give clear advice on how to use ADO.NET.

Intended Audience

This book is squarely aimed at developers who have a basic understanding of .NET and of databases. It is intended to help day-to-day developers get their job done. It does not assume prior experience with ADO, though it does build somewhat on that knowledge if it exists.

Part I   The Basics of ADO.NET

Part I is intended to get you started with the basics.

Chapter 1   Why ADO.NET

Before the book explains how to work with ADO.NET, it explains why ADO.NET was written. Chapter 1 discusses the history of Microsoft data access to explain how we got to ADO.NET.

Chapter 2   Getting Connected with ADO.NET

Before we can do anything with a database, we must know how to connect to it. Chapter 2 is all about getting connected to databases through ADO.NET. This includes a discussion of how connection strings work, connection pooling in a variety of managed providers, patterns for connection creation, and how to minimize connections to the database.

Chapter 3   Commanding the Database

Our only interface with the database is to issue commands and deal with the results of those commands. This chapter focuses on how to get the database to do work for us by using `Command` objects. This includes explanation of how to use the `Command` objects with simple SQL statements, parameterized queries, stored procedures, and batch queries.

Chapter 4   Reading Data

DataReaders are ADO.NET's method for getting tables from the database. In Chapter 4, the book explains how to use DataReaders to access database information and shows an example of writing a class that uses the DataReader as its data source.

Part II   All about DataSets

The DataSet is the heart of ADO.NET. To use the DataSet effectively, we must examine how it can be used to solve our day-to-day problems.

Chapter 5   Constructing DataSets

This chapter explains exactly what DataSets are and why you should use them. It covers the many ways to make DataSets, including using DataAdapters, XML, and code to create them. A complete discussion of how to use DataSet schema is also included in this chapter.

Chapter 6 Typed DataSets

Typed DataSets are a useful tool that allows you to have code that adapts to changing schema. Chapter 6 explores this new programming model where we create typed DataSets and use them as the basis for business logic layers that are typically all handwritten. This chapter also shows how to create typed DataSets from within Visual Studio .NET as well as from the command line.

Chapter 7 Working with DataSets

Now that we know how to create DataSets, we need to understand how to use them to manipulate data and how the data are structured inside them. Chapter 7 explains how the DataSet model works and how you can use it to get your job done.

Chapter 8 Updating the Database

Once we have manipulated data within a DataSet, we have to have a way to update the database with those changes. Chapter 8 walks you through how to plan for disconnected concurrency. It includes examples of using the built-in optimistic concurrency and how to implement pessimistic and destructive concurrency. In addition, the chapter discusses how to handle concurrency violations and gives concrete examples of one solution for dealing with concurrency violations.

Part III ADO.NET in Action

Now that we know how to access data, manipulate it, and update the database with the changes, we need to know how we can get ADO.NET to interact with the rest of the .NET framework.

Chapter 9 ADO.NET and XML

XML is just data. ADO.NET is the data framework for .NET. These two facts come together to show why ADO.NET is so tightly integrated with the XML framework to allow for database data to be commingled with database data. Chapter 9 explores the way to treat each type of data like their brethren.

Chapter 10 Data Binding with ADO.NET

In .NET, there are two forms-based technologies: Windows Forms and Web Forms. Luckily, ADO.NET containers (DataReaders, DataSets, and Data-Tables) all support direct data binding. Chapter 10 shows you how.

Chapter 11 Scalability and Performance

This chapter brings it all together with concrete design suggestions for how to build scalable, high-performance systems. In addition, the chapter lists a set of best practices for using ADO.NET and database development in general.

Appendix ADO Migration Strategies

We cannot pretend that all .NET code will be all new development. There are many developers out there who have code to migrate to .NET. This appendix lists a number of strategies for living in a mixed system where you need to have ADO.NET data structures reading ADO structures, and vice versa.

Acknowledgments

I WANT TO THANK everyone who has helped me get this book written. First and foremost, I want to thank Chris Sells for his help at every stage of this project. From getting started with the proposal, to reviewing every chapter more times than I can count, his gift for understanding that the story comes first was invaluable to getting every chapter right. In addition, he was my coach and cheerleader, helping me understand what was important to cover and encouraging me every step of the way. I also want to thank the countless individuals on the DevelopMentor .NET mailing list (discuss.develop.com) who have answered my questions and asked questions that I never thought to cover in this book until they asked. Furthermore, I want to thank everyone at OneSource Information Systems for their patience during the writing of this book.

Lastly, I would like to thank the following individuals for making this book possible: Tricia Palese, Stephanie Thomas, Chris Tavares, Bob Beauchemin, Peter Zaleksy, Cristof Falk, Scott Juranek, Purush Rudrakshala, Glenn Thimmes, Edward Hinton, Mark Israel, Joseph Ficara, David Avakian, Todd Clemetson, Steven Wright, Marshall Harrison, Kristin Erickson, Jennifer Allen, and Omri Gazitt.

Shawn Wildermuth
Tewksbury, MA
June 2002
www.adoguy.com

PART I
The Basics of ADO.NET

■ 1 ■
Why ADO.NET

WELCOME TO THE world of ActiveX Data Objects for .NET, or ADO.NET, as we will hereafter refer to it. Luckily for us, ADO.NET is not just another data access layer—it is a better way of thinking about data access. But before I start getting you excited about ADO.NET, I think a history lesson is in order.

1.1 A Short History of Universal Data Access

To get a clear picture of what Microsoft has in mind with ADO.NET, you need to look at their previous database APIs. In the past ten years, Microsoft has tried over and over again to solve the problem of universal data access. For developers the need has always been to balance simplicity with performance. Unfortunately, these needs are often at odds with each other.

In the beginning (1990), Microsoft knew that database access would be an issue for their developers and they had a plan. Microsoft knew that developers were creating applications that needed to talk to databases on other platforms, mostly UNIX minicomputers or mainframes. Their solution was to use the Open Database Connectivity (ODBC) application program interface (API). This API let developers access data in these back-end systems.

But Microsoft knew that many developers were looking for solutions for desktop databases as well. So in 1992 they released Visual Basic 2.0 and VT Objects, which provided Visual Basic (VB) with access to the ODBC

API. VT Objects was a very simple interface that allowed access to these back-end databases, but little else. The entire ODBC API was not exposed, only what was necessary to get the VB developers going with their data access needs.

Microsoft also knew that developers were grappling with the need for local storage of relational data in the form of desktop databases. In order to facilitate desktop databases, Microsoft released Access 1.0. Access 1.0 included Jet, a data access technology in its own right, and a new version of VT Objects, now renamed Data Access Objects (DAO). This version of DAO introduced the concepts of a `Connection` and a `Recordset` that persist today. DAO had its share of problems as the technology matured; for example, because DAO was not thread-safe, it failed to perform well under load or in large client-server settings.

Microsoft tried reinventing data access again with OLE DB (OLE for Databases). OLE DB tied database development directly to Microsoft's Component Object Model (COM). OLE DB is a set of COM interfaces that exposes a consumer/provider model of accessing data throughout an enterprise. OLE DB makes no distinction as to whether the data is in a desktop database (like Access), an enterprise database (like SQL Server or Oracle), or a nondatabase source (like an Excel spreadsheet). If developers wanted to expose their data to OLE DB they needed to develop an OLE DB provider. Unfortunately, development of OLE DB providers proved to be difficult for all but the most talented C++ developers. Developing data consumers in OLE DB was much simpler, but tied developers directly to Visual C++, therefore losing any language independence.

In the most recent past, Microsoft developed ActiveX Data Objects (ADO) as a COM wrapper around OLE DB. ADO was developed specifically to make OLE DB easier to use. Soon after the release of ADO, the Internet revolution exploded. Developers craved an easy-to-use API to make their Web sites and Web applications database driven. ADO's scriptability fit perfectly into Microsoft's Internet Information Server (IIS) and Active Server Pages (ASPs). ADO soon became the *lingua franca* of Internet Web sites. For small Web sites, ADO shined; it was easy to understand and simple to code. Unfortunately, ADO bent under the load of larger Web sites. All the Web pages hitting the database to retrieve the same information over and over, millions of times a day, exposed ADO's dependence on connectivity to the database.

In ADO, you created a connection to the database and then queried the database for information. In Listing 1.1, you can see that the connection has the lifetime of the query action.

Listing 1.1: *Classic ADO Database Access*

```
Option Explicit

' Create Connection
Dim conn as Object
Set conn = CreateObject("ADODB.Connection")
Dim sConn as String
sConn = "DSN=LocalServer;UID=someuser;Database=ADONET;"
conn.connectionString = sConn

' Connection opened here
conn.Open

' Create Command
Dim cmd as Object
Set cmd = CreateObject("ADODB.Command")
cmd.ActiveConnection = conn
cmd.CommandText = "SELECT * FROM CUSTOMER"

' Query the database to get a Recordset
Dim rs as Object
Set rs = cmd.Execute()

' Run through the Recordset
Do While not rs.EOF

    Dim sRecord as String
    Dim field as Object
    For Each field in rs.Fields
        sRecord = sRecord & field.name & ": " & field.value
    Next
    MsgBox sRecord
    rs.MoveNext

Loop

' Connection closed after all the database work is complete
conn.Close
```

In most cases a connection to the database is kept open while the Recordset is walked through or rows are inserted. Even bulk gets in ADO had a bad habit of keeping their connection to the database. ADO also tended to lock records or pages to handle concurrency of the data. Databases were swamped with requests and ran out of connections, especially in large Web applications. ADO addressed this connection problem by allowing users to disconnect their Recordsets from their connection. This was a powerful paradigm. The problem was that only the most experienced ADO developers ever used this feature. The complexities of reconnecting the Recordset with a connection and the even greater complexity of reconciling it with the database proved very difficult.

Recently, Microsoft released its .NET platform. With this platform came ADO.NET—but why? Microsoft allows .NET applications to communicate with older systems and to provide a migration path by talking with COM through their Interop layer. A simple C# application using ADO and Interop would look like that shown in Listing 1.2.

Listing 1.2: *Using ADO in Managed Code*

```csharp
using System.Runtime.InteropServices;
using ADODB;

// Open our Connection
Connection conn = new Connection();
conn.Open("Provider=SQLOLEDB;Server=localhost;" +
          "Database=ADONET","someuser", "", 0);

// Query the database
Command cmd = new Command();
cmd.ActiveConnection = conn;
cmd.CommandText = "SELECT * FROM CUSTOMER";
object recaffected = null;
object prms = new object();
_Recordset rs = cmd.Execute(out recaffected, ref prms, 0);

// Dump all the records to the standard output
while (!rs.EOF)
{
  for (int x = 0; x < rs.Fields.Count; x++)
  {
    Console.Write(rs.Fields[x].Value.ToString() + ":");
  }
```

```
    Console.WriteLine(""); // Endline
    rs.MoveNext();
}

// Clean up
conn.Close();
```

This should look very similar to our earlier example of ADO before .NET. This works and many people will take this path in their migration to .NET. Unfortunately this solution does not address the central problem with ADO.NET's data access predecessors: the difficulty working with disconnected data. ADO.NET simplifies that complexity.

1.2 Why ADO.NET Is a Better Data Access Layer

In the old philosophy of data access, we did not worry too much about hanging on to database connections. We wrote code to minimize our connection time because we knew that connections were precious commodities, but we did not have many options if we were actively changing the data.

Keeping the open connection worked well enough in the world of desktop applications because it was clear how long the user would want to hold on to the connection. Everything changed several years ago when we shifted into Web development and distributed computing. We could no longer make assumptions about when a user was done with the data.

We tried to use our old methodologies for data access by opening up connections and caching them until the user was finished, but in a Web application there is no way to know when the user is finished. For example, closing a browser does not alert the Web site that the user is finished. So, we closed the connections after the cached data timed out, and all was well. We were successful and everyone loved our work. But then our little 1,000-hits-a-day Web site took off, and we were processing 100,000 or 1 million hits a day—our database servers slowed to a crawl or crashed entirely. Like pouting children, they started refusing connections.

The Hypertext Transfer Protocol (HTTP) that we relied on so heavily for our Web clients provided a clue that our methods would not work in the long run. HTTP is stateless; we needed a data access method that copied this behavior. We devised mechanisms to minimize the need for database connections and page locks on our data, but the code was hard to write and was fraught with peril because it was difficult to test. We could use ADO's disconnected Recordsets and change deltas, but this was also cumbersome and difficult to write. There had to be a better way.

With ADO.NET you can feel free to continue being tied to your database's connections. Listing 1.3 is a C# example using ADO.NET to mimic the behavior of our ADO examples earlier in the chapter.

Listing 1.3: *ADO-like Connection Usage in ADO.NET*

```csharp
// Open our Connection
OleDbConnection conn = new
                       OleDbConnection("Provider=SQLOLEDB;" +
                                       "Server=localhost;" +
                                       "Database=ADONET;" +
                                       "UID=someuser;");
conn.Open();

// Query the database
OleDbCommand cmd = new OleDbCommand();
cmd.Connection = conn;
cmd.CommandText = "SELECT * FROM CUSTOMER";

// Execute the Command to create the DataReader
OleDbDataReader reader = cmd.ExecuteReader();

// Dump all the records to the standard output
while (reader.Read())
{
  for (int x = 0; x < reader.FieldCount; x++)
  {
    Console.Write(reader.GetValue(x).ToString());
  }
  Console.WriteLine(""); // Endline
}

// Clean up
conn.Close();
```

In this form, ADO.NET is not unlike its Microsoft data access brethren. The key point here is that ADO.NET alone will not solve your scalability issues. Converting your old ADO code to ADO.NET will not make it any better than your current code. ADO.NET was designed from the ground up to be disconnected. The tried and true notion of keeping that vital connection to the database is vaguely supported but not encouraged. This is not your father's data access. ADO.NET encourages us to think about disconnected data up front and forces us to think in a disconnected world.

In ADO.NET we can shorten the time we have our connection open, as shown in Listing 1.4.

Listing 1.4: *Shorter Connection Life in ADO.NET*

```
using System;
using System.Data;
using System.Data.OleDb;

// Open our Connection
OleDbConnection conn = new
                       OleDbConnection("Provider=SQLOLEDB;" +
                                       "Server=localhost;" +
                                       "Database=ADONET;" +
                                       "UID=someuser;");

// Connection opened here
conn.Open();

// Create DataSet and Command objects
OleDbCommand cmdAuthors = new OleDbCommand(
                          "SELECT COUNT(*) FROM CUSTOMER",
                          conn);

// Execute the command
int count = cmdAuthors.ExecuteScalar();

// Closed this fast!
conn.Close();
```

1.3   A Short Course in ADO.NET

ADO.NET is a set of .NET classes that allow for the connection and manipulation of data. Although our examples in this book primarily use C#, .NET's Common Language Runtime allows for the code to be exceptionally similar, whether you are developing in Visual Basic .NET, C#, Managed C++, or any managed language.[1]

1.3.1   ADO.NET Namespaces

.NET classes are separated into namespaces to help segment their specific functionality. Figure 1.1 shows the relationships of these namespaces and the classes within them.

In ADO.NET, namespaces provide segregation between different parts of the managed provider model. In Figure 1.1, the `System.Data` namespace has common data structures that are completely independent of the provider. This namespace includes the `DataSet` and its entire family of related classes (`DataTable`, `DataColumn`, `DataRow`, `DataRelation`, `Constraint`, and so on). Within the `System.Data` namespace is `System.Data.Common`, which provides base class for managed providers. These classes define a calling convention that an ADO.NET managed provider must expose in order to be called an ADO.NET managed provider. Other managed providers can be written by creating a set of classes that implement these interfaces. The `Your Provider` namespace depicted in Figure 1.1 is an example of a custom managed provider namespace.

1.3.2   ADO.NET Data Structures

ADO.NET supports three different ways of accessing database information directly: `Commands`, `DataReaders`, and `DataSets`.

Command classes (`SqlCommand` for the SQL Managed Provider and `OleDbCommand` for the OLE DB Managed Provider) can be used directly to retrieve results from database queries. Command classes always support the `IDbCommand` interface, which can get a scalar result (the first column of the first row of a result set) or out parameters of a stored procedure. This sort of data is retrieved using `IDbCommand.ExecuteScalar()` and `IDbCommand.ExecuteNonQuery()`.

DataReaders (`SqlDataReader` and `OleDbDataReader`) are classes that provide something similar to ADO's Recordset using a forward-only

---

1.   Initially Microsoft will provide compilers for Visual Basic, JScript, C#, and C++. In addition third-party developers have written compilers for Eiffel, Perl, Python, Scheme, Smalltalk, COBOL, Component Pascal, APL, Standard ML, Mercury, and Oberon.

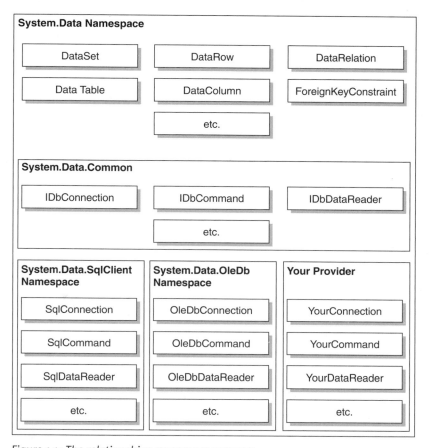

Figure 1.1: *The relationships among namespaces*

cursor. In ADO, we need to be careful and make sure we call `MoveNext()` and check for the end-of-record indicator. The `DataReader` uses a less error-prone system that just requires that you read the current record into memory and check for the end-of-record indicator in one step. For cases where you will need to simply get a query and spew out the results, the `DataReader` is the perfect vehicle. In fact, Microsoft uses DataReaders within the managed providers' `DataAdapters` to fill `DataSet`. See Listing 1.3 in Section 1.2 for an example of how to use `DataReaders`.

As far as I am concerned, the center of the ADO.NET universe is a new data structure called the `DataSet`. At first glance, the `DataSet` looks much like an OLE DB `RowSet` or an ADO `Recordset`. The `DataSet`, however, is much more than that. It is a complex data structure that allows for an

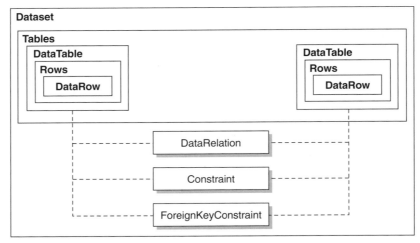

Figure 1.2: *Using ADO.NET's classes to connect to a database*

in-memory representation of almost any relational model. The `DataSet` holds a collection of tables that can have optional `DataRelations`, `Constraints`, or even `ForeignKeyConstraints`. Figure 1.2 shows these relationships.

What this means for the day-to-day developer is that the `DataSet` provides the facilities for modeling your relational data in memory. ADO.NET is all about disconnection from the database, and the DataSet allows you to continue to think of your data in the same database-centric view. Our new version of Listing 1.4 using a DataSet is shown in Listing 1.5.

Listing 1.5: *Using a DataSet*

```
using System;
using System.Data;
using System.Data.OleDb;

// Open our Connection
OleDbConnection conn = new
                    OleDbConnection("Provider=SQLOLEDB;" +
                                    "Server=localhost;" +
                                    "Database=ADONET;" +
                                    "UID=someuser;");

// Open the connection
conn.Open();
```

```
// Create Dataset and Command Objects
DataSet ds = new DataSet();
OleDbDataAdapter daAuthors = new OleDbDataAdapter(
                             "SELECT * FROM CUSTOMER",
                             conn);

// Fill the DataSet
daAuthors.Fill(ds);

// We can close the connection without any ramifications!
conn.Close();

// Get the table out of the DataSet
DataTable tbl = ds.Tables["Table"];

// Walk all the rows
foreach (DataRow row in tbl.Rows)
{
  // Walk all the fields in the row
  foreach (Object val in row.ItemArray)
  {
    Console.Write(val.ToString());
  }
  Console.WriteLine(""); // End of line
}
```

This code is not substantially more complex than our earlier example that used the `DataReader`. This code introduces us to the `DataAdapter` class (`OleDbDataAdapter` in this example) and the first use of the `DataSet`.

`DataAdapters` are a special type of compound command that holds four separate Command objects. The four commands allow us to define separate commands for select, insert, update, and delete operations. This may not seem all that important until you understand how the `DataSet` handles change operations to the database.

You may be thinking, "Using `DataSets` to refer to data in memory is fine if they are read-only, but what about changing or adding data?" Not to worry, the `DataSet` provides the ability to get subsets of the data that have been changed, deleted, or inserted, so you can do the validation of the data before routing the changes back to the database. In the normal use of `DataSets`, we would add, change, and delete records. We have already set up our `DataAdapter` class, so we can simply tie in a CommandBuilder class and call the `DataAdapter.Update()` call to update, insert, and delete changed or added records. The call does this by using the `Insert-Command`, `UpdateCommand`, and `DeleteCommand` contained within the `DataAdapter`. This can be seen in Listing 1.6.

Listing 1.6: *Simple Updating the Database from a DataSet*

```
using System;
using System.Data;
using System.Data.OleDb;

// Create the connection
OleDbConnection conn = new
                    OleDbConnection("Provider=SQLOLEDB;" +
                                    "Server=localhost;" +
                                    "Database=ADONET;" +
                                    "UID=someuser;");

// Create DataSet and Command objects
DataSet ds = new DataSet();
OleDbDataAdapter daAuthors =
        new OleDbDataAdapter("SELECT * FROM CUSTOMER", conn);

// Create an OleDbCommandBuilder to wrap
// the DataAdapter to support dynamic
// generation of update/insert/delete
// commands
OleDbCommandBuilder bldr =
                    new OleDbCommandBuilder(daAuthors);

// Fill the DataSet
daAuthors.Fill(ds);

// Get the table out of the DataSet
DataTable tbl = ds.Tables["Table"];

// Set up the primary key
DataColumn[] colArr = new DataColumn[1];
colArr[0] = tbl.Columns[0];
tbl.PrimaryKey = colArr;

// Insert a row
object[] rowVals = new object[3];
rowVals[0] = Guid.NewGuid();
```

```
rowVals[1] = "Greg";
rowVals[2] = "Maddux";
DataRow insertedRow = tbl.Rows.Add(rowVals);

// Delete a row
tbl.Rows[0].Delete();

// Change a row
tbl.Rows[1].BeginEdit();
tbl.Rows[1]["FirstName"] = "New Name";
tbl.Rows[1].EndEdit();

// Save changes
conn.Open();
daAuthors.Update(ds);
```

There are a few things to note in this example. First, we never set the InsertCommand, UpdateCommand, or DeleteCommand. We did, however, create an OleDbCommandBuilder object. When we create the Command-Builder object, we send our DataAdapter, which registers itself with the DataAdapter and creates the update, delete, and insert commands on the fly, as necessary. In addition, we set up the PrimaryKey so that the CommandBuilder knows how to create the Command objects on the fly. Also, we closed the connection after we queried the database (in Fill) and reopened the command just before we did the Update().

1.3.3   ADO.NET Managed Provider Object Model

In the initial release of ADO.NET there are two managed providers: OLE DB and SQL Server. The SQL Server Managed Provider enables native access to Microsoft's SQL Server. ADO.NET has the OLE DB Managed Provider to access databases through the OLE DB data access abstraction layer. OLE DB provides access to myriad data stores, including SQL Server, Oracle, DB2, Access, dBase, FoxPro, and even delimited text files.

The OLE DB Managed Provider specifically prohibits OLE DB's ODBC provider. In response, Microsoft released a separate ODBC Managed Provider, which allows ADO.NET to access any data source that supplies an ODBC driver. The decision of whether to use an existing OLE DB provider or an ODBC driver really depends on the particular database vendor. In many cases OLE DB is faster, whereas in others ODBC is the performance winner.

You can access SQL Server with both the SQL Server Managed Provider and the OLE DB Managed Provider. This begs the question "Which one is better for accessing SQL Server?" Let me show you how the providers differ so you can answer the question for yourself. Following are two examples of the same operation—Listing 1.7 uses the OLE DB Managed Provider and Listing 1.8 uses the SQL Server Managed Provider.

Listing 1.7: *SQL Server Access through OLE DB*

```
// OLE DB Managed Provider

using System;
using System.Data;
using System.Data.OleDb;

// Create the connection
OleDbConnection conn =
                new OleDbConnection("Provider=SQLOLEDB;" +
                                    "Server=localhost;" +
                                    "Database=ADONET;" +
                                    "UID=someuser;");

// Create DataSet and Command objects
DataSet ds = new DataSet();
OleDbDataAdapter daAuthors = new OleDbDataAdapter(
                                "SELECT * FROM CUSTOMER",
                                conn);

// Fill the DataSet
daAuthors.Fill(ds);

// Get the table out of the DataSet
DataTable tbl = ds.Tables["Table"];

// Walk all the rows
foreach( DataRow row in tbl.Rows)
{
    // Walk all the fields in the row
    foreach (Object val in row.ItemArray)
    {
        Console.Write(val.ToString());
    }
```

```
        Console.WriteLine(""); // End of line
}
```

Listing 1.8: *SQL Server Access through the SqlClient Managed Provider*

```
// SQL Server Managed Provider

using System;
using System.Data;
using System.Data.SqlClient;

// Create the connection
SqlConnection conn = new SqlConnection();
conn.ConnectionString = "Server=localhost;" +
                        "Database=ADONET;" +
                        "UserID=someuser;";

// Create DataSet and Command objects
DataSet ds = new DataSet();
SqlDataAdapter daAuthors = new SqlDataAdapter(
                        "SELECT * FROM CUSTOMER",
                        conn);

// Fill the DataSet
daAuthors.Fill (ds);

// We can close the connection without any ramifications!
conn.Close();

// Get the table out of the DataSet
DataTable tbl = ds.Tables["Table"];

// Walk all the rows
foreach( DataRow row in tbl.Rows)
{
    // Walk all the fields in the row
    foreach (Object val in row.ItemArray)
    {
        Console.Write(val.ToString());
    }
    Console.WriteLine(""); // End of Line
}
```

You will notice that the only change we made in the SQL version, other than the renaming of classes for the SQL namespace, is that we no longer need to set the provider on the connection. The exact syntax of each of these connection strings is strikingly similar, but not identical. This is a simple example and there are changes that are necessary to switch providers, but not systemic ones. Because the ADO.NET world revolves around the `DataSet`, most of the code you will write is not provider-specific.

The general rule of thumb is to use the SQL Server Managed Provider if you can guarantee that you will always use SQL Server. In theory, the SQL Server Managed Provider should perform better. The SQL Server Managed Provider uses the SQL Server wire protocol Tabular Data Stream (TDS) instead of using OLE DB to call the database, which should improve performance.

My tests, however, show that the performance of the two managed providers is very similar. The real reason to use the SQL Server Managed Provider is if you need SQL Server–specific functionality (such as XML query results) or if you prefer to work with SQL Server data types instead of the OLE DB mapped types. As you will see in Chapter 9, the SQL Server Managed Provider provides a set of classes to optimize the retrieval of XML from the database and then read it with the .NET XML classes.

In ADO.NET, the managed provider's classes communicate with the data storage. Most projects using ADO.NET are communicating with databases, so the managed provider supplies the basic methodology to open a connection to the database and request actions by the database. As seen in Figure 1.3, there are relationships between the `Connection`, `Command`, and `Parameters` classes. By creating connections, commands, and, optionally, parameters, the managed provider allows you to connect to the database and get your work done.

All of the ADO.NET providers live within the `System.Data` namespace. The `System.Data.Common` namespace contains all of the base classes for the managed providers. The classes in this namespace are not creatable, but are primarily abstract classes that define the expected base functionality of the managed providers. This means that you will never use these classes directly. Each managed provider is also segmented into its own namespace. The SQL Server Managed Provider is in the `System.Data.SqlClient`

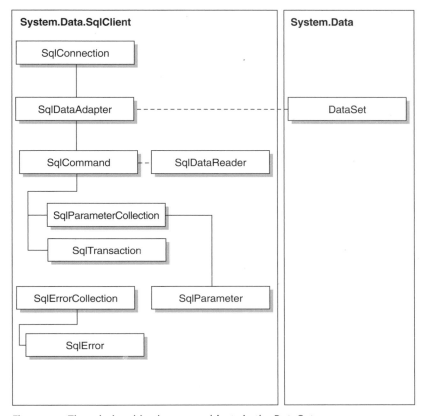

Figure 1.3: *The relationships between objects in the DataSet*

namespace, the OLE DB Managed Provider is in `System.Data.OleDb`, Microsoft's Oracle Managed Provider is in the `System.Data.Oracle-Client` namespace, and the ODBC Managed Provider is in `System.Data.Odbc`. I would not be surprised to find that Sybase and IBM have written their own providers by the time this book hits the shelves.

In order to write an ADO.NET provider, a developer needs to create a namespace and a set of classes that exposes the common interfaces as specified in the `System.Data.Common` namespace. The namespace does not need to carry only classes that implement interfaces defined in `System.Data.Common`. In fact, the SQL Server Managed Provider has a number of specialty classes that deal with SQL Server–specific functionality. In Chapters 2 and 3, I will elaborate on these relationships between the managed providers and the `Common` namespace.

1.4 Conclusion

I hope that this chapter has thoroughly convinced you of the merits of moving from the connection-rich method of data access and taking up the disconnected ADO.NET religion. Any developer who keeps a connection longer than necessary is just greedy. Luckily, ADO.NET helps you think in a disconnected world. You will write better code, your databases will stop pouting, and one day your stock options will allow you to buy that boat you have been eyeing.

■ 2 ■
Getting Connected with ADO.NET

I OFTEN LIKE TO compare disconnected database programming to ordering a pizza for dinner. First I have to call the pizza place and tell them what I want on my pizza. Once the pizza arrives, I pay the delivery guy and send him on his way, so he can deliver more pizzas. I would never think of asking him to wait while I eat the pizza. Database programming is usually just a series of pizza deliveries. First, establish the connection (call the pizza place). Next, issue a command (order the pizza). And last, close the connection and consume the data returned (send the delivery guy on his way and consume the pizza). In ADO.NET, connections are used to dial the phone, and commands are used to order your pizza. We will cover commands in Chapter 3, and in Chapters 4 through 8 we will get to eat the pizza.

2.1 First Impressions

Before we jump into the heart of how connections work, we should look at the simplest of examples: Hello ADO.NET. Listing 2.1 is a very simple example of how to use ADO.NET. It queries a single table and lists the contents of the database to the console.

Listing 2.1: *Using a Connection*

```
using System;
using System.Data;
using System.Data.SqlClient;

// Create the connection
SqlConnection conn =
              new SqlConnection("Server=localhost;" +
                                "Database=ADONET;" +
                                "Integrated Security=true;");

// Open the connection
conn.Open();

// Create the command object
SqlCommand cmd = new SqlCommand("SELECT * FROM Customers",
                                conn);

// Execute the query
SqlDataReader reader = cmd.ExecuteReader();

// Dump the results to the console
while (reader.Read())
{
  Console.WriteLine(reader["FirstName"] + " " +
                    reader["LastName"]);
}

// Close the connection
conn.Close();
```

This example is extremely similar to Listing 1.4 in Chapter 1. We create a connection to the database and open it. We command the database to return the entire Customers table to us. Finally we iterate through all of the rows of the table, dumping each record out to the console as a separate line. This example explains the core functionality of the Connection and Command relationship: Establish a connection; issue a command.

2.2 Connections

Connections in ADO.NET are modeled as a single Connection class within each managed provider. The Connection classes represent a single connection to a data source, but not necessarily a single call. ADO.NET is geared toward disconnected data, so the Connection classes must provide for repeated opening and closing of the connection. Listing 2.2 shows the recommended life cycle of a `Connection` object:

Listing 2.2: *Connection Life Cycle*

```
// Create and set up the server
SqlConnection conn =
            new SqlConnection("Server=localhost;" +
                              "Database=ADONET;" +
                              "Integrated Security=true;");

// Use the connection
SqlCommand cmd = new SqlCommand("SELECT COUNT(CustomerID)" +
                              " FROM Customer",
                              conn);

// Open the Connection
conn.Open();

// Execute a command
int result = (int) cmd.ExecuteScalar();

// Close the Connection
conn.Close();

// Do some work with the data retrieved
// ...

// Change the command information
cmd.CommandText = "SELECT MAX(Discount)" +
                " FROM Customer;";

// Reopen the Connection
conn.Open();

// Execute the new work
float maxDiscount = (float) cmd.ExecuteScalar();
```

```
// Close the Connection
conn.Close();
```

This code illustrates the fact that the Connection object can live longer than a single open/close cycle. The opening and closing of a connection are not analogous with creation and destruction of an instance of the Connection class. A connection is expected to be opened and closed a number of times throughout its life.

After we create the Connection object, we set the connection string, which describes the location of the data source (in this case our local database server). Next, we open the connection and issue a command on the ADO.NET database. Once we have retrieved the pertinent data, we close the connection. After manipulating the data, we can reopen the connection and continue working with the same data source. Notice that we reuse the command object instead of creating a new one—there is no need to create a command object for each operation. While we're manipulating the data, the database's connection is freed. Because this precious resource is freed during the intervening cycles, the database server's load is reduced. We are incurring a bit of overhead from re-establishing the connection when we need it, but ADO.NET connection pooling (discussed later in this chapter in Section 2.2.4) should minimize that cost.

2.2.1 Connection Strings

The Connection classes are ADO.NET's way of making a phone call to the database. Like making a phone call, there is a protocol for initiating the conversation. You must know the phone number and to whom you want to talk, and sometimes you need to have access to personal information (like a PIN code, your mother's maiden name, or a Social Security number). After you have all of this information, making the call is usually trivial. Connection strings are the way to specify that information to a managed provider.

No rules govern the syntax of all providers. Each managed provider is free to define whatever syntax it wants for the connection string. Luckily, all of the Microsoft-supplied managed providers use a fairly consistent syntax. This syntax is a list of settings (in the form of name/value pairs) separated by semicolons. Each setting consists of a name, the equal (=) sign, and the value to be specified for the name. In these connection strings, case and space are not significant. A typical connection string is made up of several settings, as shown in Figure 2.1.

At a minimum, connection strings for managed providers require you to specify where the provider can find the database and provide enough information to figure out what security credentials to present when connecting to the database. Aside from these minimum settings, each provider has additional information associated with a connection that can be set with the connection string. If a connection string does not specify every possible setting, the managed provider assumes the default. These defaults are covered very nicely in the documentation so I will not belabor the default behavior here. Please see Carl Prothman's great site at www. able-consulting.com/ado_conn.htm, where he has compiled a huge number of connection string examples.

In managed providers, it is very common to expose read-only properties of values specified in connection string settings. Whether you specify the settings in the connection string or not, these properties will expose what the values of the settings are. For example, if you omit specifying the `ConnectionTimeout` in a SQL Server connection string, you can still retrieve the connection timeout by looking at the `SqlConnection.ConnectionTimeout` property.

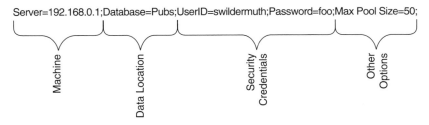

Figure 2.1: *A typical connection string*

In the following sections, I explain how each managed provider handles connection strings and what the most common settings for each managed provider are.

2.2.1.1 *SQL Server Connection Strings*

SQL Server Managed Provider connection strings contain a variety of elements, but only a handful are used in most development. (A complete reference of the supported settings can be found at Microsoft Developer Network [MSDN]).[1] The most common settings are:

- **Server**: The name or address of the SQL Server machine (for example, `192.168.0.1`, `myserver.mydomain.com`, or `localhost`).
- **Database**: The database within the server (for example, Pubs or Master).
- **Integrated Security**: A Boolean flag that indicates whether the SQL Server will be using NT Authentication or Username/Password validation. By setting Integrated Security to true, SQL Server will use the current NT Security descriptor for authentication to the database. The default is false. See Section 2.2.2, "Understanding Integrated Security," for more information on how to use integrated security.
- **User ID**: The user ID that should be used to authenticate with the database server (when Integrated Security is turned off).
- **Password**: The password that should be used to authenticate with the database server (when Integrated Security is turned off).
- **Connection Timeout**: The number of seconds for which the connection should attempt to connect before failing. The default is 15 seconds.

2.2.1.2 *OLE DB Connection Strings*

The OLE DB Managed Provider connection string is similar to the SQL Server connection string syntax. Syntactically, the OLE DB Managed Provider's connection string is an OLE DB connection string. Other than the Provider setting in the connection string, all settings are defined by the specific (OLE DB) provider. For an exhaustive list of supported settings, please consult the OLE DB provider's specific documentation. For all Microsoft-supplied OLE DB providers, consult MSDN (msdn.microsoft.

---

1.   See msdn.microsoft.com/library/en-us/cpref/html/
frlrfSystemDataSqlClientSqlConnectionClassConnectionStringTopic.asp.

com). A complete reference to the supported settings for the OLE DB Managed Provider is in MSDN.[2] The most common name/value pairs that you need for a connection string are:

• **Provider**: A ProgID for a particular OLE DB provider. Common providers are:

ProgID	Data Source
SQLOLEDB.1	SQL Server
MSDASQL.1	The ODBC OLE DB provider is specifically not supported (it generates a runtime error). Please use the ODBC Managed Provider if ODBC is required.
MSDAORA.1	Oracle
Microsoft.Jet.OLEDB.4.0	Microsoft Access Files (.mdb)

• **Server**: The name, network address to the database server, or file name of a database file (for file-based OLE DB providers like Microsoft Access and FoxPro). For example, `192.168.0.1`, `myserver.mydomain.com`, `localhost`, or `c:\access\northwind.mdb`.

• **Database**: In the case of database servers (such as SQL Server or Oracle), this is the specific database's name. This is not used for file-based OLE DB providers such as Microsoft Access.

• **UID**: The user ID that should be used to authenticate with the database server.

• **PWD**: The password that should be used to authenticate with the database server.

• **Integrated Security**: The type of integrated security (if any) to use. To enable integrated security in your connection string, use Integrated Security=SSPI. See Section 2.2.2, "Understanding Integrated Security," for more information on how to use integrated security.

• **Connection Timeout**: The number of seconds for which the connection should attempt to connect before failing. If not specified, the default is 15 seconds.

---

2. See msdn.microsoft.com/library/en-us/cpref/html/
frlrfSystemDataOleDbOleDbConnectionClassConnectionStringTopic.asp.

2.2.1.3 *Oracle Connection Strings*

The Oracle Managed Provider[3] supports a connection string syntax that is very similar to that of SQL Server. In fact, the connection string is a subset of that syntax. A complete reference of the supported settings for this managed provider is included in the provider's documentation. The most common settings are:

- **Server**: The name or network address of the Oracle database.
- **Integrated Security**: A Boolean flag that indicates whether the managed provider should send the Oracle server the current NT Authentication information or expect Username/Password validation. By setting Integrated Security to true, the Oracle server will use the NT Security descriptor for authentication to the database.
- **User ID**: The user ID that should be used to authenticate with the database server (when Integrated Security is turned off).
- **Password**: The password that should be used to authenticate with the database server (when Integrated Security is turned off).

2.2.1.4 *ODBC Connection Strings*

The ODBC Managed Provider's connection strings are a bit different than either SQL Server or OLE DB. There are two different methods of creating a connection string with the ODBC Managed Provider:

- Connect using a Data Source Name (DSN).
- Connect using a dynamic connection string.

DSNs are connection attributes that are dedicated and stored on a local machine. A DSN can be created by simply opening the ODBC Data Source Administrator, which is found either in the Control Panel or in Administrative Tools as "Data Sources." Specifying your connection string can be as simple as the following:

```
OdbcConnection conn = new OdbcConnection();
conn.ConnectionString = "DSN=MyDSN;";
```

---

3. As of this writing, the Oracle Managed Provider from Microsoft is in beta. Please consult the documentation that comes with the Oracle Managed Provider to make sure that the connection string syntax has not changed since the publication of this book.

The drawback of using a DSN is that each machine must either be specifically set up with a DSN or have access to the file-based DSN. This can be particularly problematic in large installations like Web farms. On the other hand, by using a DSN you keep a certain amount of control over the connection string. If the server moves or needs new authentication information, all you need to do is change the DSNs; no code changes are necessary if you change the DSN or DSN file.

Another approach to using DSNs is to dynamically create the connection information for the connection string. You can specify the connection string settings by providing them directly to the connection string (instead of hiding them in a DSN). This is very similar to how we specify these settings in the SQL Server and Oracle Server Managed Providers. A complete reference to the supported settings for the managed provider are included in its documentation. The most common settings are:

- **DSN**: A data source name or file path.
- **Driver**: The name of an ODBC driver, usually surrounded by curly brackets to delimit the name. These are some of the most common drivers:

DRIVER	Data Source
SQL Server	SQL Server
Oracle ODBC Driver	Oracle
Microsoft Access Driver (*.mdb)	Microsoft Access Files (.mdb)

- **Server**: The name or URL to the database server. For example, `192.168.0.1`, `myserver.mydomain.com`, or `(local)` for the localhost.
- **Database**: In the case of database servers (such as SQL Server or Oracle), this is the specific database's name. This is not used for file-based ODBC drivers such as Microsoft Access.
- **UID**: The user ID that should be used to authenticate with the database server.
- **PWD**: The password that should be used to authenticate with the database server.

2.2.1.5 *Connection Timeout*

Sometimes the database server is just too busy to take your request. Luckily it is up to you to decide how long to wait until you give up trying to connect. The idea behind the connection timeout is to provide a more graceful way to bow out when the database server is overloaded. For both the SQL Server and OLE DB providers, the default is 15 seconds. The connection timeout can be set to zero, which means to wait indefinitely, but this is not recommended because failure to connect to a server may not be recoverable.

You may need to use a custom setting for connection timeout, depending on your need for responsiveness and your proximity to the database server. For example, if you are writing pages for a Web server you may want to limit the timeout to a very short time so the Web server can let the user know it's overburdened. It is better to let users know that they cannot get to your page than force them to wait 30 seconds just to find out that the database server is unavailable.

The connection timeout is set within the connection string, but ADO.NET has exposed a read-only property of the Connection class to allow us to get at the value without parsing the connection string. It is important to realize that you cannot change the connection timeout without changing the connection string and reopening the connection.

2.2.2 Understanding Integrated Security

The SQL Server Managed Provider, the OLE DB Managed Provider, and the Oracle Managed Provider all support the concept of integrated security. Integrated Security is simply a shortcut that allows ADO.NET or OLE DB to infer the database security based on the current user's Windows security settings. In the case of interactive applications, the current network-authenticated user is specified to authenticate with SQL Server or Oracle.

Integrated security can be problematic when using connections on ASP.NET pages—unless you use impersonation or ADO.NET within the COM+ catalog, the current user is usually a fairly weak entity (MACHINE or other weakly privileged user). This user account is generated when IIS is installed and has enough security to access only the file system where the

Web site lives. I do not suggest giving these users access to the SQL Server, which is a potentially huge security hole. Creating a new user to use for authentication to the database makes much more sense. This requires that either the managed provider not use integrated security or the ASP.NET page use impersonation, but that is a small price to pay for security. In Web applications I would not use integrated security but instead put security information into the connection strings. In the case of desktop applications, using integrated security is perfectly acceptable.

2.2.3 Changing Databases

Connection objects represent a connection to a single data source, not a single database. The database value is special because we can switch which section or partition of a database server we are using during the time a connection is open. Other values (like User ID and Password) do allow for changing of the connection string values because changing databases provides the user the convenience of changing the logical area of data that the connection is working against. For all other types of connection information, you must close and change the connection string to change the values.

The following example illustrates the use of the `ChangeDatabase()` call. After we create the connection object and set the connection string, we open the connection and issue a command on the ADO.NET database. Afterward we need to get more information from this same server, but not the same database. To accomplish this feat, we issue a `ChangeDatabase()` call to change the database to the master database.

One thing to be careful of when using the `ChangeDatabase()` call is that your connection must be open. If you want to change the database with a closed connection, you may want to change the connection string to point to the new database to reduce the time it takes to bind to the database (see Listing 2.3).

Listing 2.3: *Changing the Database*

```
using System;
using System.Data;
using System.Data.SqlClient;

namespace EmptyProject
{
  class ShowDatabaseChange
```

```csharp
{
  static void Main(string[] args)
  {
    // Create and setup the server
    SqlConnection conn = new SqlConnection();
    conn.ConnectionString = "Server=localhost;" +
                            "Database=ADONET;" +
                            "Integrated Security=True;" +
                            "ConnectionTimeout=5;";

    // Use the connection
    SqlCommand cmd = new SqlCommand(
                "SELECT COUNT(au_id) FROM CUSTOMER;");
    cmd.Connection = conn;

    // Open the Connection
    conn.Open();

    // Execute a command
    int result = (int) cmd.ExecuteScalar();

    // Change the Database that we're using
    conn.ChangeDatabase("master");

    // Change the Command information
    cmd.CommandText =
            "SELECT COUNT(name) FROM dbo.sysdatabases;";

    // Execute the new work
    int nDatabases = Convert.ToInt32(cmd.ExecuteScalar());

    // Close the Connection
    conn.Close();

    // Clean up our Resources
    conn.Dispose();
  }
}
}
```

The point I am trying to make is that creating new connections (as opposed to opening existing connections) is a waste of time and code. If you think about connection objects as connections to a data source (that is, a specific server) and not as connections to a specific database (a data store within that server), you should be able to better reuse connection objects.

2.2.4 Connection Pooling

Connections are precious commodities, and writing code to minimize the stress on the server of having too many connections open concurrently will help with overall database performance. Fortunately, ADO.NET (like its predecessors) tries to help manage those connections with a facility called Connection Pooling. Connection Pooling is the process of managing connections as shared resources that can be doled out from a pool of recently used connections. Connection pooling takes advantage of the fact that many different parts of most applications require connections for a short amount of time as well as the fact that building and tearing down connections is an inherently expensive operation. Connection pooling is a method of reusing connections. The real magic occurs when connections are closed, because the pool hangs on to the connection for some short time (the pooling timeout) before actually closing the connection. If another connection is requested before that short amount of time has elapsed, it hands the open connection to the requestor. This saves the actual work of tearing down the connection and opening a new one. By utilizing connection pooling, you reduce the likelihood of making a round trip to the database only to find out that the database is out of connections. The connection pool reduces the time it takes to determine the out-of-connections state. In fact, with the connection pool, the additional requests can block to wait for a new connection to be available. This allows a machine to throttle its actual usage of the database so as not to swamp a particular database server with requests.

Each of the managed providers handles connection pooling differently. Although connection pooling is mostly transparent to the database developer, understanding how the different pooling mechanisms work allows you to write code that will take advantage of the connection pooling.

2.2.4.1 *SQL Server Managed Provider's Connection Pooling*

The SQL Server Managed Provider creates a pool of connections that have identical connection strings—these connection strings must be byte-for-byte identical. The managed provider simply matches identical connection strings in the pool. It uses the connection strings that a connection has after it has been set, not the connection strings you set. For example, if I create a connection with the connection string of `"Server=localhost; Database=ADONET;"`, after I set it the connection will have all of the defaults in the connection string, including security information (unless you have specified not to persist it). What this means is that if you are trying to pool connections and you are using integrated security, your connections will not pool because the security information in the connection string will be different from that in the pool (because the different users each will have their own security identity and credentials embedded into the connection string, so they can't be identical to another user's connection string).

SQL Server's Managed Provider implements the pooling facilities down in the bowels of the `System.Data` namespace.[4] If you want to watch the pooling, use the SQL Server Profiler to see the connections created and destroyed. The SQL Server Managed Provider gives us limited influence over how the pooling works. It exposes the pool settings through the connection string. These additional properties are shown in Table 2.1.

2.2.4.2 *OLE DB Managed Provider's Connection Pooling*

The OLE DB Managed Provider handles connection pooling much differently than the SQL Server Managed Provider. With the `OleDbConnection` class, the underlying OLE DB provider (not the ADO.NET managed provider) handles the connection pooling. This process is transparent to the ADO.NET developer with the exception of the `OleDbConnection.ReleaseObjectPool()` static method, which alerts the underlying provider that your code will not be using data access for some period of time and that it can destroy the object pool after all the connections are returned. This helps OLE DB shut down more effectively. Because the pool and the connections have a specific amount of time to live, these connections normally will not be destroyed for that period of time. By calling the `ReleaseObjectPool()` method, this destruction will be more timely.

---

4. **Note**: The SQL Server Managed Provider's connection pooling is not enabled while running under Visual Studio .NET's debugger.

TABLE 2.1 SQL Server Managed Provider Pooling Settings

Attributes	Description
Pooling	A Boolean expression that determines whether a connection is pooled. The default is true.
Min Pool Size	The minimum number of connections in the pool that will exist at all times. The default is zero.
Max Pool Size	The maximum number of connections in the pool. If the maximum number of connections in the pool are in use, the next client will wait either until a connection is available or until the connection timeout has expired. The default is 100.
Enlist	A Boolean expression that determines whether a connection is automatically enlisted in the thread's current transaction context. The default is true.
Isolation Level	The connection's transaction isolation level. The default is ReadCommitted.
Connection Lifetime	Determines how many seconds elapse before the connection being held open in the pool is closed and removed from the pool. When a connection is returned to the pool, a check is made between the creation time of the connection and the current time. If the Connection Lifetime's time has elapsed and the connection has not been requested, the connection is closed.

An OLE DB provider enables a number of services including connection pooling (which it calls *resource pooling*), transaction auto-enlistment, and client-side cursors. These services are enabled or disabled based on the provider's OLEDB_SERVICES Registry key. Because changing this Registry key would cause all applications on that machine to be affected by that change, the preferred method is to use the OLE DB Services connection string attribute to modify the behavior. The possible values are shown in Table 2.2.

For example, if I wanted to disable pooling and automatic transaction enlistment, I would do the following:

TABLE 2.2 Values for the OLE DB Services Connection String

Services Provided	OLE DB Services Value
All services (default)	−1
All except pooling and automatic transaction enlistment	−4
All except Client Cursor Engine	−5
All except pooling, automatic transaction enlistment, and Client Cursor Engine	−8
Pooling and automatic transaction enlistment only, session level aggregation only	3
No services	0

```
OleDbConnection conn = new
OleDbConnection("Server=localhost;" +
                         "OLE DB Services=-4;" +
                         "Integrated Security=true");
conn.Open();
```

Other than in the connection string, there is no way to control this behavior. The `IDataInitialize::GetDataSource()` OLE DB call can initialize it with specific values, but this is really only useful when you are calling OLE DB directly or within an OLE DB provider.

2.2.4.3 *Oracle Managed Provider's Connection Pooling*
The Oracle Managed Provider implements connection pooling much like the SQL Server Managed Provider. In other words, connections are pooled by identical connection strings within a single process. Several settings can be specified in the connection string to change the default behavior of Oracle Managed Provider's connection pooling, as shown in Table 2.3.

2.2.4.4 *ODBC Managed Provider's Connection Pooling*
The ODBC Managed Provider has no native support for connection pooling; however, in ODBC 3.0 and above there is support for connection pooling. There are two methods for enabling ODBC connection pooling;

TABLE 2.3 Oracle Managed Provider's Connection String Settings

Attributes	Description
Pooling	A Boolean expression that determines whether a connection is pooled. The default is true.
Min Pool Size	The minimum number of connections in the pool that will exist at all times. The default is zero.
Max Pool Size	The maximum number of connections in the pool. If the maximum number of connections in the pool are in use, the next client will wait either until a connection is available or until the connection timeout has expired. The default is 100.
Enlist	A Boolean expression that determines whether a connection is automatically enlisted in the thread's current transaction context. The default is true.
Connection Lifetime	Determines how many seconds elapse before the connection being held open in the pool is closed and removed from the pool. When a connection is returned to the pool, a check is made between the creation time of the connection and the current time. If the Connection Lifetime's time has elapsed and the connection has not been requested, the connection is closed.

neither of them has anything to do with ADO.NET. First, if you have the ODBC Data Source Administrator 3.5 or above, you can use the Connection Pooling tab (see Figure 2.2). Simply double-click the driver name and enable or disable the connection pooling (see Figure 2.3). This will affect all software on the computer.

The other method for enabling ODBC connection pooling is to call the ODBC API to enable connection pooling during your process. You do this by importing the ODBC call with DLLImport. Listing 2.4 shows how I have wrapped the calls into a simple class.

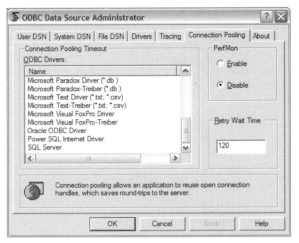

Figure 2.2: *The Connection Pooling tab of the ODBC Data Source Administrator*

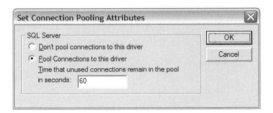

Figure 2.3: *Enabling connection pooling*

Listing 2.4: *Enabling ODBC Connection Pooling*

```
/*

  Example Usage:

    ODBCPooling.Enable();

*/

public class ODBCPooling
{
  [System.Runtime.InteropServices.DllImport
      ("odbc32.dll",
       CharSet=System.Runtime.InteropServices.CharSet.Auto)]

  private static extern int SQLSetEnvAttr(
                                long Environment,
```

```
                                   long EnvAttribute,
                                   long ValuePtr,
                                   long StringLength);

    const long SQL_ATTR_CONNECTION_POOLING = 201;
    const long SQL_CP_ONE_PER_DRIVER = 1;
    const long SQL_IS_INTEGER = -6;
    const long SQL_CP_OFF = 0;

    static int Enable()
    {
      return SQLSetEnvAttr( 0,
                            SQL_ATTR_CONNECTION_POOLING,
                            SQL_CP_ONE_PER_DRIVER,
                            SQL_IS_INTEGER);
    }
    static int Disable()
    {
      return SQLSetEnvAttr( 0,
                            SQL_ATTR_CONNECTION_POOLING,
                            SQL_CP_OFF,
                            SQL_IS_INTEGER);
    }
}
```

You only need to do this once per process to enable the pooling of connections. You can turn pooling for ODBC on and off by enabling or disabling it with this class. Unfortunately, there is no support for configuring the pooling beyond just enabling or disabling it.

2.2.5 Connection Events

During the life of a connection object, its status and role may change many times. Having the connection let you know when these changes occur is useful. Connection classes from all three standard managed providers support notification events for both information messages and connection state changes. In order to capture these events you must interact with the events that the Connection classes specify. These events are shown in Table 2.4.

Listing 2.5 shows a simple way to capture the events.

TABLE 2.4 Connection Class Events

Event	Description
Disposed	Called when the connection has called Dispose. This usually is used to clean up resources that are not handled automatically by the garbage collector.
InfoMessage	Called when the provider has information or warning messages. This is called at the discretion of the managed provider. Some providers make good use of this, others do not.
StateChanged	Called when the connection changes between closed and open. The event allows the user to see both the new and the old state.

Listing 2.5: *Connection Events (C#)*

```csharp
public class ShowEvents
{
  public void Show()
  {
    // Create Connection
    OleDbConnection conn = new OleDbConnection();
    conn.ConnectionString = "Provider=SQLOLEDB.1;" +
                            "Server=localhost;" +
                            "Database=Northwind;" +
                            "Integrated Security=SSPI;";

    // Set Events
    conn.InfoMessage +=
            new OleDbInfoMessageEventHandler(this.ConnInfo);
    conn.StateChange +=
            new StateChangeEventHandler(this.ConnChange);

    // Open Database
    conn.Open();

    // Create the Command Object
    OleDbCommand cmd = conn.CreateCommand();
    cmd.CommandText = "SELECT * from [Order Details];" +
                    "SELECT * from orders;";

    // Get the Reader Object by Executing the Query
    OleDbDataReader rdr = cmd.ExecuteReader();
```

```
   // Dump All Results
   do
   {
     Console.WriteLine("Result:");
     // Iterate through all the records of the result
     while (rdr.Read())
     {
       Console.WriteLine(rdr[0]);
     }
   }
   while (rdr.NextResult());
 }


 // Info Event Handler
 void ConnInfo(object sender, OleDbInfoMessageEventArgs e)
 {
   Console.WriteLine("Connection Info Message:" +
                      e.Message);
 }


 // State Change Event Handler
 void ConnChange(object sender, StateChangeEventArgs e)
 {
   Console.WriteLine(   "Connection State Changed: From: " +
                        e.OriginalState.ToString() +
                        " to " +
                        e.CurrentState.ToString());
 }


}
```

The VB .NET syntax for handling events and delegates is a bit different from C#. VB .NET does not support the += syntax for adding an event handler. In VB .NET you would use AddHandler. Listing 2.6 is the same code in VB .NET.

Listing 2.6: *Connection Events (VB.NET)*

```
Public Class ShowEvents

   Public Sub Show()

     ' Create connection
     Dim conn As OleDbConnection = New OleDbConnection()
```

```
                        conn.ConnectionString = "Provider=SQLOLEDB.1;" & _
                                                "Server=localhost;" & _
                                                "Database=Northwind;" & _
                                                "Integrated Security=SSPI;"

             ' Set events
             AddHandler(conn.InfoMessage, AddressOf ConnInfo)
             AddHandler(conn.StateChange, AddressOf ConnChange)

             ' Open database
             conn.Open()

             ' Create the command object
             Dim cmd As OleDbCommand = conn.CreateCommand()
             cmd.CommandText = "SELECT * from [Order Details];" +
                               "SELECT * from orders;"

             ' Get the reader object by executing the query
             Dim rdr As OleDbDataReader = cmd.ExecuteReader()

             ' Dump all results
             Do

               Console.WriteLine("Result:")
               ' Iterate through all the records of the result
               While rdr.Read()

                 Console.WriteLine(rdr.Item(0))

               End While

             Loop While rdr.NextResult()

        End Sub


        ' Info Event Handler
        Public Sub ConnInfo(ByVal sender As Object,
                            ByVal e As OleDbInfoMessageEventArgs)

            Console.WriteLine("Connection Info Message:" +
                              e.Message)
        End Sub

        ' State Change Event Handler
        Public Sub ConnChange(ByVal sender As Object,
                              ByVal e As StateChangeEventArgs)
```

```
        Console.WriteLine("Connection State Changed: From: " & _
                          e.OriginalState.ToString() & _
                          " to " + _
                          e.CurrentState.ToString())
    End Sub
End Class
```

The `InfoMessage` event is sporadically supported in the standard managed providers as well as in OLE DB providers. Some provide a lot of info messages, whereas others never report anything. The `InfoMessage` event reports warnings and information to the user, but if the provider does not report them, then the managed provider has nothing to report.

The `StateChange` event is a bit more conventional. Because of connection pooling, the last `StateChange` event is usually not called because the connection will not be closed until the connection times out of the pool. I have used the `InfoMessage` event to help with trace logging, but overall these events are of limited value.

2.2.6 Connection Factories

As you build ADO.NET applications, I suggest that you ensure connection uniformity to enable pooling and simplify connection creation. Unfortunately, Microsoft has decided to seal the Connection classes, so creating an inherited class is not an option. Creating a `ConnectionFactory` class is a common way to facilitate this uniformity in ADO.NET. By using the `ConnectionFactory` pattern, you can dole out new connections wherever you need them and reduce the amount of duplicated code. A connection factory could be implemented as simply as Listing 2.7.

Listing 2.7: *Connection Factory*

```
public class ConnectionFactory
{

  static public OleDbConnection CreateOleDbConnection()
  {
    return CreateOleDbConnection("ADONET");
  }

  static public OleDbConnection CreateOleDbConnection(
                                string sDatabase)
```

```
  {
    OleDbConnection conn = new OleDbConnection();

    // Set the Connection string
    conn.ConnectionString = "Provider=SQLOLEDB.1;" +
                            "Data Source=localhost;" +
                            "Database=" + sDatabase + ";" +
                            "UID=sa;" +
                            "Pwd=password;" +
                            "ConnectionTimeout=5;";
    return conn;
  }
```

The power of a connection factory is that the details of the connection are hidden from the developer. If the goal were abstraction from the details of which managed provider was to be used, the factory could return an IDbConnection interface instead of a specific provider object. In this way the implementation details of which managed provider was used could be further isolated, while still allowing the user to open and close the connection without regard to which provider is used.

This connection factory is simple and to the point, but a more likely scenario is a dynamic factory that could pull the connection information from the machine it's being run on, as shown in Listing 2.8.

Listing 2.8: *Dynamic Connection Factory*

```
public class ConnectionFactory
{
  static public OleDbConnection CreateRegisteredConnection()
  {
    try
    {
      // You could store the connection string information
      // in the Registry, app.config, or even machine.config

      // Get it from the Registry
      string sKey =
            "Software\\AW\\ADO.NET\\Chapter2\\ConnFactory";
      RegistryKey fac =
                  Registry.LocalMachine.OpenSubKey(sKey);
      string sSrc = fac.GetValue("Data Source").ToString();
      string sDB = fac.GetValue("Database").ToString();
```

```
        string sUID = fac.GetValue("Database").ToString();
        string sPwd = fac.GetValue("Pwd").ToString();

        // Create a new connection
        OleDbConnection conn = new OleDbConnection();

        // Set the connection string
        conn.ConnectionString = "Provider=SQLOLEDB.1;" +
                                "Data Source=" + sSrc +
                                ";Database=" + sDB +
                                ";UID=" + sUID +
                                ";Pwd=" + sPwd +
                                ";ConnectionTimeout=5;";

        fac.Close();
        return conn;
    }
    catch(Exception e)
    {
        // ...
        return null;
    }
  }
}
```

This dynamic connection object factory is powerful because it abstracts the details of both the OLE DB provider and the server. This allows the integrator or IS department to make the changes without affecting the code at all. This example, however, is not very representative because we would expect a .NET application to store its settings in a .config file of some sort (app.config, web.config, machine.config, or even enterprise.config).

2.3 Getting OLE DB Database Schema Information

OLE DB supports the retrieval of schema information from databases using *schema rowsets*. The OLE DB Managed Provider exposes this functionality with the `OleDbConnection.GetOleDbSchemaTable()` call. To get the schema information, you need to specify both a schema type you are looking for and a restriction list (to limit the number of schema to retrieve). For example, see Listing 2.9.

Listing 2.9: *Getting OLE DB Schema Information*

```
// Connect to the database
OleDbConnection conn = new OleDbConnection();
conn.ConnectionString = "Provider=SQLOLEDB;" +
                        "Server=localhost;" +
                        "Database=ADONET;" +
                        "Integrated Security=SSPI;";
conn.Open();

// Create a DataSet
DataSet ds = new DataSet();

// Get the tables in the database
ds.Tables.Add(conn.GetOleDbSchemaTable(
            OleDbSchemaGuid.Tables,
            new object[] {null, null, null, "TABLE"}));

// Add a new table to the DataSet per table in the database
foreach (DataRow row in ds.Tables[0].Rows)
{
    // Get a Table with the Columns of each table
    DataTable tbl =
            conn.GetOleDbSchemaTable(OleDbSchemaGuid.Columns,
            new object[] {null, null, row["TABLE_NAME"], null});

    // Change the TableName (since it will be named Columns
    // and we can't add multiple tables with the same name)
    tbl.TableName = row["TABLE_NAME"].ToString();

    // Add to it DataSet
    ds.Tables.Add(tbl);
}
```

When you call GetOleDbSchemaTable, you will specify one of the Guids in the OleDbSchemaGuid class. This will allow you to specify the type of schema you need. The first call gets a complete list of tables from the database, whereas the second call gets the columns for a specific table. The format that GetOleDbSchemaTable returns is a DataTable with the specified data about the database's schema. For more information on how to use this, please consult the specific OleDbSchemaGuid member (for example, OleDbSchemaGuid.Tables for how to get tables from the connection) and Appendix B of the OLE DB Programmer's Reference.

2.4 Error Handling in .NET

Unfortunately, the above examples are not representative of real use of ADO.NET. At its heart, database connectivity is network programming. Making requests across a wire complicates even the most benign of functions. Not to say this has to be difficult, but we have to take some precautions and deal with failures. Anything can happen when you get a wire involved: The server you are trying to contact could suddenly go silent, your security credentials may not be sufficient, or the cable could get disconnected because the cleaning lady just unplugged the hub.

In order to deal with these unforeseen circumstances, we must be ready to handle errors gracefully. The .NET platform deals with this by throwing exceptions. For some developers this is a very familiar topic, but for the Visual Basic developers out there, this may be new territory. Visual Basic developers can think of exception handling as being somewhat like the On Error Goto syntax.

The general idea behind exceptions is that when a process attempts to do some piece of work and fails to do so, it will throw an exception object that can be caught by calling code. In order to catch these exceptions (and deal with them), .NET has the try-catch-finally construct. A typical try-catch-finally scenario looks like Listing 2.10.

Listing 2.10: *Error Handling in .NET*

```
public void Test()
{
  int nResult = 0;

  try
  {
    // Try to call SomeFunction() to get the nResult
    SomeFunction();
  }
  catch (SqlException exception)
  {
    // Whoops . . . if we got here, we must have a
    // problem with our SQL provider so show the user
    // what the error was and tell them that it is a
    // SQL provider error
    MessageBox.Show("SQL Provider Error: " +
                    exception.Message);
  }
```

```
catch (Exception exception)
{
  // Whoops . . . if we got here, we must have a
  // problem, so show the user what the error was
  MessageBox.Show(exception.Message);
}
finally
{
  // This gets called whether an exception was
  // thrown or not
  nResult = -1;
}
return nResult;
}
```

This is the basic construct for `try-catch-finally`. If you need to understand this more thoroughly, please consult the .NET documentation. In real-world ADO.NET development, you will need to be prepared for exceptions to be thrown when ADO.NET cannot talk with the database server correctly. Exceptions do not mean there is a bug, just an unexpected condition (like an unplugged hub). Catching the exception gives you the power to wait and try again or exit gracefully while letting the user know what is going on. With exception handling you can specify the type of exception to catch, which allows you to catch provider errors but let system errors fall through.

Listing 2.11 is the `HelloADONET` example rewritten to handle exceptions.

Listing 2.11: *Using Finally Block*

```
namespace BetterHelloADONET
{
  using System;
  using System.Data;
  using System.Data.SqlClient;

  class Class1
  {
    static void Main(string[] args)
    {
      SqlConnection conn =
              new SqlConnection("Server=localhost;" +
                                "Integrated Security=true");
```

```
      try
      {
        conn.Open();

        SqlCommand cmd =
              new SqlCommand("SELECT * FROM Teams", conn);

        SqlDataReader reader = cmd.ExecuteReader();

        while (reader.Read())
        {
          Console.WriteLine(reader.GetString(2) +
                      " " + reader.GetString(1));
        }
      }
      catch (Exception ex)
      {
        Console.WriteLine(
                    "An Error Occurred: " + ex.Message);
      }
      finally
      {
        // Close the connection if it was opened
        // correctly.
        if (conn.State == ConnectionState.Open)
        {
          conn.Close();
        }
      }
    }
  }
}
```

This code is longer than the first example, but the logic flow is not much more complicated. Except for the `catch` block and an additional check before the `conn.Close()`, the code is intact.

Throughout this book I have removed the error handling for clarity. Developing production code without this error handling will expose the exceptions directly to the user, which is not usually very productive. Catching exceptions, at least at the highest level of your software, is a good idea, even if it is only to put a pretty logo next to the error message.

2.4.1 ADO.NET Exceptions

The SQL Server and OLE DB Managed Providers both expose specialized exception classes. In each of these classes, they expose an `Errors` property that is a collection of Error objects (of type `SqlError` and `OleDbError`). The errors contain additional information from the database about the specific exception. You can go through these errors to get the full description of why the exception was thrown, as shown in Listing 2.12.

Listing 2.12: *SqlException Handling*

```
public void Test()
{
  int nResult = 0;

  try
  {
    // Try to call SomeFunction() to get the nResult
    SomeFunction();
  }
  catch (SqlException ex)
  {
    string error = "";

    // Get the exception's message
    error += ex.Message + "\n";

    // Tack on each of the errors
    foreach (SqlError err in ex.Errors)
    {
      error += err.Message + "\n";
    }

    // Whoops . . . if we got here, we must have a
    // problem with our SQL provider so show the user
    // what the error was and tell them that it is a
    // SQL provider error
    MessageBox.Show("SQL Provider Error: " + error);
  }
  finally
  {
    // This gets called whether an exception was
    // thrown or not
    nResult = -1;
  }
  return nResult;
}
```

2.5 **Conclusion**

Connections are the alpha and omega. They are the first to be created and the last to be destroyed. They are also the key to providing scalability. By utilizing smart creation and connection pooling, you can aid your system's performance and availability. In addition, I hope I have helped you understand the arcane black magic of connection strings. Even though they may contain dozens of settings, knowing what is available should help you find the settings that will help you get your job done.

3
Commanding the Database

FINALLY, WE CAN start to do actual work with the database. In this chapter I will help you learn how to use command objects for your most basic tasks. In addition, I will help you reduce the network traffic associated with database commands. In most systems, the database development is the largest piece of networking code that is written. Optimizing those operations will help you reduce the overall network throughput of your system.

3.1 Commands

If dialing the phone is the connection, then the phone conversation is a set of commands. The database cannot do anything without ADO.NET Command classes. Whether we want to ask the database to give us information about data or simply insert or update data, it all starts with a Command object.

3.1.1 Command Object Creation

There are two common ways to create a Command object. First, you can use the standard syntax to create a command, as shown in Listing 3.1.

Listing 3.1: *Creating a Command*

```
SqlConnection conn = new SqlConnection();

//...
```

```
SqlCommand cmd = new SqlCommand();
cmd.Connection = conn;
cmd.CommandText = "SELECT * FROM Customer;";
```

Alternatively you can create your commands directly from the Connection objects, as shown in Listing 3.2.

Listing 3.2: *Creating a Command from a Connection*

```
SqlConnection conn = new SqlConnection();

//...

SqlCommand cmd = conn.CreateCommand();
cmd.CommandText = "SELECT * FROM Customer;";
```

This syntax simply creates a new command and assigns the connection in one step. In either case, you are not tied to keeping the connection to a particular command.

3.1.2 Command Types

Commands are powerful entities that are capable of complex database manipulation. According to ADO.NET, there are only three types of commands:

- **Text**: A text command is made up of instructions to a managed provider to do some work at the database level. In most cases this is a dialect of SQL for a specific database (T-SQL for SQL Server, PL/SQL for Oracle, and so on). A text command will usually be passed through to the database without any special handling, with the exception of sending parameters. The SQL Server, OLE DB, Oracle, and ODBC Managed Providers all support this type of command.
- **Stored Procedure**: A stored procedure is a command that calls a procedure located within the database itself. The SQL Server, OLE DB, Oracle, and ODBC Managed Providers all support this type of command.
- **TableDirect**: A TableDirect command is a special command type that returns a complete table from the database. This is identical to calling a command of type text with SELECT * FROM TABLENAME. This command is

supported by the OLE DB Managed Provider only. In general, I would avoid using this command type.

These three command types cover the entire spectrum of commands you can send to the database. By default, the `CommandType` is set to a text command. To set the command type, you will use the `CommandType` enumeration that resides within the `System.Data` namespace, as shown in Listing 3.3

Listing 3.3: *Specifying the Command Type*

```
SqlConnection sqlconn = new SqlConnection();

//...

SqlCommand sqlcmd = sqlconn.CreateCommand();

// You could set the CommandText to text, but it is
// unnecessary
sqlcmd.CommandText = "SELECT * FROM Customer;";

OleDbConnection odbconn = new OleDbConnection();

//...

OleDbCommand odbcmd = odbconn.CreateCommand();
odbcmd.CommandType = CommandType.StoredProcedure;
odbcmd.CommandText = "spMyStoredProc";
```

3.2 Executing Commands

After you have everything in place, you want to execute the command. You can execute ADO.NET commands in a number of ways; the results differ only in how data is returned from the database. The following execution methods are supported by all managed providers:

• **ExecuteNonQuery()**: Calling this method executes the query and returns the number of rows the command affected. This is used to execute commands for which you do not care what the results are. Because the call returns the number of rows affected, `ExecuteNonQuery()` can be used to determine success in many instances.

- **ExecuteScalar()**: This method executes the command and returns the first column of the first row of the first result set. This is useful for retrieving analysis information from the database (for example, `SELECT COUNT(userid) FROM USERS;`).

- **ExecuteReader()**: This method executes the command and returns a DataReader object. DataReaders are forward-only streams of records from a database. DataReader objects are discussed in detail in the next chapter. Each of the managed providers' versions of `ExecuteReader` returns a DataReader object from its namespace (`OleDbDataReader`, `SqlData-Reader` or `OdbcDataReader`), as shown in Listing 3.4.

Listing 3.4: *Using ExecuteReader*

```
//...
SqlDataReader sqlrdr = sqlcmd.ExecuteReader();

while (sqlrdr.Read())
{
  //...
}

//...
OleDbDataReader odbrdr = odbcmd.ExecuteReader();

while (odbrdr.Read())
{
  //...
}
```

In addition, the SQL Server Managed Provider supports the `XmlReader` execution method:

- **ExecuteXmlReader()**: This method executes the command and returns an `XmlReader` derived object that can be used to navigate through the data. This execution type is valid only for SQL Server 2000 and later and requires that the query or stored procedure return the results as XML, as shown in Listing 3.5.

Listing 3.5: *Using ExecuteXmlReader()*

```
SqlConnection sqlconn = new SqlConnection();

//...

SqlCommand sqlcmd = sqlconn.CreateCommand();
sqlcmd.CommandType = CommandType.Text;
sqlcmd.CommandText = "SELECT * FROM Customer FOR XML AUTO;";

//...

XmlTextReader xml = sqlcmd.ExecuteXmlReader();
```

Ultimately, we need to understand what our commands are doing for us. If our goal is to modify the database, there may be little need to deal with the results of a command except to ensure that it succeeded.

3.2.1 Result Sets Defined

The most common use of commands is when we issue a single command to the database and get a single set of data. Most of the commands that we execute are for reading data. When we use the DataReader to read data, we usually deal with a single rectangular piece of data as the result of a query or stored procedure. This single result is called a result set.

But if we issue multiple queries or a stored procedure does multiple queries, can we actually get back all the results from each of these queries? The database returns each of these as a separate result set. As we will see in more detail in Chapter 4, the DataReader has specific support for retrieving each of these result sets.

3.2.2 Using Parameters

Database parameters are essentially the same as parameters in Visual Basic, C++, or C#. Parameters are used to transfer mutable pieces of information to and from the database server. Parameter objects can be used with both stored procedures and parameterized queries. ADO.NET allows you to set up parameter objects when executing either of these types of database commands. Listing 3.6 is an example of calling a simple stored procedure using SQL Server.

Listing 3.6: *Using Parameters*

```csharp
// Connect to the database
SqlConnection conn = new SqlConnection(
                        "Server=localhost;Database=master;" +
                        "Integrated Security=true;");
conn.Open();

// Create the command for the stored procedure
SqlCommand cmd = conn.CreateCommand();
cmd.CommandText = "sp_stored_procedures";
cmd.CommandType = CommandType.StoredProcedure;

// Set up the parameters
SqlParameter param =
                new SqlParameter("@RETURN", SqlDbType.Int);
param.Direction = ParameterDirection.ReturnValue;
cmd.Parameters.Add(param);

param = new SqlParameter("@sp_name", SqlDbType.NVarChar);
param.Direction = ParameterDirection.Input;
cmd.Parameters.Add(param);

param = new SqlParameter("@sp_owner", SqlDbType.NVarChar);
param.Direction = ParameterDirection.Input;
param.Value = "dbo";
cmd.Parameters.Add(param);

param =
    new SqlParameter("@sp_qualifier", SqlDbType.NVarChar);
param.Direction = ParameterDirection.Input;
cmd.Parameters.Add(param);

// Execute the stored procedure
SqlDataReader rdr = cmd.ExecuteReader();

// Run through the records and show
// the stored procedure names
while (rdr.Read())
{
  Console.WriteLine("Proc: {0}", rdr["PROCEDURE_NAME"]);
}

// Clean up
conn.Dispose();
```

We set up the four parameters that `sp_stored_procedure` requires. You should notice that we set up some input parameters without giving them a value—these receive the default value of parameter objects, which is `DBNull`. If you want to send a null parameter, you do not need to set a value. You will notice that we need to set up several different properties for each parameter. Not every parameter will need to specify all these parameter attributes:

• **`ParameterName`**: The name of the parameter. Each database vendor has its own intricacies about the naming of parameters. In the SQL Server Managed Provider and Access through OLE DB, the parameters are named (using an @ sign followed by a name). In contrast, most other OLE DB providers and all ODBC and Oracle providers use position to determine where each parameter belongs. In this case, you must create the parameters in order as they appear in the stored procedure or parameterized query.

• **`DbType`**: Parameter type determines what type of data the parameter holds. The `DbType` enumeration has .NET types that can be specified for the `DbType`. In addition, each provider has a property that matches closer to the actual database datatypes. For example, the SQL Managed Provider has the `SqlDbType` enumeration. When the managed provider–specific enumeration is set, the corresponding `DbType` is also set. This is how the mapping between database datatypes and managed types is made. For example, setting a `SqlParameter`'s `DbType` to `DbType.Boolean` will also set the `SqlDbType` to `SqlDbType.Bit`.

• **`Size`**: Depending on the type, the size is usually used to show the maximum length of a parameter's data. For string types (`NVarChar`, `VarChar`, `Char`) this is the maximum string size. Default is inferred from the `DbType` of the parameter. In most cases the inferred size can be used without a problem. If your stored procedure code is very stable, setting the size can reduce the chance of sending parameters that are larger than the stored procedure can accept. In this case, a database error will occur.

• **Direction**: This determines how to transport the parameter. `ParameterDirection` is the enumeration that details all the direction types—`Input`, `Output`, `InputOutput`, or `ReturnValue`. The default is `Input`.

• **`IsNullable`**: This determines whether the parameter can accept a null value. The default is false.

- **Value**: The value of the parameter. For `Input` or `InputOutput` parameters, this should be set before the command is executed. For `InputOutput`, `Output`, or `ReturnValue` parameters, the value can be retrieved after the command has completed execution. If you want to send an empty input parameter, either don't set the value or set the value to `DBNull`. This defaults to `DBNull`.
- **Precision**: Determines the number of digits used to represent the value. Precision is the number of digits to the left of the decimal point. This defaults to 0.
- **Scale**: Determines how many decimal places the value should resolve. Scale is the number of digits to the right of the decimal point. This defaults to 0.
- **SourceColumn**: This refers to how the parameter is used with the `Data-Adapter`. Please see Chapter 8 for more information.
- **SourceVersion**: This also refers to how the parameter is used with the `DataAdapter`. Please see Chapter 8 for more information.

3.2.2.1   *Wrapping Stored Procedures*

Writing ADO.NET code to access a stored procedure can be tedious and repetitious. Usually it requires that you create each parameter separately. Listing 3.7 shows how you can do this verbosely or concisely.

Listing 3.7: *Creating Parameters*

```
// The verbose way
SqlParameter param = new SqlParameter();
param.ParameterName = "@RETURN_VALUE";
param.DbType = DbType.Int32;
param.Direction = ParameterDirection.ReturnValue;
_cmd.Parameters.Add(param);

// The concise way
_cmd.Parameters.Add("@RETURN_VALUE",
                    DbType.Int32).Direction =
                    ParameterDirection.ReturnValue;
```

The verbose way has advantages in that it is very clear to the reader of the code. On the other hand, the concise is, well, concise. To eliminate some of the tedium, you can hide the details of the parameters entirely by encapsulating the entire stored procedure into a wrapper class, as shown in Listing 3.8.

Listing 3.8: *Wrapping Stored Procedures*

```
public class spAddMember : IDisposable
{
  public spAddMember(SqlConnection conn)
  {
    ConstructCommand();
    _cmd.Connection = conn;
  }

  public SqlCommand Command
  {
    get
    {
      return _cmd;
    }
  }

  public Int32 Execute( string firstName,
                        string lastName,
                        string address,
                        string city,
                        string state,
                        string zip,
                        string phone,
                        string fax)
  {
    FirstName = firstName;
    LastName = lastName;
    Address = address;
    City = city;
    State = state;
    Zip = zip;
    Phone = phone;
    Fax = fax;
    _cmd.ExecuteNonQuery();
    return RETURN_VALUE;
  }

  // IDisposable
  public void Dispose()
  {
    _cmd.Dispose();
  }
```

```csharp
// Parameter Access
public  Int32 RETURN_VALUE
{
  get
  {
    return (Int32) _cmd.Parameters["@RETURN_VALUE"].Value;
  }
}
public  String FirstName
{
  set
  {
    _cmd.Parameters["@FirstName"].Value = value;
  }
}
public  String LastName
{
  set
  {
    _cmd.Parameters["@LastName"].Value = value;
  }
}
public  String Address
{
  set
  {
    _cmd.Parameters["@Address"].Value = value;
  }
}
public  String City
{
  set
  {
    _cmd.Parameters["@City"].Value = value;
  }
}
public  String State
{
  set
  {
    _cmd.Parameters["@State"].Value = value;
  }
}
public  String Zip
{
  set
```

```
    {
      _cmd.Parameters["@Zip"].Value = value;
    }
  }
  public  String Phone
  {
    set
    {
      _cmd.Parameters["@Phone"].Value = value;
    }
  }
  public  String Fax
  {
    set
    {
      _cmd.Parameters["@Fax"].Value = value;
    }
  }
  public  Int32 Key
  {
    get
    {
      return (Int32) _cmd.Parameters["@Key"].Value;
    }
  }
  // Protected member that constructs the command object
  protected void ConstructCommand()
  {
    _cmd = new SqlCommand("spAddMember");
    _cmd.CommandType = CommandType.StoredProcedure;

    // RETURN_VALUE parameter
    SqlParameter _RETURN_VALUE = new SqlParameter();
    _RETURN_VALUE.ParameterName = "@RETURN_VALUE";
    _RETURN_VALUE.DbType = DbType.Int32;
    _RETURN_VALUE.Direction =
                        ParameterDirection.ReturnValue;
    _RETURN_VALUE.SourceVersion = DataRowVersion.Current;
    _cmd.Parameters.Add(_RETURN_VALUE);

    // FirstName parameter
    SqlParameter _FirstName = new SqlParameter();
    _FirstName.ParameterName = "@FirstName";
    _FirstName.DbType = DbType.String;
    _FirstName.Direction = ParameterDirection.Input;
    _FirstName.SourceVersion = DataRowVersion.Current;
    _cmd.Parameters.Add(_FirstName);
```

```csharp
// LastName parameter
SqlParameter _LastName = new SqlParameter();
_LastName.ParameterName = "@LastName";
_LastName.DbType = DbType.String;
_LastName.Direction = ParameterDirection.Input;
_LastName.SourceVersion = DataRowVersion.Current;
_cmd.Parameters.Add(_LastName);

// Address parameter
SqlParameter _Address = new SqlParameter();
_Address.ParameterName = "@Address";
_Address.DbType = DbType.String;
_Address.Direction = ParameterDirection.Input;
_Address.SourceVersion = DataRowVersion.Current;
_cmd.Parameters.Add(_Address);

// City parameter
SqlParameter _City = new SqlParameter();
_City.ParameterName = "@City";
_City.DbType = DbType.String;
_City.Direction = ParameterDirection.Input;
_City.SourceVersion = DataRowVersion.Current;
_cmd.Parameters.Add(_City);

// State parameter
SqlParameter _State = new SqlParameter();
_State.ParameterName = "@State";
_State.DbType = DbType.String;
_State.Direction = ParameterDirection.Input;
_State.SourceVersion = DataRowVersion.Current;
_cmd.Parameters.Add(_State);

// Zip parameter
SqlParameter _Zip = new SqlParameter();
_Zip.ParameterName = "@Zip";
_Zip.DbType = DbType.String;
_Zip.Direction = ParameterDirection.Input;
_Zip.SourceVersion = DataRowVersion.Current;
_cmd.Parameters.Add(_Zip);

// Phone parameter
SqlParameter _Phone = new SqlParameter();
_Phone.ParameterName = "@Phone";
_Phone.DbType = DbType.String;
_Phone.Direction = ParameterDirection.Input;
_Phone.SourceVersion = DataRowVersion.Current;
_cmd.Parameters.Add(_Phone);
```

```
      // Fax parameter
      SqlParameter _Fax = new SqlParameter();
      _Fax.ParameterName = "@Fax";
      _Fax.DbType = DbType.String;
      _Fax.Direction = ParameterDirection.Input;
      _Fax.SourceVersion = DataRowVersion.Current;
      _cmd.Parameters.Add(_Fax);

      // Key parameter
      SqlParameter _Key = new SqlParameter();
      _Key.ParameterName = "@Key";
      _Key.DbType = DbType.Int32;
      _Key.Direction = ParameterDirection.Output;
      _Key.SourceVersion = DataRowVersion.Current;
      _cmd.Parameters.Add(_Key);
   }

   // Data members
   protected SqlCommand _cmd;
}
```

I have included a tool on the ADOGuy Web site (www.adoguy.com/book) that will allow you to generate this class for any stored procedure. This should simplify the creation of the stored procedure wrapper classes. The usage of this class is deceptively simple, as shown in Listing 3.9.

Listing 3.9: *Using Wrapper Stored Procedure*

```
SqlConnection conn = new SqlConnection("Server=localhost;" +
                                        "Database=ADONET;" +
                                        "Integrated Security=true;");
conn.Open();

// Create the stored procedure wrapper
spAddMember sp = new spAddMember(conn);

// Call the procedure
spAddMember.Execute("Maddux",
                    "Greg",
                    "123 Main Street",
                    "Atlanta",
                    "GA",
                    "30307",
                    "404-555-1212",
                    "404-555-1213");
```

```
// If the query worked, then get the key
Int32 key;
if (spAddMember.RETURN_VALUE == 0)
{
  key = spAddMember.Key;
}
```

You may also find it useful to set each of the parameters separately and deal with the command class directly, as shown in Listing 3.10.

Listing 3.10: *Calling Wrapper Stored Procedure's Parameters*

```
SqlConnection conn = new SqlConnection("Server=localhost;" +
                                "Database=ADONET;" +
                                "Integrated Security=true;");
conn.Open();

// Create the stored procedure wrapper
spAddMember sp = new spAddMember(conn);

// Add the member variables
spAddMember.FirstName = "Greg";
spAddMember.LastName = "Maddux";
spAddMember.Address = "123 Main Street";
spAddMember.City = "Atlanta";
spAddMember.State = "GA";
spAddMember.Zip = "30307";
spAddMember.Phone = "404-555-1212";
spAddMember.Fax = "404-555-1213";

// Execute the stored procedure
spAddMember.Command.ExecuteNonQuery();

// If the query worked, then get the key
Int32 key;
if (spAddMember.RETURN_VALUE == 0)
{
  key = spAddMember.Key;
}
```

Sometimes you will find it necessary to craft reusable queries that are ad hoc and therefore do not make sense to create as stored procedures. For these cases, you can use parameterized queries.

3.2.2.2 *Parameterized Queries*

For the simplest parameterized queries, you can write a query that returns the number of records that match a certain criteria:

```
SELECT COUNT(*) FROM CUSTOMER WHERE STATE = 'MA'
```

This query is simple enough and will return a result set with a single record containing the single value of the count. Using a parameter in the query will allow you to specify what contract value you are counting. For example:

```
SELECT COUNT(*) FROM CUSTOMER WHERE STATE = ?
```

In this example, we can call this query with a parameter, which allows us to change the value of the state.

Using parameters in parameterized queries is identical to using them with stored procedures, but there is no need to create a parameter for the return value, because parameterized queries do not have return values.

An important peculiarity that must be noted is that the format of parameterized queries is different for the native SQL Server Managed Provider than both OLE DB and ODBC. Table 3.1 details the appropriate syntax with different provider/vendor combinations. For example, see Listing 3.11.

Listing 3.11: *Calling Parameterized Queries*

```
. . .

// Create the command with the parameterized query
SqlCommand cmd = conn.CreateCommand();
cmd.CommandText =
        "SELECT * FROM Customer Where CustomerID = @CustID";

// Create the parameter
cmd.Parameters.Add("@CustID", DbType.Guid).Direction =
                                ParameterDirection.Input;
cmd.Parameters["@CustID"].Value = Guid.NewGuid();

. . .
```

TABLE 3.1 Parameter Syntax for Various Providers and Vendors

Managed Provider	Database Vendor	Parameter Syntax
SQL Client	SQL Server	@Name
OLE DB	SQL Server	?
OLE DB	Oracle	?
OLE DB	MS Access (Jet 4.0)	? or @Name
ODBC	SQL Server	?
ODBC	Oracle	?
ODBC	DB2	?
ODBC	MS Access	?

3.2.2.3 *Alternatives to Using Parameter Objects*

Building commands does not need to be an arduous task. In most cases, constructing strings of the database commands is just as appropriate, as shown in Listing 3.12.

Listing 3.12: *Calling a Query without Using Parameters*

```
SqlConnection conn = new SqlConnection("...");

SqlCommand cmd = conn.CreateCommand();

// Our CustomerID
int custID = 12345;

// Create the command with a string.Format()
cmd.CommandText = string.Format("SELECT * FROM Customer
                         WHERE CustomerID = {0}", custID);

// Or with a StringBuilder
StringBuilder bldr = new StringBuilder();
bldr.Append("SELECT * FROM Customer WHERE CustomerID = ");
bldr.Append(custID);
cmd.CommandText = bldr.ToString();
```

Usually, managed providers simply take the contents of a command and build a string to send to the database server. By using parameters, you end up writing more code than necessary and may even cause a performance penalty.

Why use parameter objects at all? After all, we can call stored procedures or parameterized queries just as easily with straight SQL, as shown in Listing 3.13.

Listing 3.13: *Calling a Stored Procedure without Parameter Objects*

```
// Connect to the database
SqlConnection conn = new SqlConnection("Server=localhost;" +
                                "Database=master;" +
                                "Integrated Security=true;");
conn.Open();

// Create the command for the stored procedure
SqlCommand cmd = conn.CreateCommand();
cmd.CommandText =
            "EXEC sp_stored_procedures NULL, 'dbo', NULL";

// Execute the stored procedure
SqlDataReader rdr = cmd.ExecuteReader();

...

// Clean up
conn.Close();
```

This works perfectly well for input parameters. However, if you need to extract values (other than result sets) from the database, you should use parameter objects. The rule of thumb is to use parameters if you need to handle output, input/output, or return value parameters. If all you are doing is handling the input values, you are probably wasting effort using parameter objects when building strings is just as appropriate.

3.3 **Database Transactions in ADO.NET**

A common problem in database programming is the requirement for a set of discrete operations to all work together. For example, if you were working on a medical records system and your database failed to write the new patient record but succeeded in writing the new patient visit records, you would have an inconsistent state. This is the problem that database transactions are meant to solve. Database transactions allow you to wrap a set of database operations in a wrapper that forces all operations to either fail or succeed. This is typically done within a stored procedure or straight SQL statements. For example, this SQL statement shows how the database uses transactions to roll back from an inconsistent state:

```
BEGIN TRAN

    INSERT INTO Customer
      (CustomerID, LastName, FirstName, Phone, Zip)
    VALUES (newid(), 'Smoltz', 'John', '503-432-4565',
                                         '12345');
    IF @@ERROR <> 0
    BEGIN
      ROLLBACK TRAN
      RETURN @@ERROR
    END

    INSERT INTO Invoice
      (InvoiceID, InvoiceNumber, InvoiceDate, Terms)
    VALUES (newid(), '123456', '05/01/2001', 'Net 20');

    IF @@ERROR <> 0
    BEGIN
      ROLLBACK TRAN
      RETURN @@ERROR
    END

  COMMIT TRAN
  RETURN 0
```

In this query we attempt to add an author, a new title, and a record in the author-to-title linkage table in the pubs database. If there is a problem (for instance, if the author ID is already used), then the entire set of commands will roll back as if they were never made. If all three commands succeed, then we commit the transaction to tell the database to actually save it. We can test to see if the transaction was committed by looking at the return code of the call—zero means it was committed, as shown in Listing 3.14.

Listing 3.14: *Calling a Stored Procedure without a Transaction*

```
// We can call this method to call the statement and let us
// know if it was committed or not
bool RunCommand(SqlConnection conn, string sqlStatement)
{
  // Create the command
  SqlCommand cmd = conn.CreateCommand();
  cmd.CommandText = sqlStatement;

  // Set up the return parameter
  cmd.Parameters.Add("@RETURN", DbType.Integer).Direction =
                          ParameterDirection.ReturnValue;
  // Open the connection
  conn.Open();

  // Execute the command
  cmd.ExecuteScalar();

  // Close the connection
  conn.Close();

  // if result is zero, we committed so return true
  int result = (int) cmd.Parameters["@RETURN"];
  return (result == 0);
}
```

ADO.NET permits you to have the same control over your database code as you would have with raw SQL. In ADO.NET, the transaction is represented by a transaction object (SqlTransaction, OleDbTransaction, or OdbcTransaction). Listing 3.15 illustrates how to rewrite the above SQL in ADO.NET.

Listing 3.15: *Using a Transaction*

```
// Open the connection
SqlConnection conn = new SqlConnection("Server=localhost;" +
                          "Database=ADONET;" +
                          "Integrated Security=true;");

conn.Open();

// Create the command
SqlCommand cmd = conn.CreateCommand();
```

```
// Create the transaction
cmd.Transaction = conn.BeginTransaction();

try
{
  // Add the customer
  cmd.CommandText = "INSERT INTO Customer " +
                    "(CustomerID, LastName, FirstName,
                      Phone, Zip) " "VALUES (newid(),
                     'Smoltz', 'John', '503-432-4565',
                     '12345');";
  cmd.ExecuteNonQuery();

  // Add the invoice
  cmd.CommandText = "INSERT INTO Invoice " +
                    "(InvoiceID, InvoiceNumber,
                      InvoiceDate, Terms) " +
                    "VALUES (newid(), '123456',
                     '05/01/2001', 'Net 20');";
  cmd.ExecuteNonQuery();

  // If we got this far then commit it
  cmd.Transaction.Commit();
}
catch(Exception ex)
{
  cmd.Transaction.Rollback( );
  Console.WriteLine("Command failed: " +
                    ex.Message +
                    "\nTransaction Rolled back");
}
```

This code is functionally identical to the SQL statement earlier in the section. The drawback of using client-side transaction objects is that they require many more database roundtrips than straight SQL. Server-based transactions (like the SQL version) are usually preferable because they are more efficient than client-based transactions. You would want to use client transactions (as in Listing 3.15) if you need to tie the transaction in the database to some external system. For example, if your code saved the changes in a database and updated a Web service at the same time, the call to the Web service could fail and allow you to roll back the database transaction from the client.

If you need only transactional support within the database, you probably should use server-based transactions. On the other hand, if you want some isolation from the specifics of the database engine, you can choose to do all your transactions on the client side. Keep in mind that performance is affected negatively when using all client-side transactions.

You will notice that the transaction is created by calling `BeginTransaction` on the connection. This call returns a newly created transaction object. After a transaction has been created, none of the commands to the database on that connection are committed until the `Commit` method is called on the transaction. In the case of failure, the `Rollback` method can be called to cancel all the database work since the transaction was started.

After a transaction has been started you must either commit it or roll back. If the transaction is not committed or rolled back, then during cleanup of the transaction, a rollback will occur. This means that if the connection closes or is disposed, or if the transaction is garbage collected, an automatic rollback will occur. Because this automatic rollback is observed, but not documented, I would not depend on this behavior; it is an implementation detail and may change in new versions of .NET. In addition, the finalization of the object may not happen until very late in the process because the Garbage Collector does not clean up objects in a timely fashion. If you do not want to save the changes to the database, please roll back your changes immediately.

3.3.1 Isolation Levels

When starting a transaction, you will need to specify the level of isolation the transaction will have. The isolation level specifies how the database can be locked while the transaction is still in process. The supported isolation levels are:

• **Chaos**: Your transaction cannot overwrite other uncommitted transactions that have a higher isolation level, but changes will overwrite other changes that are made without a transaction. No lock is made to the data, so writes that occur while the transaction is in process will be overwritten when the transaction commits.

- **ReadCommitted**: Reads within your transaction may not read data in other transactions. This level isolates you from dirty reads because the data that the transaction is manipulating is locked during the transaction.
- **ReadUncommitted**: Reads within your transaction may read data in other transactions. Choosing this option may cause unrepeatable reads and phantom rows because other transactions may be rolled back after you read data from their transaction.
- **RepeatableRead**: Your transaction cannot read data in other uncommitted transactions and your data is locked during the transaction.
- **Serializable**: Your transaction is completely isolated from other transactions.

Even though this isolation level enumeration has a `FlagsAttribute` that would allow a bitwise combination of multiple members, the use of these levels does not support this behavior. The default behavior of Read-Committed is usually your best bet for transaction isolation, but this needs to be considered on a case-by-case basis.

3.3.2　SQL Server Transaction SavePoints

While you are in the process of making multiple changes to a SQL Server database, there may be instances when you would like to support partial rollbacks of changes without abandoning the entire transaction. The current versions of SQL Server do not support nested transactions, but they have implemented SavePoints, which allow for similar behavior. A Save-Point is a SQL Server facility that allows for partial rollback of a transaction. A SavePoint is a bookmark that you can specify by calling the `Save` method of the `SqlTransaction` class when you are at a point that you might want to rollback to (without rolling back the entire transaction). In Listing 3.16 we create a SavePoint and roll the transaction back to the SavePoint.

Listing 3.16: *Rolling Back a Transaction*

```
// Open the connection
SqlConnection conn = new SqlConnection("Server=localhost;" +
                        "Database=ADONET;" +
                        "Integrated Security=true;");
conn.Open();
```

```csharp
// Create the command
SqlCommand cmd = conn.CreateCommand();

// Create the transaction
cmd.Transaction =
        conn.BeginTransaction(IsolationLevel.ReadCommitted);

try
{
  // Add the customer
  cmd.CommandText = "INSERT INTO Customer " +
          "(CustomerID, LastName, FirstName, Phone, Zip) " +
          "VALUES (newid(), 'Smoltz', 'John',
            '503-432-4565', '12345');";
  cmd.ExecuteNonQuery();

  // Create a SavePoint
  cmd.Transaction.Save("New Customer");

  try
  {

    // Add the invoice
    cmd.CommandText = "INSERT INTO Invoice " +
        "(InvoiceID, InvoiceNumber, InvoiceDate, Terms) " +
        "VALUES (newid(), '123456', '05/01/2001',
          'Net 20');";
    cmd.ExecuteNonQuery();

  }
  catch(Exception ex)
  {
    // Roll back to after saving of the new customer
    cmd.Transaction.Rollback("New Customer");
  }

  // If we got this far then commit it
  cmd.Transaction.Commit();
}
catch(Exception ex)
{
  cmd.Transaction.Rollback( );
  Console.WriteLine("Command failed:
                {0}\nTransaction Rolled back", ex.Message);
}
```

In this code we have created a SavePoint called "New Customer." If the creation of the new customer succeeds, but then the creation of a new invoice fails, we do not want to fail to create the customer in the database. After the customer is saved, if the transaction needs to roll back, we simply roll back to this saved point and commit the transaction.

3.3.3 COM+ and Enterprise Services

Sometimes database transactions are not large enough in scope, such as when you need to wrap a set of operations across several servers. For transactions such as this or anything larger, you would use .NET's Enterprise Services, which is the .NET wrapper to COM+. However, I will not be covering Enterprise Services in this book. If you need some information on transactional programming, I suggest Tim Ewald's excellent book, *Transactional COM+ Programming*, or his MSDN article, "COM+ Integration: How .NET Enterprise Services Can Help You Build Distributed Applications," found at msdn.microsoft.com/msdnmag/issues/01/10/complus/complus.asp.

3.4 Batch Queries

While sending commands to the database, many times you will need to ask the database to perform a series of jobs. You may simply set the `Command-Type` and `Execute` the commands one after another; however, you will end up paying a cost in roundtrips to the database. For every command, a database roundtrip is required. To optimize this sort of work, batch queries are often used. For example, let's assume that you need to do the following sets of work:

```
INSERT INTO Customer
   (CustomerID, LastName, FirstName, Phone, Zip)
VALUES (newid(), 'Smoltz', 'John', '503-432-4565', '12345');

INSERT INTO Invoice
   (InvoiceID, InvoiceNumber, InvoiceDate, Terms)
VALUES (newid(), '123456', '05/01/2001', 'Net 20');
```

You could instruct the database to perform the queries as in Listing 3.17.

Listing 3.17: *Executing a Query without Batching*

```
string sQuery1 = "INSERT INTO Customer " +
        "(CustomerID, LastName, FirstName, Phone, Zip) " +
        "VALUES (newid(), 'Smoltz', 'John',
         '503-432-4565', '12345');";

string sQuery2 = "INSERT INTO Customer " +
        "(CustomerID, LastName, FirstName, Phone, Zip) " +
        "VALUES (newid(), 'Maddux', 'Greg',
         '503-432-4566', '12345');";

// Connect to the database
SqlConnection sqlconn = new SqlConnection();

//...

SqlCommand sqlcmd = sqlconn.CreateCommand();
sqlcmd.CommandType = CommandType.Text;

// First query
sqlcmd.CommandText =  sQuery1;
sqlcmd.ExecuteNonQuery();

// Second query
sqlcmd.CommandText =  sQuery2;
sqlcmd.ExecuteNonQuery();
```

This would definitely work, but it is inefficient because the code requires three roundtrips to the database. Alternatively you can simplify the code and make it more efficient by utilizing a batch query as in Listing 3.18.

Listing 3.18: *Executing a Batch Query*

```
string sQuery = "INSERT INTO Customer " +
        "(CustomerID, LastName, FirstName, Phone, Zip) " +
        "VALUES (newid(), 'Smoltz', 'John',
         '503-432-4565', '12345'); " +
        "INSERT INTO Customer " +
        "(CustomerID, LastName, FirstName, Phone, Zip) " +
        "VALUES (newid(), 'Maddux', 'Greg',
         '503-432-4566', '12345');";

SqlConnection sqlconn = new SqlConnection();
```

```
//...
SqlCommand sqlcmd = sqlconn.CreateCommand();
sqlcmd.CommandType = CommandType.Text;

// Batch query
sqlcmd.CommandText =  sQuery;
sqlcmd.ExecuteNonQuery();
```

In this example, we used `ExecuteNonQuery()` to execute the batch. This method is fine, but doesn't provide any real support for error handling. To enable error handling, you will need to sprinkle your SQL code with error checking and optional transactional support, as we did in our transaction example, like this:

```
BEGIN TRAN

    INSERT INTO Customer
        (CustomerID, LastName, FirstName, Phone, Zip)
    VALUES (newid(), 'Smoltz', 'John', '503-432-4565',
            '12345');

    IF @@ERROR <> 0
    BEGIN
      ROLLBACK TRAN
      RETURN
    END

    INSERT INTO Invoice
        (InvoiceID, InvoiceNumber, InvoiceDate, Terms)
    VALUES (newid(), '123456', '05/01/2001', 'Net 20');

    IF @@ERROR <> 0
    BEGIN
      ROLLBACK TRAN
      RETURN
    END

COMMIT TRAN
```

We can have the batch query do the work of both inserts and make sure that the entire transaction succeeds or fails. If it fails, roll back all the work; otherwise, commit it all. Batch queries are nothing more than simply putting several queries together into a single command call. ADO.NET under-stands how to handle multiple result sets, so there is no real reason for not using batch queries. For example, see Listing 3.19.

Listing 3.19: *Retrieving Multiple Result Sets with a DataReader*

```
...

// Create a command with two selects to return
// two Result Sets
SqlCommand cmd = conn.CreateCommand();
cmd.CommandText = "SELECT * FROM Customer;" +
                  " SELECT * FROM Invoice;";

// Get a DataReader to go through the Result Sets
SqlDataReader rdr = cmd.ExecuteReader();

// Go through each row and ResultSet
do
{
  // while we have more rows in a ResultSet
  while (rdr.Read())
  {
    Console.WriteLine(rdr[0]);
  }
// After we're through the first ResultSet
// Move to the next one and do it again
} while (rdr.NextResult());
```

3.5 Conclusion

ADO.NET may allow for disconnected data, but you are still going to need to connect to the data. The information in this chapter will be used in *every* database application you write—there is no getting around issuing com-mands to the database. In subsequent chapters we will delve into how to consume the actual data.

◤ 4 ◼

Reading Data

M Y FIRST JOB in programming was to write reports for a CP/M[1] system against a long-forgotten relational database called FMS-80. In those days, writing reports consisted of simply reading the database and dumping a bunch of lines of text out to the console. The job of database reporting has become more complex in today's systems, but at its core it is still just reading data and dumping it somewhere.

One of the first rules in some database access layers that I have used was to "fire hose" database reads to lessen the load on the database. *Fire hose* is a term that usually means asking the database for a cursor that allows for iterating through the result in only one pass. By telling the database what we intend to do, the reading of the result is faster and uses less resources. ADO.NET has abstracted this concept into a set of classes called DataReaders. DataReaders are what this entire chapter is about.

4.1 Reading Data

Reading and reporting data is the most common and mundane task of the database developer. Whether you are retrieving stock quotes, listing a doctor's patients, or reporting monthly sales, reading data and reporting it to the user should be the simplest of tasks. Unfortunately, in database

---

1. I guess I am just showing my age. To see CP/M in action, see jfrace.sourceforge.net/ appletCPM.html.

development the most difficult part of reading data is constructing the query required to retrieve it.

The Structured Query Language (SQL) is a language of databases. The SQL-86, SQL-92, and SQL1999 languages are American National Standards Institute (ANSI) standards that most database vendors use. In fact, SQL is used to retrieve data from all the managed providers from Microsoft. The SQL in this book is based on SQL-92.

4.1.1 A Very Short Course in SELECT Statements

SQL is too large a topic to cover adequately in this book, but I will try to give you a short primer in the basics of querying data from a database. For a more thorough explanation, I suggest you refer to www.sql.org to get you started with SQL. In addition, take a look at Joe Celko's excellent books. For beginners, refer to *Instant SQL Programming* (ISBN: 1874416508). For more advanced SQL programmers, see Joe Celko's *SQL for Smarties: Advanced SQL Programming* (ISBN: 1558605762).

In reading data with a SQL query, you will need to get comfortable with the SELECT statement. SELECT is used to get a set of data from the database. Let's assume that we have the four tables shown in Figure 4.1 (taken from a database that you can build from the examples available at www. adoguy.com/book).

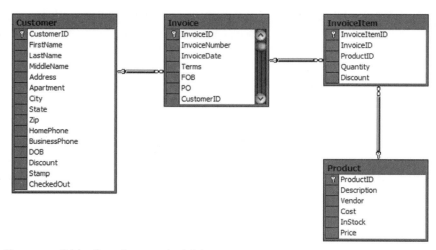

Figure 4.1: *Tables from the sample database*

The following example shows the simplest of queries:

```
SELECT * FROM Customer
```

This query asks the database to give us all the rows from the `Customer` table inside the database. The asterisk (*) is a wildcard that tells the database that we want all the columns in the table. The `FROM` clause instructs the database as to which table in the database we want to read from. The name, `Customer`, refers to a table in the database.

In most cases, not only will we not need every column in a table, but we will want to make sure the columns we do want are returned to us in a specific order. In this case, we would simply replace the asterisk with the column names we needed. The following example will instruct the database to give us every row from the `Customer` table, but only the `FirstName`, `LastName`, and `Phone` columns of the table:

```
SELECT FirstName, LastName, Phone FROM Customer
```

SQL also supports aggregation functions like `COUNT`, to get a count of the records that would be returned in a query, and `MAX`, to get the maximum value for a specified field:

```
SELECT COUNT(*) FROM Customer
SELECT MAX(Price) FROM Product
```

In addition, you will often want to get only a subset of the data in a table; to do this you will use a `WHERE` clause of the `SELECT` statement. For example, the following query tells the database to return every row from the `Customer` table that matches customers that live in Massachusetts:

```
SELECT FirstName, LastName, HomePhone FROM Customer
  WHERE State = 'MA'
```

Another clause that you will use often is the `JOIN` clause. `JOIN` allows you to retrieve related data from different tables. Using `JOIN` would allow us to retrieve not only the customer's data, but also every invoice for that customer. Here is an example of a simple `JOIN`:

```
SELECT FirstName, LastName, HomePhone, InvoiceNumber FROM
Customer
    JOIN Invoice
       ON Customer.CustomerID = Invoice.CustomerID
```

This example JOINs the Customer and Invoice tables by linking the two tables using their matching CustomerID fields. We can complete the linkage to the invoice by adding another JOIN to link the Invoice table to the InvoiceItem table:

```
SELECT FirstName, LastName, HomePhone,
       InvoiceNumber, Quantity, ProductID
  FROM Customer
    JOIN Invoice
      ON Customer.CustomerID = Invoice.CustomerID
    JOIN InvoiceItem
      ON Invoice.InvoiceID = InvoiceItem.InvoiceID
```

To limit our search to only the invoices for customers with the last name of Maddux, we then add a WHERE clause:

```
SELECT FirstName, LastName, HomePhone,
       InvoiceNumber, Quantity, ProductID
  FROM Customer
    JOIN Invoice
      ON Customer.CustomerID = Invoice.CustomerID
    JOIN InvoiceItem
      ON Invoice.InvoiceID = InvoiceItem.InvoiceID
  WHERE Customer.LastName = 'Maddux'
```

Lastly, we use the ORDER BY clause to sort our returned list by the invoice date. To use the clause, simply end your SELECT with ORDER BY and list a column by which to order. For example:

```
SELECT FirstName, LastName, HomePhone,
       InvoiceNumber, Quantity, ProductID
  FROM Customer
    JOIN Invoice
      ON Customer.CustomerID = Invoice.CustomerID
    JOIN InvoiceItem
      ON Invoice.InvoiceID = InvoiceItem.InvoiceID
```

```
WHERE Customer.LastName = 'Maddux'
ORDER BY InvoiceDate
```

If you would like the order to be descending instead of ascending (the default), end the clause with DESC:

```
SELECT FirstName, LastName, HomePhone, InvoiceNumber,
Quantity, ProductID
  FROM Customer
    JOIN Invoice
      ON Customer.CustomerID = Invoice.CustomerID
    JOIN InvoiceItem
      ON Invoice.InvoiceID = InvoiceItem.InvoiceID
  WHERE Customer.LastName = 'Maddux'
ORDER BY InvoiceDate DESC
```

All of these examples use SQL-92 syntax. Pretty much all database vendors (including Microsoft, IBM, and Oracle) are compliant with the SQL-92 syntax, although each vendor has extended the language into its own flavor (such as T-SQL for SQL Server and PL/SQL for Oracle). Writing vendor-independent SQL code is difficult and fraught with land mines. If you absolutely have to write database vendor–neutral code, be aware that your performance will suffer; because all vendors have their own peculiarities, tuning SQL statements is a bit art and a bit magic.

4.2 The DataReader

Now that you know how to write a query, how do you get ADO.NET to issue that query? Unlike most other data access methodologies where there is a single object that can read and modify the database, ADO.NET separates reading from changing the database. Much of the time you will be writing code that simply reads the database and presents that data to the user. ADO.NET provides a basic object whose sole job is to read the database. This object is the DataReader.

The DataReader is a read-only representation of the data returned by a SQL query. The DataReader is a class that exists in all of the providers: OleDbDataReader, SqlDataReader, OracleDataReader, and OdbcDataReader. Listing 4.1 is an example of a SqlDataReader in action.

Listing 4.1: *Using a DataReader*

```
// Create the command object
SqlCommand cmd = conn.CreateCommand();
cmd.CommandText = "SELECT * FROM CUSTOMER";

// Get the reader object by executing the query
SqlDataReader rdr = cmd.ExecuteReader();

// Iterate through all the records
while (rdr.Read())
{
  Console.WriteLine(rdr[0]);
}
```

This example shows the simplest usage of a DataReader. The Data-Reader uses the `Read()` method to move down the records of the result set. Please notice that `Read()` must be called before reading your first record. This design makes the DataReader less error prone because the moving of the row cursor and the validation that we are not at the end of a result are done in the same statement. When the DataReader reaches the end of the results, it simply returns a false.

4.2.1 DataReader Construction

A DataReader is not constructed directly by the client code that uses it; instead, command objects create them as part of executing a command. Specifically, by calling the `IDbCommand.ExecuteReader(...)` method, a DataReader is constructed and passed back to the client code. Note that the constructor of the DataReader is hidden to prevent you from trying to create a new DataReader object. This can be seen here:

```
SqlCommand cmd = new SqlCommand();
...

// Good
SqlDataReader rdr = cmd.ExecuteReader();

// Bad (will not compile)
SqlDataReader rdr = new SqlDataReader();
```

4.2.2 How the DataReader Works

It is important for you to understand how the DataReader does its job underneath the covers. In Chapter 1, I stressed the importance of disconnected data, but this does not apply at all to the DataReader. When you execute a DataReader, the entire time you are reading or even just iterating through rows and result sets, the connection must continue to be valid. In reality, the DataReader is more like its predecessors that dealt with data in a completely connected way.

Because the DataReader is continually connected, it has the advantage of not needing to retrieve all the data from a query at once. This is an advantage for large databases found in financial houses or data warehousing projects. Asking the database to return a million records into memory at once would be a daunting task. The DataReader simplifies this by storing a small amount of the result set in memory at once.

In addition, because DataReaders are connected by nature, some developers are hesitant to use them because they are trying to keep their data disconnected. Many developers opt for using the DataSet instead. In Chapter 7 we discuss when to use DataReaders and when to use DataSets.

4.2.3 Accessing Data from a DataReader

As shown in Listing 4.1, the DataReader allows you to retrieve individual columns by treating the DataReader as an array. The indexer (the [] syntax) allows you to specify either ordinal number or field name, as shown in Listing 4.2.

Listing 4.2: *Retrieving DataReader Columns*

```
. . .

// Create the command object
SqlCommand cmd = conn.CreateCommand();
cmd.CommandText = "SELECT * FROM CUSTOMER";

// Get the reader object by executing the query
SqlDataReader rdr = cmd.ExecuteReader();

// Iterate through all the records
while (rdr.Read())
```

```
{
    Console.WriteLine(rdr[0]);        // These lines are identical
    Console.WriteLine(rdr["CustomerID"]);// in functionality
}
```

Because the indexer returns an object, you can either cast it to the type of the column or call the DataReader's type-safe accessors, as shown in Listing 4.3.

Listing 4.3: *Type-Safe DataReader Access*

```
// Create the command object
SqlCommand cmd = conn.CreateCommand();
cmd.CommandText = "SELECT * FROM CUSTOMER";

// Get the reader object by executing the query
SqlDataReader rdr = cmd.ExecuteReader();

// Iterate through all the records
while (rdr.Read())
{
    Console.WriteLine((string) rdr[0]);   // Identical
    Console.WriteLine(rdr.GetString(0));  // Functionality
}
```

The type-safe accessors do not do any conversions—they simply do the cast for you. If you attempt to retrieve a column whose type is not a valid cast to the type you have requested, the accessor will throw an Invalid-CastException, just like a cast would. In the above example, if the first column was an integer, the InvalidCastException would be thrown. If you want to do a conversion, use the System.Convert class shown in Listing 4.4.

Listing 4.4: *Using the System.Convert Class with the DataReader*

```
...
cmd.CommandText = "SELECT * FROM PRODUCT";

// Get the reader object by executing the query
SqlDataReader rdr = cmd.ExecuteReader();

// Iterate through all the records
while (rdr.Read())
```

```
{
    Console.WriteLine(Convert.ToString(rdr["Price"]));
}
```

All of these type-safe methods require the ordinal number of the column to retrieve the data; however, this may not be as convenient as retrieving the data by column name. To get around this you can use the `GetOrdinal()` method to retrieve the column number, as shown in Listing 4.5

Listing 4.5: *Using GetOrdinal with Type-Safe Accessors*

```
// Create the command object
SqlCommand cmd = conn.CreateCommand();
cmd.CommandText = "SELECT * FROM INVOICE";

// Get the reader object by executing the query
SqlDataReader rdr = cmd.ExecuteReader();

// Iterate through all the records
while (rdr.Read())
{
    // These lines are identical in functionality
    Console.WriteLine(rdr.GetDateTime(
                        rdr.GetOrdinal("InvoiceDate")));
    Console.WriteLine((DateTime) rdr["InvoiceDate"]);
}
```

The `GetOrdinal()` and `GetName()` methods of the DataReaders are complementary to each other. You should be able to determine the column ordinal or name with these functions.

4.2.3.1 **ExecuteReader** *Options*

In most cases, calling the `Command` class's `ExecuteReader` method without any parameters is the right thing to do. For more complex scenarios, `ExecuteReader` can be called with a `CommandBehavior` flag. The `CommandBehavior` flag modifies how the DataReader is generated and also affects the types of data that the DataReader will contain. The `CommandBehavior` flag can contain one or more of the following values (they can be combined bitwise):

- **Default**: No special behavior is associated with this value. Therefore, the command will be executed on the server without any special code for locking or unlocking rows. The connection is not manipulated in any way. This is the default for `ExecuteReader()` when you call without specifying the `CommandBehavior`.

- **CloseConnection**: Automatically closes the associated `Connection` object when the DataReader reaches the end of all result sets or the DataReader is closed.

- **KeyInfo**: Returns the data requested without locking any of the rows. This is useful when you are only reading data. If this is used, you should expect that you will not update any data in the result sets the DataReader has returned. This is important because if you do not lock the rows while the DataReader is open, any rows you have not yet retrieved can be changed and may result in unexpected results. In addition, the SQL Server Managed Provider interprets this as instructing it to put the FOR BROWSE clause on the command. This can have unintended side effects in SQL Server. Please see the SQL Server Books Online for more information.[2]

- **SchemaOnly**: The `Schema` metadata information is returned in the DataReader, but the query is not executed and does not affect the database state.

- **SequentialAccess**: The rows are read sequentially at the column level. This is used with `GetChars` or `GetBytes` to retrieve long binary data from a row in the DataReader. Not choosing this will cause all the long binary data to be read into the DataReader, whether or not it will be used. This will help optimize large binary data queries where not all data is needed.

- **SingleResult**: The query is expected to return only a single result set.

- **SingleRow**: The query is expected to return only a single row.

4.2.3.2 *Dealing with* Null *Columns*

The type-safe methods of the DataReaders (such as `GetString`, `Get-Boolean`, and so on) are very useful in retrieving column values from the DataReader. In a perfect world these would be all you ever need. The trouble is that in database development there is no guarantee that a column has

---

2. See msdn.microsoft.com/library/en-us/tsqlref/ts_sa-ses_9sfo.asp#_from_clause.

ever been written. For beginning database developers this often causes confusion. For example, if the customer table has a record of a customer who has never reported his address, then the address field of the customer table may be null. What is stored there is entirely up to the original developer's code. If he or she chose to not insert that field in the customer record (instead of inserting an empty string), then the field would be null.

When walking through the records of DataReader, if you try to retrieve a value from a null field, ADO.NET will throw an exception. This exception is caused when attempting to convert the null field to the requested type. To avoid throwing the exception, the DataReader supports calling the `IsDBNull()` method, which informs the caller as to whether the field is null. Listing 4.6 is `IsDBNull()` in action.

Listing 4.6: *Dealing with Null Values in a DataReader*

```
// Assumes that cmd is a SqlCommand
SqlDataReader rdr = cmd.ExecuteReader();

while (rdr.Read())
{
  // Write the field if the field is not null
  if (!rdr.IsDBNull(0))
  {
    // Write the first field
    Console.WriteLine(rdr.GetString(0));
  }
}
```

This certainly works, but in most applications it creates a huge amount of ugly code. Take a look at Listing 4.7 as an example of typical usage of copying the contents of a DataReader to a local class's storage.

Listing 4.7: *Verbose Checking for Null in a DataReader*

```
public Invoice(IDataReader rdr)
{

  // If the columns are not null, then fill our Invoice Info
  if (!rdr.IsDBNull(rdr.GetOrdinal("InvoiceID")))
  {
    InvoiceID = rdr.GetString(rdr.GetOrdinal("InvoiceID"));
  }
```

```
if (!rdr.IsDBNull(rdr.GetOrdinal("InvoiceNumber")))
{
  InvoiceNumber = rdr.GetString(
                        rdr.GetOrdinal("InvoiceNumber"));
}

if (!rdr.IsDBNull(rdr.GetOrdinal("InvoiceDate")))
{
  InvoiceDate = rdr.GetString(
                        rdr.GetOrdinal("InvoiceDate"));
}

if (!rdr.IsDBNull(rdr.GetOrdinal("Terms")))
{
  Terms = rdr.GetString(rdr.GetOrdinal("Terms"));
}

if (!rdr.IsDBNull(rdr.GetOrdinal("PO")))
{
  PO = rdr.GetString(rdr.GetOrdinal("PO"));
}

if (!rdr.IsDBNull(rdr.GetOrdinal("FOB")))
{
  FOB = rdr.GetString(rdr.GetOrdinal("FOB"));
}
}
```

That is a lot of work to simply copy the values of six fields! I looked at this code and knew there had to be a better way. This `Field` class is part of the example code that can be downloaded at my site (www.adoguy.com/book). Listing 4.8 is an excerpt of the source for the `Field` class.

Listing 4.8: *The Field Class*

```
public class Field
{

  // By number
  static public string GetString(IDataRecord rec,
                                  int fldnum)
  {
    if (rec.IsDBNull(fldnum)) return "";
    return rec.GetString(fldnum);
  }
```

```
static public decimal GetDecimal(IDataRecord rec,
                                 int fldnum)
{
  if (rec.IsDBNull(fldnum)) return 0;
  return rec.GetDecimal(fldnum);
}


...


}
```

The purpose of this helper class is to provide a simpler, reusable way to determine the acceptable default for null fields. By using the `Field` class, I am able to make our code more readable. Listing 4.9 is the example from Listing 4.7, rewritten to use the `Field` class.

Listing 4.9: *Using the Field Class in a DataReader*

```
public Invoice(IDataReader rdr)
{

    // If the columns are not null, then fill our Invoice Info
    InvoiceID = Field.GetGuid(rdr, "InvoiceID");
    InvoiceNumber = Field.GetInt(rdr, "InvoiceNumber");
    InvoiceDate = Field.GetDateTime(rdr, "InvoiceDate");
    Terms = Field.GetString(rdr, "Terms");
    PO = Field.GetString(rdr, "PO");
    FOB = Field.GetString(rdr, "FOB");
}
```

There are genuine cases where we may want to expect that the field cannot be null; typical examples of these are primary keys and required fields. In fact, we could use the database schema to make these determinations for us. If the database schema says that the field is required, then checking `IsDbNull()` is a waste of time. If the field is required, but ADO.NET reports it as null, the exception thrown is perfectly appropriate because it is an unexpected situation that we are unlikely to recover from. In any case, if you decide to use my `Field` class, you can get around this requirement at the risk of allowing null rows where a genuine exception would be thrown.

4.2.3.3 *Database Locks*

Every multi-user database on the market today supports locking the database. Locking database records has to do with how to alert the database that the data you are reading may be changed soon and not allowing other systems or users to change those records. ADO.NET's DataReaders do not support a complex level of database locking. When calling `IDbCommand.ExecuteReader()` you can tell the command whether to lock the records you are reading. Locking of the records is the default behavior, as shown in Listing 4.10.

Listing 4.10: *Using the DataReader with Database Locks*

```
// Locks the records
SqlDataReader rdr = cmd.ExecuteReader();

// Does not lock the records
SqlDataReader rdr =
                cmd.ExecuteReader(CommandBehavior.KeyInfo);
```

There are two reasons for locking the records in a DataReader:

• You will be modifying the records and do not want other systems or users changing the data until you've made your changes.
• You want your data to not be changed while you are analyzing data you have read. This is usually used if there is a critical need for consistency in the data for statistical analysis or other high-risk reporting.

In most every other case where you are simply reporting on the data, you will want to use the `CommandBehavior.KeyInfo` option. Locking the database where you do not need the lock simply ties up those rows and may reduce the performance of other processes working with the database.

4.2.4 What Are Result Sets?

Whenever you make a request (or query) to the database, it packages up the answer or response to the request into something called a result set. If your query requested one piece of information (i.e., a single query), then you can expect to get only a single result set. When you are calling a stored procedure or a batch query, you can expect more than one result set. In its simplest form you can expect to receive two result sets if you call:

```
SELECT * FROM CUSTOMER
SELECT * FROM INVOICE
```

4.2.5 Handling Multiple Result Sets

Retrieving multiple result sets from a single DataReader is perfectly valid. To iterate through multiple result sets, call the `NextResult()` method of the DataReader to move to the next result set. Unlike the `Read()` method, this should not be called before reading data. The most common usage can be seen in Listing 4.11.

Listing 4.11: *The DataReader with Multiple Result Sets*

```
. . .

// Create the command object
SqlCommand cmd = conn.CreateCommand();
cmd.CommandText = "SELECT * FROM CUSTOMER\n" +
                  "SELECT * FROM INVOICE";

// Get the reader object by executing the query
SqlDataReader rdr = cmd.ExecuteReader();

// Do all result sets
do
{
  // Iterate through all the records of the result
  while (rdr.Read())
  {
    Console.WriteLine(rdr[0]);
  }
}
while (rdr.NextResult());
```

As you can see from this example, we are calling the `NextResult()` method only after we are done with the first result set.

4.2.6 Working with DataReader Metadata

Most of the time you will know the exact type of data you are expecting from the database, but this is not always the case. Luckily, the Data-Reader also provides type information for each and every result set. All DataReader classes are required to expose a `GetSchemaTable()` method. This method returns a `DataTable` object that contains information about the type information of the result set. `DataTables` are discussed in detail in Chapter 6, but Listing 4.12 is a simplified example of how to retrieve information about the columns of the result set.

Listing 4.12: *Working with DataReader MetaData*

```
...

// Create the command object
SqlCommand cmd = conn.CreateCommand();
cmd.CommandText = "SELECT * FROM CUSTOMER\n" +
                  "SELECT * FROM INVOICE";

// Get the reader object by executing the query
SqlDataReader rdr = cmd.ExecuteReader();

// Do all Result Sets
do
{

  // Get a DataTable of the schema from this Result Set
  DataTable schema = rdr.GetSchemaTable();

  // Show the Result Set Header
  Console.WriteLine("Result Set");

  // Dump the schema information
  foreach (DataRow row in schema.Rows)
  {
    Console.WriteLine("  Column:");
    Console.WriteLine("    {0} : ", row["ColumnName"]);
    Console.WriteLine("      Type:       {0}",
                row["DataType"]);
    Console.WriteLine("      IsUnique:   {0}",
                row["IsUnique"]);
    Console.WriteLine("      AllowDBNull: {0}",
                row["AllowDBNull"]);
  }
```

```
        }
        while (rdr.NextResult());
```

When we run this, we get a listing for the metadata about the customer and invoice tables. Here is an excerpt of what we found:

```
Result Set
  Column:
    CustomerID :
      Type:        System.Guid
      IsUnique:    False
      AllowDBNull: False
  Column:
    FirstName :
      Type:        System.String
      IsUnique:    False
      AllowDBNull: False
  Column:
    LastName :
      Type:        System.String
      IsUnique:    False
      AllowDBNull: False

    ...

Result Set
  Column:
    InvoiceID :
      Type:        System.Guid
      IsUnique:    False
      AllowDBNull: False
  Column:
    InvoiceNumber :
      Type:        System.Int32
      IsUnique:    False
      AllowDBNull: False
  Column:
    InvoiceDate :
      Type:        System.DateTime
      IsUnique:    False
      AllowDBNull: False
```

The columns of the schema relate different information about the data being returned. The following lists all the metadata available regarding a `Result Set`:

- **`ColumnName`**: The name of the column as best as the provider can determine. If the column name is specified in the `Command` object, that name is used. There is no guarantee that this name will be either unique or not null, depending on the individual provider's implementation of the `GetSchemaTable()` method.
- **`ColumnOrdinal`**: This is the numeric order of the columns. The ordinals start with one.
- **`ColumnSize`**: If the datatype supports a fixed-length size, then the maximum size of the column's data.
- **`NumericPrecision`**: If the column is numeric, this specifies the amount of precision that the number can hold. This is null for non-numeric columns.
- **`NumericScale`**: If the column is numeric, this specifies the number of digits to the right of the decimal place that the numeric value can hold. This is null for non-numeric columns or numeric datatypes that do not support scale.
- **`DataType`**: This is the Common Language Runtime type of the column.
- **`DbType`**: This is the provider-specific type of the column.
- **`IsLong`**: Boolean expression that indicates whether the data in this column can contain long binary data (such as BLOBs).
- **`AllowDBNull`**: Boolean expression that indicates whether the column can hold a null value.
- **`IsReadOnly`**: Boolean expression that indicates whether the column is read only.
- **`IsRowVersion`**: Boolean expression that indicates whether the column holds a value whose sole purpose is to identify the row. This usually is used to indicate whether a SQL Server database is using a GUID as the key to the table.
- **`IsUnique`**: Boolean expression that indicates whether the column is unique. If `IsKeyColumn` is true, then `IsUnique` is guaranteed to be true.
- **`IsKeyColumn`**: Boolean expression that indicates whether the column is either the primary key or some part of the primary key for the table.

- **IsAutoIncrement**: Boolean expression that indicates whether the column's value is automatically assigned by the database in fixed increments.
- **BaseSchemaName**: The name of the schema in the database that the column's table exists in. If this cannot be determined the column is null.
- **BaseCatalogName**: The name of the catalog in the database that the column's table exists in. If this cannot be determined the column is null.
- **BaseTableName**: The name of the database table that this column belongs to. If this cannot be determined the column is null.
- **BaseColumnName**: The name of the column in the database table. This is irrespective of how the Command object is used to rename a column.

If you need to retrieve more-sophisticated schema information, please see Section 2.3, "Getting OLE DB Database Schema Information," in Chapter 2.

4.3 Putting It All Together

Now how can we put this all together to work in harmony? I wrote a simple Windows Forms application that lets the user browse the invoices for a customer. The application is shown in Figure 4.2.

You can download this example application from my Web site (www. adoguy.com/book). The following sections highlight how I am using the DataReader.

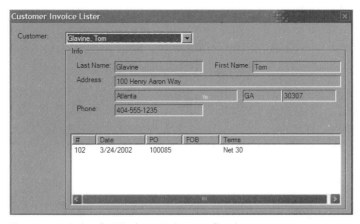

Figure 4.2: *A simple Windows Forms application*

4.3.1 **Database Access**

We could have approached getting all the information about the customers and their invoices in several ways. One way would be to get the entire `Customer` table as well as the entire `Invoice` table (where invoices are stored). By doing this we would have to match up the customers to their invoices. This complexity was unnecessary.

Ultimately, I wrote a query that would get all the information we needed in one resultset. What we need is to have the query select each of the fields that we need from the `Customer` and `Invoice` tables. Here is the `SELECT` portion of the query:

```
SELECT Customer.CustomerID, FirstName, LastName, HomePhone,
       Address, City, State, Zip, DOB,
       InvoiceNumber, InvoiceDate, FOB, PO, Terms
```

Note that the only field that I have qualified with a table name is the `CustomerID` field because it exists in more than one table. Because we are asking the database to give us data from more than one table, we need to join the tables together. This `JOIN` looks like this:

```
FROM Customer
   JOIN Invoice on Customer.CustomerID = Invoice.CustomerID
```

Last of all, in order to allow us to construct our objects in an orderly fashion, we need to add an `ORDER BY` clause to make sure that customers' invoices are not intermingled. To do this, we add `ORDER BY Customer.CustomerID, Invoice.InvoiceID`. Here is the query in its entirety:

```
SELECT Customer.CustomerID, FirstName, LastName, HomePhone,
       Address, City, State, Zip, DOB,
       InvoiceNumber, InvoiceDate, FOB, PO, Terms
   FROM Customer
     JOIN Invoice on Customer.CustomerID = Invoice.CustomerID
   ORDER BY Customer.CustomerID, Invoice.InvoiceID
```

4.3.2 **Data Objects**

I decided early on that I wanted to create classes that represented both the customers and their invoices. These classes would simply store the basic information that I was retrieving from the database. Because I wanted to use a DataReader to get the information, this would be an in-memory copy of the data so that I could read the data and close the database as soon as I read all the data in.

The other requirements were that I wanted the objects to use the DataReader to construct themselves and I wanted them to be managed provider–unspecific. To achieve this, I used constructors that took an `IDataReader` interface so that I could change the managed provider if necessary. I was able to pass this `IDataReader` interface throughout the object hierarchy to allow for the objects to be constructed straight from the DataReader.

4.3.2.1 *The* `Customer` *Class*

We start with the `Customer` class. It would contain demographic data about the customer straight from the database. In addition, the `Customer` class needed to hold a list of all the customer's invoices. The `InvoiceList` class serves this purpose and is described in Listing 4.16.

After spending some time getting this class right, I realized that I wanted to use a combo box to store all the customers. To customize the look of the customer's name, I overrode the `ToString()` method of the `Object` class to return the first and last name of the customer. When I insert `Customer` objects into a combo box, it automatically calls `ToString()` on the object to determine what to show in the user interface. Listing 4.13 shows the `Customer` class.

Listing 4.13: *Customer Class*

```
public class Customer
{

  public Customer(IDataReader rdr)
  {

    // If the column is not null, get the member data
    // from the DataReader
    CustomerID = Field.GetGuid(rdr,     "CustomerID");
    LastName =   Field.GetString(rdr,   "LastName");
    FirstName =  Field.GetString(rdr,   "FirstName");
    HomePhone =  Field.GetString(rdr,   "HomePhone");
```

```
            Address =       Field.GetString(rdr,    "Address");
            City =          Field.GetString(rdr,    "City");
            State =         Field.GetString(rdr,    "State");
            Zip =           Field.GetString(rdr,    "Zip");
            DOB =           Field.GetDateTime(rdr,  "DOB");

            // Create the BookList
            Invoices = new InvoiceList(rdr);
        }
        // Member data
        public Guid      CustomerID;
        public string    LastName;
        public string    FirstName;
        public string    HomePhone;
        public string    Address;
        public string    City;
        public string    State;
        public string    Zip;
        public DateTime DOB;
        public InvoiceList Invoices;

        // Override object.ToString() to support formatting of
        // the name in the ComboBox
        public override string ToString()
        {
          return LastName + ", " + FirstName;
        }
    }
```

4.3.2.2 *The* `CustomerList` *Class*

The `CustomerList` class is a thin wrapper around the `ArrayList` class to provide a simple sequential collection for storing the customers. The reason I wrapped the class was to provide a constructor that would take a DataReader, and therefore be able to read itself from a DataReader. Listing 4.14 is the `CustomerList` class.

Listing 4.14: *CustomerList Class*

```
// Wrapper for ArrayList to support creation
// from a DataReader
public class CustomerList : ArrayList
{

  public CustomerList(IDataReader rdr)
  {
```

```
      // Add each customer to the collection
      while (rdr.Read())
      {
        Customer cust = new Customer(rdr);
        Add(cust);
      }
    }
}
```

4.3.2.3 *The* Invoice *Class*

The Invoice class is modeled much like the Customer class. It is a simple class that holds the information about a single invoice for a customer. In the user interface for this utility I decided to use a ListView to show a small grid of the invoices. The most efficient way to construct each of the lines in the ListView was to generate an array. I decided to let my Invoice class do this for me, using the ToStringArray() method of that class. Listing 4.15 is the Invoice class.

Listing 4.15: *Invoice Class*

```
public class Invoice
{

  public Invoice(IDataReader rdr)
  {

    // If the columns are not null, then fill our
    // Invoice Info
    InvoiceID     = Field.GetGuid(rdr,     "InvoiceID");
    InvoiceNumber = Field.GetInt32(rdr,    "InvoiceNumber");
    InvoiceDate   = Field.GetDateTime(rdr, "InvoiceDate");
    PO            = Field.GetString(rdr,   "PO");
    FOB           = Field.GetString(rdr,   "FOB");
    Terms         = Field.GetString(rdr,   "Terms");

  }

  // Our Data...it is public in case we need to
  // access it directly
  public Guid       InvoiceID;
  public Int32      InvoiceNumber;
  public DateTime   InvoiceDate;
  public string     PO;
  public string     FOB;
  public string     Terms;
```

```
    public string[] ToStringArray()
    {
        // Create an array of strings for the book info so we
        // can more easily show them in a ListView
        string[] values = new string[6];
        values[0] = InvoiceNumber.ToString();
        values[1] = InvoiceDate.ToString();
        values[2] = PO;
        values[3] = FOB;
        values[4] = Terms;
        return values;
    }
}
```

4.3.2.4   *The* `InvoiceList` *Class*

The `InvoiceList` class (like the `CustomerList` above) is a simple wrapper around the `ArrayList` class to support construction from an `IDataReader`. The important piece of code in this class is how I handled the adding of the invoices. If you look back to the query we are using, you'll notice that every row has the customer information as well as the information about the invoices. Both of these are used to add the invoices for a specific customer. In the beginning of the constructor I cache the customer ID (`CustomerID`). In the `do . . . while` construct, I add all the invoices, as long as the customer ID of the row matches the cached customer ID. You may notice that when I cache the customer ID, I choose not to check for a null field. This is because the customer ID is the table primary key. If the customer ID were null, that would indicate an unexpected and unrecoverable error, so if the field is null, the thrown exception is appropriate. Listing 4.16 is the `InvoiceList` class.

Listing 4.16: *InvoiceList Class*

```
public class InvoiceList : ArrayList
{

    public InvoiceList(IDataReader rdr)
    {
        // Cache the current customer
        Guid customerID = rdr.GetGuid(
                            rdr.GetOrdinal("CustomerID"));
```

```
  // Add new invoice for the customer until the customer
  // changes or we reach the end of the DataReader
  do
  {
    Invoice inv = new Invoice(rdr);
    Add(inv);
  }
  while (rdr.Read() &&
    customerID == rdr.GetGuid(
                        rdr.GetOrdinal("CustomerID")));

  }

}
```

4.3.3 The Windows Forms Code

Now that we have seen the query and the classes that will hold the data, let's look at the code that actually is used to construct the object model, as shown in Listing 4.17.

Listing 4.17: *Windows Forms Code for Our Example*

```
// Required for Windows Form Designer support
InitializeComponent();

// Our Query
string query =
  "SELECT Customer.CustomerID, FirstName, LastName, " +
  "       HomePhone, Address, City, State, Zip, DOB, " +
  "       InvoiceNumber, InvoiceDate, FOB, PO, Terms " +
  " FROM Customer " +
  "   JOIN Invoice on Customer.CustomerID = " +
  "        Invoice.CustomerID " +
  "  ORDER BY Customer.CustomerID, Invoice.InvoiceID ";
// Attach to the database and execute the query
SqlConnection conn = new SqlConnection(
                    "Server=localhost;" +
                    "Database=ADONET;" +
                    "Integrated Security=true;");
conn.Open();

// Make a new command for our query
SqlCommand cmd = conn.CreateCommand();
cmd.CommandText = query;
```

```
// Get the DataReader
SqlDataReader rdr =
  cmd.ExecuteReader(CommandBehavior.KeyInfo |
  CommandBehavior.CloseConnection);

// Use the DataReader to construct our object model
customerList = new CustomerList(rdr);

// Clean up the DataReader, we are done with it
rdr.Close();

// Fill the combobox
cbCustomers.Items.AddRange(customerList.ToArray());

// Set the selected to the first item
// in the Combo Box
cbCustomers.SelectedIndex = 0;
```

Because we have put together a decent object model, the construction is accomplished by simply creating a new `CustomerList` object and passing in the DataReader. Feel free to download the code from my Web site to see it in action.

4.4   Conclusion

At this point you should understand how powerful this "fire hose" mentality is. Because ADO.NET has abstracted the forward-only cursors into an entirely separate type of entity (the DataReader), reading data with the fire hose should be more natural than in older data access layers. In addition, you should understand how to use DataReaders to write simple data access for your own classes. As we enter Part II, you will build on this knowledge to see how the DataSet fits into this overall scheme.

PART II
All about DataSets

■ 5 ■
Constructing DataSets

W<small>HAT THE HECK</small> are DataSets anyway? Try not to get too hung up on the buzz and complication of disconnected data. The DataSet is simply an in-memory relational data structure. But how can that help you in your day-to-day work? If you remember my soap-box ranting about the cost of network roundtrips and database connections, you may start to understand that holding the data and rules about that data in the client or middle tier can reduce the cost of applying those rules to the data.

5.1 What Is a DataSet?

If you are familiar with other data access layers, you may try to find an object from them that is analogous with the DataSet. This is a futile search. Is the DataSet about database development, XML development, or something entirely different? The DataSet has been described as:

- A disconnected set of database data
- An in-memory database
- A complex, relational data structure with built-in support for XML serialization

Frankly, the DataSet is all three of these. The DataSet's role in ADO.NET is to provide disconnected storage for database data and to provide some in-memory database facilities to .NET. The DataSet is simply a collection of data structures that is used for disconnected data storage.

5.1.1 DataSet Composition

The DataSet is made up of a number of related data structures. Conceptually, the DataSet is a complete set of relational data. Within the DataSet are five major objects that can be stored:

- **DataTable**: A rectangular set of data organized into columns and rows. This is analogous with ADO's Recordset or OLE DB's RowSet.
- **DataColumn**: A collection of rules that describes what data is allowed to be stored in a DataRow.
- **DataRow**: A collection of data that makes up a single row of the DataTable's data. This is the actual data storage.
- **Constraint**: A rule that determines the admissibility of certain data into the DataTable. This is used to enforce business rules in the DataSet.
- **DataRelation**: A description of how different DataTables are associated. This is a navigable link between tables. In most cases a DataConstraint will accompany DataRelations to enforce the relationship.

As Figure 5.1 illustrates, within the DataSet is a collection of one or more DataTables. Within each DataTable are collections of DataRows, DataColumns, and Constraints and two collections of DataRelations. The collections of DataRelations within the DataTable correspond to the parent relations and the child relations, which form the linkage between DataTables that is the basis for their relationship. The DataRelations collection within the DataSet is an aggregate view of all the DataRelations in all DataTables.

5.1.2 The DataSet and Managed Providers

In previous chapters, we explored methods for interacting with data stores (usually databases). From this perspective it would be easy to assume that there is some relation between the DataSet and data access. Unfortunately, this assumption would be completely wrong. Microsoft designed the namespaces to try to clarify this disconnect:

- **System.Data**: Contains classes that make up the DataSet as well as the interfaces that are used to define managed providers

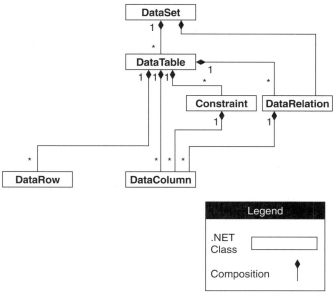

Figure 5.1: *The structure of a DataSet*

- **System.Data.Common**: Base managed provider classes and interfaces
- **System.Data.SqlClient**: The SQL Server Managed Provider
- **System.Data.OleDb**: The OLE DB Managed Provider
- **System.Data.Odbc**: The ODBC Managed Provider
- **System.Data.OracleClient**: The Oracle Managed Provider

Unlike older database access layers from Microsoft, the DataSet does not have any internal knowledge of the data source for the data. The DataSet is completely disconnected, not only from the data, but also from the knowledge of where the data originated. We must have something that connects the DataSet to data sources.

5.2 **Filling DataSets**

Because DataSets are not tied to database data in any way, you may think of DataSets as simply relational data stores. There is no requirement that you use database data to fill in a DataSet. In practice, there are three ways to construct DataSets: from a DataAdapter (usually from a database), from XML, and by constructing the DataSet manually.

5.2.1 Introducing DataAdapters

DataAdapters are the glue that connects DataSets to the underlying data stores. With DataAdapter, you can fill the DataSet and update the data store from the DataSet. DataAdapters are essentially meta-Command objects. The `DataAdapter` is composed of up to four `Command` objects. Each of these `Command` objects does a specific job:

- **`SelectCommand`**: Retrieves data from the data store
- **`InsertCommand`**: Adds new records created in the DataSet to the underlying data store
- **`UpdateCommand`**: Changes existing records in the data store based on changes in the DataSet
- **`DeleteCommand`**: Deletes existing records in the data store based on deletions in the DataSet

The DataAdapter is used whenever the DataSet needs to interact directly with the data source. The important concept here is that the DataAdapter holds `Command` objects for each of the basic database operations, SELECT, INSERT, UPDATE, and DELETE. The idea behind the DataAdapter is for it to be the bridge between the DataSet and the database. If the DataAdapter is that bridge, then it must have the ability to do all the necessary database operations. As we continue to discuss the DataSet throughout this chapter and the rest of Part 2 of this book, you will see how the DataAdapter is used as a bridge.

One important job of the DataAdapter is to minimize the time a connection is open. You will notice that throughout our use of DataAdapters, we never open and close the connection associated with our DataAdapter. The DataAdapter knows that the connection needs to be as short-lived as possible and handles all opening and closing of the connection. If we are using an already opened connection when we use our DataAdapter, it will preserve the state of the connection (it will not open or close the connection).

5.2.2 Creating a DataSet from a Database

In the most basic case, you would use the DataSet to hold a single table, as shown in Listing 5.1.

Listing 5.1: *Creating a DataSet from the Database*

```
. . .

// Create a Command object to query the entire Customer
table
SqlCommand cmd = conn.CreateCommand();
cmd.CommandText = "SELECT * FROM CUSTOMER";

// Create a DataAdapter for use with filling a DataSet
SqlDataAdapter dataAdapter = new SqlDataAdapter(cmd);

// Create your blank DataSet
DataSet dataSet = new DataSet();

// Fill it with the DataAdapter
dataAdapter.Fill(dataSet);


. . .
```

This example simply creates a DataSet with the results of the CUSTOMER table. You should be familiar with the creation of the Connection and Command objects by now, so we can ignore that and walk through the highlighted code:

1. We create an instance of the SqlDataAdapter class. SqlDataAdapter is a specialized class that is a container for commands that are responsible for reading and writing data to and from the database.
2. Next we need to create a new instance of the DataSet. After creation, the DataSet is completely empty.
3. Lastly, we call the Fill() method of the DataAdapter to fill the DataSet with data from the query that we defined in the earlier Command object.

This very simple example will fill a DataSet with a single table based on a single SQL query. In this chapter we will cover the many complexities associated with creating all sorts of DataSets; however, we are not going to cover any database updates. Please see Chapter 8 for information on updating the database.

5.2.2.1 *Multiple DataTables*

You will soon find out that the real power of the DataSet is in its use as an in-memory relational data store. In that case, you will need to create DataSets with more than one DataTable. You can do this in several different ways. Let's walk through each of these and discuss their merits and pitfalls. Listing 5.2 shows how we can use batch queries[1] to retrieve more than one table from the database.

Listing 5.2: *Using a Batch Query*

```
. . .

// Create a query string
// In order to get all tables, we are using a batch query
// that returns multiple resultsets
string query = "";
query += "SELECT * FROM CUSTOMER;";
query += "SELECT * FROM INVOICE;";
query += "SELECT * FROM INVOICEITEM;";

// Create a DataAdapter to retrieve the data
SqlDataAdapter dataAdapter = new SqlDataAdapter(query,
                                                conn);

// Create and fill the DataSet
DataSet dataSet = new DataSet();
dataAdapter.Fill(dataSet);
```

This is fine except for the fact that the tables will be automatically assigned generic names. In this example, the DataTables are named `Table`, `Table1`, and `Table2`, respectively. These names work, but are not very descriptive. If you want to have meaningful table names, you can use a DataAdapter per table to fill the DataSet, as shown in Listing 5.3.

---

1. Please note that not all database vendors support batch queries. Please make sure to read the entire section to see all of the different methods of filling multi-table DataSets. Other methods are more database vendor–independent.

Listing 5.3: *Filling a DataSet with Meaningful Table Names*

```
. . .

// Create a DataAdapter for each of the tables we're filling
SqlDataAdapter daCustomers = new
  SqlDataAdapter("SELECT * FROM CUSTOMER;",
  conn);
SqlDataAdapter daInvoices = new
  SqlDataAdapter("SELECT * FROM INVOICE;",
  conn);
SqlDataAdapter daInvoiceItems = new
  SqlDataAdapter("SELECT * FROM INVOICEITEM;",
  conn);

// Create your blank DataSet
DataSet dataSet = new DataSet();

// Fill the DataSet with each DataAdapter
// and assign the DataTable name
daCustomers.Fill(dataSet, "Customers");
daInvoices.Fill(dataSet, "Invoices");
daInvoiceItems.Fill(dataSet, "InvoiceItems");
```

We now have our tables named significantly, but we're doing three database roundtrips, which is inefficient. If you want to use a batch query and want significant DataTable names, you will have to use the `TableMappings` property of the DataAdapter.

5.2.2.2 *Using* `TableMappings`

The `DataAdapter`'s `TableMappings` property is a collection of `Data-TableMapping` objects. `DataTableMappings` are used to tell the Data-Adapter how to name DataTables within a DataSet and how to name columns within each table. To use the `TableMappings` property to name the tables, just add mappings to the `TableMappings` with the old table name and the new table name, as shown in Listing 5.4.

Listing 5.4: *Using TableMappings*

```
...

// Create a query string
// In order to get all tables, we are using a batch query
// that returns multiple resultsets
string query = "";
query += "SELECT * FROM CUSTOMER;";
query += "SELECT * FROM INVOICE;";
query += "SELECT * FROM INVOICEITEM;";

// Create a DataAdapter to retrieve the data
SqlDataAdapter dataAdapter = new SqlDataAdapter(query,
                                                conn);
// Set up table mappings
dataAdapter.TableMappings.Add("Table", "Customers");
dataAdapter.TableMappings.Add("Table1", "Invoices");
dataAdapter.TableMappings.Add("Table2", "InvoiceItems");

// Create your blank DataSet
DataSet dataSet = new DataSet();

// Fill the DataSet with each DataAdapter
dataAdapter.Fill(dataSet);
```

As we discussed earlier, the `DataAdapter.Fill()` call creates tables named `Table`, `Table1`, and `Table2`. Because we know this is the algorithm, we simply have to create mappings to rename `Table` to `Customers`, `Table1` to `Invoices`, and `Table2` to `InvoiceItems`. You can also tell the `DataAdapter.Fill()` method to name your DataTables with a more useful name by including a table name, as shown in Listing 5.5.

Listing 5.5: *Using TableMappings while Filling the DataSet with a Custom Table Name*

```
...

// Create a query string
// In order to get all tables, we are using a batch query
// that returns multiple resultsets
string query = "";
query += "SELECT * FROM CUSTOMER;";
query += "SELECT * FROM INVOICE;";
query += "SELECT * FROM INVOICEITEM;";
```

```
// Create a DataAdapter to retrieve the data
SqlDataAdapter dataAdapter = new SqlDataAdapter(query,
                                                conn);

// Set up TableMappings
dataAdapter.TableMappings.Add("ADONET", "Customers");
dataAdapter.TableMappings.Add("ADONET1", "Invoices");
dataAdapter.TableMappings.Add("ADONET2", "InvoiceItems");

// Create your blank DataSet
DataSet dataSet = new DataSet();

// Fill the DataSet while using the temporary name
dataAdapter.Fill(dataSet, "ADONET");
```

Here we tell the `DataAdapter.Fill()` method to name our tables with
`"ADONET"` and when we execute the batch query, it names them `ADONET`,
`ADONET1`, and `ADONET2`. In effect, when you call `DataAdapter.Fill()`
without specifying a table name, you are defaulting the name to `Table`. In
practice, you will not really need to do both `TableMappings` and specifying the name in the `Fill` command.

In addition to naming the tables, the `TableMappings` property can be
used to change the name of the columns from the original queries to different columns in the resulting DataTables. To facilitate this, the `Data-
TableMapping` class contains a collection of `DataColumnMapping` objects
that are used to map between field names in the query and field names in
the DataSet (see Listing 5.6).

Listing 5.6: *Using ColumnMappings*

```
...

// Create a query string
// In order to get all tables, we are using a batch query
// that returns multiple resultsets
string query = "";
query += "SELECT * FROM CUSTOMER;";
query += "SELECT * FROM INVOICE;";
query += "SELECT * FROM INVOICEITEM;";

// Set up table mappings
dataAdapter.TableMappings.Add("ADONET", "Customers");
```

```
dataAdapter.TableMappings.Add("ADONET1", "Invoices");
dataAdapter.TableMappings.Add("ADONET2", "InvoiceItems");

// Set up column mappings
dataAdapter.TableMappings["ADONET"].
                    ColumnMappings.Add("CustomerID", "ID");
dataAdapter.TableMappings["ADONET1"].
                    ColumnMappings.Add("InvoiceID", "ID");
dataAdapter.TableMappings["ADONET2"].
                    ColumnMappings.Add("InvoiceItemID", "ID");

// Create your blank DataSet
DataSet dataSet = new DataSet();

// Fill the DataSet with each DataAdapter
dataAdapter.Fill(dataSet, "ADONET");
```

In Listing 5.6, you can see that we are telling the DataAdapter to make sure that the CustomerID field in the Customer table and the InvoiceID field in the Invoice table are both renamed to ID. The only requirement for renaming columns in a DataTable is that a DataTableMapping exists for the DataTable. If you have no need to use a DataTableMapping for your DataTable, you can create an empty DataTableMapping to support the DataColumnMapping, as shown in Listing 5.7.

Listing 5.7: *Using ColumnMappings without Changing Table Names*

```
...

// Create a DataAdapter for each of the tables we're filling
SqlDataAdapter dataAdapter = new SqlDataAdapter(
  "SELECT * FROM CUSTOMER",
  conn);

// Add a no-op DataTableMapping
dataAdapter.TableMappings.Add("Customers", "Customers");

// Setup Column Mappings
dataAdapter.TableMappings["Customers"].
                          ColumnMappings.Add("CustomerID",
                                             "ID");

// Create your blank DataSet
DataSet dataSet = new DataSet();
```

```
// Fill the DataSet with each DataAdapter
dataAdapter.Fill(dataSet, "Customers");
```

In this example, we are creating a new `DataTableMapping` object that is not renaming the table at all. Please note that for this to work, the table name used in the `TableMappings.Add()` call must be the same as the one used in the `DataAdapter.Fill()` call.

5.2.3 Creating a DataSet from XML

Times have changed and we need to be able to integrate our data with non-database data. To create a DataSet from XML, you will avoid managed providers completely and tell the DataSet to read an XML file or URL directly, as shown in Listing 5.8.

Listing 5.8: *Loading a DataSet with an XML Document*

```
// Fill the DataSet straight from a file or URL
DataSet dsFile = new DataSet();
dsFile.ReadXml(@"c:\test.xml");

// Fill the DataSet from a TextReader
// (from which StringReader derives)
DataSet dsTextReader = new DataSet();
StringReader textReader =
          new StringReader("<xml><foo>hello</foo></xml>");
dsTextReader.ReadXml(textReader);
textReader.Close();

// Fill the DataSet from an XmlReader
// (from which XmlTextReader is derived)
DataSet dsXmlReader = new DataSet();
XmlTextReader xmlReader = new XmlTextReader(@"c:\test.xml");
dsXmlReader.ReadXml(xmlReader);
xmlReader.Close();

// Fill the DataSet from a Stream
// (from which FileStream is derived)
DataSet dsStream = new DataSet();
FileStream fs =
          new FileStream(@"c:\test.xml", FileMode.Open);
dsXmlReader.ReadXml(fs);
fs.Close();
```

The `ReadXml()` method will take any number of inputs: XML text, file path, XmlReader, StringReader, or even a `Stream` object.

Because DataSets are a relational construct, it may seem odd to create a DataSet from XML, because XML is naturally hierarchical. The DataSet may not be the perfect container for XML data, but commingling your database data with XML data in the DataSet is a powerful tool. To commingle your data with XML data, you will need to use a DataAdapter to fill some of the tables, and `ReadXml()` to fill other data, as shown in Listing 5.9.

Listing 5.9: *Commingling XML Data and Database Data*

```
. . .

// Create a query string
// In order to get all tables, we are using a batch query
// that returns multiple resultsets
string query = "";
query += "SELECT * FROM CUSTOMER;";
query += "SELECT * FROM INVOICE;";
query += "SELECT * FROM INVOICEITEM;";

// Create a DataAdapter to retrieve the data
SqlDataAdapter dataAdapter = new SqlDataAdapter(query,
                                                conn);

// Create and fill the DataSet from the database
DataSet dataSet = new DataSet();

// Add our database data
dataAdapter.Fill(dataSet);

// Add the XML data to the DataSet
dataSet.ReadXml(@"products.xml",
        XmlReadMode.InferSchema);

. . .
```

Here we read in some data from the database and then get some XML to augment our DataSet's data. We are using the `XmlReadMode.Infer-Schema` directive when we call `ReadXml()` because by default, when you read XML into a DataSet with data in it, the `ReadXml()` method will try to match the schema of the XML file to the current schema. Because the

`Product` table does not exist in the DataSet when we call this, if we do not instruct the DataSet to infer the schema, it will silently fail to add the XML data to the DataSet. We could have gotten around this by loading the XML first because by omitting the `InferSchema` directive, the DataSet would have created the schema because there was no initial schema. The default behavior of adding the schema only if it does not exist is what makes this a bit confusing. If the XML we were reading was simply more rows in tables that already existed, then we would not have needed the `Infer-Schema` directive.

Please see Chapter 9 for more information on XML integration with DataSets.

5.2.4 Creating a DataSet Programmatically

On some occasions you may want to craft a DataSet programmatically. Creating DataTables and filling them with data will help give you some insight into how DataSets are constituted. All we need to do is create the DataSet from the top down. We create the DataSet, add a DataTable, and set the schema information to the DataTable by creating DataColumns. Finally, we add data to the DataTable by adding rows to the DataTable, as shown in Listing 5.10.

Listing 5.10: *Creating a DataSet Programmatically*

```
// Create our DataSet instance
DataSet dataSet = new DataSet();

// Ask the DataSet's Tables collection for a
// new DataTable object
DataTable dataTable = dataSet.Tables.Add("Pitchers");

// Add some columns (schema information)
dataTable.Columns.Add("pitcher_id",
                    System.Type.GetType("System.Int64"));
dataTable.Columns.Add("lname",
                    System.Type.GetType("System.String"));
dataTable.Columns.Add("fname",
                    System.Type.GetType("System.String"));

// Add some data
object[] aSmoltz = {1, "Smoltz", "John"};
object[] aMaddux = {2, "Maddux", "Greg"};
```

```
object[] aGlavine = {3, "Glavine", "Tom"};
dataTable.Rows.Add( aSmoltz );
dataTable.Rows.Add( aMaddux );
dataTable.Rows.Add( aGlavine );
```

After all of this is complete, we can start dealing with the DataSet just like we created it from a database or from XML.

5.3 Defining DataSet Schema

Isn't schema great? Or is your schema getting in your way? The job of database schema is to make sure that all the data in your database are consistent with some set of rules. The problem has always been that as a programmer you have to mimic those same rules in custom code to make sure that the data that are ultimately stored in the database do not throw errors in the user's face. The DataSet can be made to enforce those rules without writing complicated custom code to do it.

After loading data into the DataSet, you are only half done with constructing the DataSet. In most examples of DataSets that I have seen, they seem to miss this important second piece. What is DataSet schema after all? After you have loaded the DataSet with data, the tables will already have the minimum of schema, mainly tables, column names, and column types. Settling for this minimum schema can make your job much harder. The missing pieces are keys, constraints, relationships, and triggers.

To make our DataSet behave like a database, we will need to set keys, relationships, constraints, and triggers. We can use a few different methods to do this: we can have a DataAdapter infer our schema from the database queries we are doing, we can load an XSD file that contains our schema, or we can create the schema programmatically. We will explore all these different ways of adding schema to DataSets in the subsequent sections.

5.3.1 Why Use Database Schema in Your DataSet?

In every DataSet that contains data, you will have a certain amount of schema. DataColumns will exist in each DataTable that contain the rules for what each column of each DataRow can hold, but what about the schema that you already have in your database? It may not be apparent

Does Your Database Have Enough Schema?

I have been in database development for longer than I care to admit. In that time I have had the pleasure to review hundreds of database designs. In a majority of cases, the only schema that seemed to be designed was the minimum needed to get the job done. What is the minimum? That depends on the case, but usually just the table and column definition. Usually primary keys are defined, too (but not always). When I have delved deeper into the actual application code, I have noticed that these database systems have written all sorts of code to do the work that the database could do for them. I do not mean to be a harsh critic. In fact, I have been guilty of this from time to time, myself.

How do you know if your database has enough schema? If you ever end up writing code (ADO.NET's DataSet notwithstanding) to handle relationships, triggers, constraints, or other database schema facilities, then take another look at your database schema design.

My point is that you should really let the database (or the DataSet by extension) do the work that it was intended to help with. For example:

• If you write code to make sure that all the rows in a table are unique, add a primary key to your table.

• If you write code to make sure an individual column in a table is unique, add a constraint to your table.

• If you write code to link parent-child tables, create a relationship.

• If you write code to make sure that related rows are modified or deleted when the parent changes, enable cascading updates and deletes in your relationships.

• If you write code to poll the database for changes, add a trigger to your database.

• If all of your calls to the database use many JOINed queries, create views.

For more information about how schema can help you, please consult any of Joe Celko's great books (www.celko.com/books.htm).

why you would want keys, relationships, constraints, and triggers in your DataSet, especially if you already have that same schema in the database. The benefit of creating the same schema in the DataSet is that you can find data problems long before you ever attempt to save the data to the database. In this way, you will reduce the number of roundtrips to the database as well as eliminate roundtrips when the result is only going to be a schema violation. The earlier we can find violations of the schema, the easier it is for us to fix them.

5.3.2 Inferring Schema with the DataAdapter

Whenever you fill a DataSet with a DataAdapter, your DataSet needs to have the DataColumn schema in place to hold the new rows. If your DataSet does not already contain the schema, the DataAdapter infers the schema from the results of the `SelectCommand` property. You have some control over how this inference happens. The DataAdapter contains a property called `MissingSchemaAction`, which you can set to determine what you want to do when the schema for your DataAdapter does not exist in the DataSet. The possible values are:

- **Add**: Adds all the columns to the schema that are necessary to let the DataAdapter fill the DataSet. This is the default value.
- **AddWithKey**: Adds all the columns to the schema that are necessary to let the DataAdapter fill the DataSet. In addition, the DataAdapter attempts to retrieve key information from the database and set the primary keys of DataTables that it fills. For the OLE DB Managed Provider, the underlying OLE DB Provider must support this functionality. See the MSDN documentation for `MissingSchemaAction` enumeration for more information.
- **Error**: An exception is generated if schema needed to add data from the DataAdapter does not already exist in the DataSet.
- **Ignore**: Extra columns that the DataAdapter knows about but are not in the DataSet's schema are ignored and lost.

These let you specify how you want to handle the fact that the schema is missing. In practice, I find it easier to specify the schema ahead of time and set the `MissingSchemaAction` to `Error`. This way, if a DataAdapter attempts to fill in data that I am not expecting, I will see the error instead of phantom rows appearing that I had no intention of supporting. (See Listing 5.11.)

Listing 5.11: *Filling a DataSet with MissingSchemaAction.Error*

```
// Create a DataAdapter for each of the tables we're filling
SqlDataAdapter dataAdapter =
          new SqlDataAdapter("SELECT * FROM CUSTOMER",conn);

// Tell the DataAdapter to throw an error if it finds
// missing schema
dataAdapter.MissingSchemaAction = MissingSchemaAction.Error;

// Create your blank DataSet
DataSet dataSet = new DataSet();

// An error will be thrown when we attempt to fill the
// DataSet because the DataSet is empty
dataAdapter.Fill(dataSet, "Customers");
```

If you want to let the DataAdapter fill the schema, you can do so using the `DataAdapter.FillSchema()` method. This method will infer the schema from the database in the same way that it would normally, except that it allows the schema to be created ahead of time. This can be a benefit if you are trying to create a DataSet to be filled later or that will be filled by user data, but that is not necessarily meant to hold data that was queried from the database. The `FillSchema()` method takes a DataSet or Data-Table and a `SchemaType`. You specify the `SchemaType` to tell the Data-Adapter whether to use the `TableMappings` to fill the schema (by using `SchemaType.Mapped`), or to ignore those mappings and fill the schema based on the schema contained in the database (by using `SchemaType.Source`). Because you have to take an active step to actually add `Table-Mappings` to your DataAdapter, the `SchemaType` should almost always be `Mapped`. If you wanted to ignore `TableMappings`, you usually just would not create any. The `MissingSchemaAction` is still used to tell the `Fill-Schema()` method how to add the schema, as shown in Listing 5.12.

Listing 5.12: *Filling a DataSet with MissingSchemaAction.AddWithKey*

```
...


// Create a DataAdapter for each of the tables we're filling
SqlDataAdapter dataAdapter =
          new SqlDataAdapter("SELECT * FROM CUSTOMER",conn);

// Tell the DataAdapter to add the Schema and include the
// primary key information
dataAdapter.MissingSchemaAction =
                              MissingSchemaAction.AddWithKey;

// Create your blank DataSet
DataSet dataSet = new DataSet();

// Create a new DataTable in the DataSet and call it
// "Customers"
dataAdapter.FillSchema(dataSet,
                       SchemaType.Mapped,
                       "Customers");
```

5.3.3 Using XSDs to Define DataSet Schema

As you will soon see, creating complete schema can take a lot of code. For performance and maintenance reasons, it would be good to have a way to serialize DataSet schema so that it could be managed separately from the code that fills the DataSet. You can accomplish this by creating your DataSets and saving an .XSD file that contains the schema for the DataSet. Whenever you instantiate the DataSet, you can use that .XSD file to set up the schema for your DataSet, as shown in Listing 5.13.

Listing 5.13: *Specifying DataSet Schema with an .XSD File*

```
...


// Create a DataAdapter for each of the tables we're filling
SqlDataAdapter dataAdapter =
          new SqlDataAdapter("SELECT * FROM CUSTOMER",conn);

// Tell the DataAdapter to throw an error if it finds
// missing schema
dataAdapter.MissingSchemaAction = MissingSchemaAction.Error;

// Create your blank DataSet
DataSet dataSet = new DataSet();
```

```
// Fill the schema from an XSD file
dataSet.ReadXmlSchema(@"customer.xsd");

// No Error should be thrown because our customer.xsd should
// contain an accurate schema for Customers
dataAdapter.Fill(dataSet, "Customers");
```

Note that this loads the schema for the entire DataSet. You cannot set up modular .XSD files to fill the schema for each DataTable separately. For more information on how the DataSet is integrated with XML, see Chapter 9.

5.3.4 Programmatically Creating DataSet Schema

There will be times when setting up the complete schema will require you to write code to actually define the schema. It may appear that creating your DataSet schema programmatically is a little daunting because of the sheer amount of code required, but there are alternatives to writing all that code. At some point, you are going to want to understand how it all comes together inside the DataSet.

In addition, even though the samples in this chapter do not create classes that inherit directly from DataSets, in practice, I would suggest doing just that. Once you create new classes that inherit from DataSet, you can create your schema during construction, as shown in Listing 5.14.

Listing 5.14: *Inheriting from the DataSet Class*

```
class PragmaticDataSet : DataSet
{
  public PragmaticDataSet()
  {
    // Create your Schema here
  }

  . . .

}
```

5.3.4.1 *Primary Keys*

Just like in the database, you can set a primary key for a table. The primary key is used to make sure no duplicate rows ever are entered into a table. By setting the `PrimaryKey` property of the DataTable, we can be assured that the system will throw an exception if a duplicate key is added to the table. This is highly effective because we do not need to make a roundtrip to the database just to find out it is a duplicate record. Listing 5.15 shows how you would add a primary key.

Listing 5.15: *Creating Primary Keys*

```
...

// Create a DataAdapter for each of the tables we're filling
SqlDataAdapter daCustomers = new
                    SqlDataAdapter("SELECT * FROM CUSTOMER",
                                        conn);
SqlDataAdapter daInvoices = new
                    SqlDataAdapter("SELECT * FROM INVOICE",
                                        conn);
SqlDataAdapter daInvoiceItems = new
                SqlDataAdapter("SELECT * FROM INVOICEITEM",
                                        conn);

// Create your blank DataSet
DataSet dataSet = new DataSet();

// Fill the DataSet with each DataAdapter
daCustomers.Fill(dataSet, "Customers");
daInvoices.Fill(dataSet, "Invoices");
daInvoiceItems.Fill(dataSet, "InvoiceItems");

// Grab our tables for simplicity
DataTable customerTable    = dataSet.Tables["Customers"];
DataTable invoiceTable     = dataSet.Tables["Invoices"];
DataTable invoiceItemTable = dataSet.Tables["InvoiceItems"];

// Set up PrimaryKeys
customerTable.PrimaryKey = new DataColumn[]
            { customerTable.Columns["CustomerID"] };
invoiceTable.PrimaryKey = new DataColumn[]
            { invoiceTable.Columns["InvoiceID"] };
invoiceItemTable.PrimaryKey = new DataColumn[]
            { invoiceItemTable.Columns["InvoiceItemID"] };
```

You will notice that in Listing 5.15, the keys are set up as new arrays of DataColumns. This is because a key is really an array of DataColumns. In many situations a single column key is the norm, but there are cases where multicolumn keys are necessary. ADO.NET gets around handling these differently by insisting that a `PrimaryKey` is really an array of columns.

If you create a `PrimaryKey` for a DataTable that has data that violates the `PrimaryKey`, an `ArgumentException` is raised. You can catch this problem by catching the `ArgumentException`, as shown in Listing 5.16.

Listing 5.16: *Testing Primary Keys*

```
// Create a DataAdapter for the Customer table
SqlDataAdapter daCustomers = new
                  SqlDataAdapter("SELECT * FROM CUSTOMER",
                                 conn);

// Create your blank DataSet
DataSet dataSet = new DataSet();

// Fill the DataSet with each DataAdapter
daCustomers.Fill(dataSet, "Customers");

// Grab our table for simplicity
DataTable customerTable   = dataSet.Tables["Customers"];

// Add a duplicate row before we set the PrimaryKey to
// allow us to handle the error
customerTable.Rows.Add(customerTable.Rows[0].ItemArray);

try
{
  // Set up PrimaryKey
  customerTable.PrimaryKey = new DataColumn[]
                  { customerTable.Columns["CustomerID"] };
}
catch (ArgumentException ex)
{
  // Show the error. If we get this exception, we can be
  // certain it is because the PrimaryKey DataColumn(s)
  // is(are) not unique.
  Console.WriteLine("Column(s) in the PrimaryKey are " +
                  "not unique.");
  Console.WriteLine("  Exception Thrown:  {0}", ex.Message);
}
```

5.3.4.2 *Primary Key Strategies*

One of the first (and most important) decisions that will need to be made in database design is how to specify the primary key for a particular table. The three usual methodologies for single column primary keys are:

- **Auto-incremented value**: A column will contain a number that indicates the identity for the row. For every row that is added to the table, the number in this column is automatically incremented by some known amount (usually one). If you are going to use server-side auto-incremented keys in SQL Server, please see Chapter 8 for more information on how to handle this situation.
- **Unique name**: The key column contains some unique piece of information about the row. This usually is used with a piece of data that is guaranteed to be unique; for example, in a patient table you might use patients' social security numbers, or in a Web site user table you might use their e-mail addresses.
- **Globally Unique Identifier (GUID)**[2]: The key column contains a GUID that uniquely identifies the column.

All three of these approaches have their pros and cons. For use in a DataSet, I would suggest either unique names or GUIDs. The chief problem with auto-incremented columns in DataSets is that if you do not decide to have one (and only one) DataSet into which all inserts are made for a particular table, you are bound to have overlapped key values. If the keys are overlapped, you will need to change them (and all references to them) once you persist the new rows to the database. By using either GUIDs or unique names, you can avoid these pitfalls. This all assumes that you have control over the schema.

There are many occasions where you have to work with older systems. If this is the case and your database is using auto-incremented fields, do not try to use auto-incremented fields in your DataSet. You can rely on the database to create the IDs and return them during the update (see Chapter 8 for details on how to return identity from a database).

---

2. GUIDs are 128-bit numbers that are practically guaranteed to be unique. In the .NET Framework, the Guid class can be used to generate, parse, and read GUIDs.

5.3.4.3 *Creating Relationships*

Now that we have the primary key set, we will want to tell the DataSet that our tables are related. Most databases in use today (SQL Server, Oracle, Microsoft Access, DB2, and so on) are *relational* databases, which means that different sets of data are related to other pieces of data. In this case, our `Customer` table is related to our `Invoice` table, which, in turn, is related to the `InvoiceItem` table, which is also related to the `Product` table (see Figure 5.2).

So if we extend the above example we would add Listing 5.17 to set up the relationships.

Listing 5.17: *Creating Relationships*

```
. . .

// Set up relations

// Create the first relationship (between Invoices and
// InvoiceItems). We tell the relation to set up a
// constraint to make sure the relationship is created
// on a unique key
dataSet.Relations.Add( "Invoices_InvoiceItems",
  dataSet.Tables["Invoices"].Columns["InvoiceID"],
  dataSet.Tables["InvoiceItems"].Columns["InvoiceID"],
  true);

// Create the second relationship
// (between Customers and Invoices)
dataSet.Relations.Add( "Customers_Invoices",
  dataSet.Tables["Customers"].Columns["CustomerID"],
  dataSet.Tables["Invoices"].Columns["CustomerID"],
  true);
```

We add a new relation with the `DataRelationCollection.Add()` method. The first parameter is the name of the relation. The next two parameters are the parent and child columns to relate. Finally, the last parameter is a Boolean to determine whether to create a constraint for this relation. Creating a constraint tells the DataSet that you expect that the parent column's unique key will be in that DataTable.

But what happens if the key of the table is a multipart key? In this case, Listing 5.18 shows how you would create an array of the key columns.

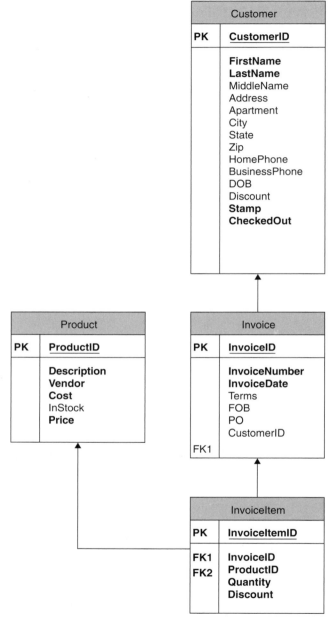

Figure 5.2: *The relationships among our four tables*

Listing 5.18: *Adding Multi-key Relationships*

```
. . .

// Create the array of parent keys
DataColumn[] aParentCols =
                    { ds.Tables["Table1"].Columns["key1"],
                      ds.Tables["Table1"].Columns["key2"]};

// Create the array of child keys
DataColumn[] aChildCols =
                    { ds.Tables["Table2"].Columns["key1"],
                      ds.Tables["Table2"].Columns["key2"]};

// Create a new relation based on the arrays of columns
ds.Relations.Add( "DualKeyRelation",
                  aParentCols,
                  aChildCols,
                  false);
```

5.3.4.4 *Constraints*

Constraints to a DataSet are rules that the DataSet must follow. There are two ready-to-use constraint types in ADO.NET:

- **UniqueConstraint**: This constraint makes sure each row is unique based on a column or set of columns.
- **ForeignKeyConstraint**: This constraint tells the DataSet that if a parent row is changed, then a child row in another table must follow a specific set of rules (such as cascade a delete).

These two constraint types are created when you set the PrimaryKey of a table and create relationships with constraints. Each ForeignKey-Constraint contains three different rules:

- **DeleteRule**: The behavior of the child rows when the parent row is deleted
- **UpdateRule**: The behavior of the child rows when the parent row is updated

- **AcceptRejectRule**: The rule that defines the behavior of changed and deleted rows when the AcceptChanges or RejectChanges methods are called on the DataSet, DataTable, or DataRow

The difference between these rules is that the DeleteRule and the UpdateRule are applied when the actual deleting and updating of rows occur in the DataSet. On the other hand, the AcceptRejectRule is applied only when the AcceptChanges and RejectChanges methods are called on the DataSet.

The DeleteRule and UpdateRule properties both hold a Rule enumeration. The values of the enumeration and their respective behaviors are:

- **Cascade**: The change to the parent row is duplicated on the child row. This is the default behavior.
- **None**: The change to the parent row will not have any discernable effect on the child row. This can leave orphaned rows in the child table.
- **SetDefault**: The change to the parent row causes the child rows to be changed to their default values. This option may leave orphaned rows in the child table, but when it orphans them, it changes the key involved in the constraint to the default value as defined in the schema.
- **SetNull**: The change to the parent row causes the child rows to be changed to DBNull values. Like SetDefault, this option may leave orphaned rows in the child table, but when it orphans them, it changes the key involved in the constraint to null.

The AcceptRejectRule enumeration has only a subset of the Delete-Rule/AcceptRule enumeration members: Cascade and None.

- **Cascade**: The change to the parent row is duplicated on the child row. This is the default behavior.
- **None**: The change to the parent row does not have any effect on the child row. This can leave orphaned rows in the child table.

If we take our earlier example, we can read out the state of the constraints (Listing 5.19 gives the entire code for clarity).

Listing 5.19: *Creating All the Schema*

```
...

// Create a DataAdapter for each of the tables we're filling
SqlDataAdapter daCustomers = new
  SqlDataAdapter("SELECT * FROM CUSTOMER;",
  conn);
SqlDataAdapter daInvoices = new
  SqlDataAdapter("SELECT * FROM INVOICE;",
  conn);
SqlDataAdapter daInvoiceItems = new
  SqlDataAdapter("SELECT * FROM INVOICEITEM;",
  conn);

// Create your blank DataSet
DataSet dataSet = new DataSet();

// Fill the DataSet with each DataAdapter
daCustomers.Fill(dataSet, "Customers");
daInvoices.Fill(dataSet, "Invoices");
daInvoiceItems.Fill(dataSet, "InvoiceItems");

// Grab our tables for simplicity
DataTable customerTable    = dataSet.Tables["Customers"];
DataTable invoiceTable     = dataSet.Tables["Invoices"];
DataTable invoiceItemTable = dataSet.Tables["InvoiceItems"];

// Set up PrimaryKeys
customerTable.PrimaryKey = new DataColumn[]
                    { customerTable.Columns["CustomerID"] };
invoiceTable.PrimaryKey = new DataColumn[]
                    { invoiceTable.Columns["InvoiceID"] };
invoiceItemTable.PrimaryKey = new DataColumn[]
            { invoiceItemTable.Columns["InvoiceItemID"] };

// Set up relations

// Create the first relationship (between Invoices and
// InvoiceItems). We tell the relation to set up a
// constraint to make sure the relationship is created
// on a unique key
dataSet.Relations.Add( "Invoices_InvoiceItems",
  dataSet.Tables["Invoices"].Columns["InvoiceID"],
  dataSet.Tables["InvoiceItems"].Columns["InvoiceID"],
  true);
```

```csharp
// Create the second relationship
// (between Customers and Invoices)
dataSet.Relations.Add( "Customers_Invoices",
  dataSet.Tables["Customers"].Columns["CustomerID"],
  dataSet.Tables["Invoices"].Columns["CustomerID"],
  true);

// Dump the contents of each DataTable's constraints
foreach (DataTable tbl in dataSet.Tables)
{
  form.WriteLine("Table: {0}", tbl.TableName);
  foreach (Constraint con in tbl.Constraints)
  {
    form.WriteLine("  Name: {0}  ", con.ConstraintName);
    if (con is UniqueConstraint)
    {
      form.WriteLine("    UNIQUECONSTRAINT");
      UniqueConstraint u = con as UniqueConstraint;
      form.WriteLine("    Is on Primary Key: {0}",
        u.IsPrimaryKey);
      DumpColumns("Columns",u.Columns, "    ");
    }
    else if (con is ForeignKeyConstraint)
    {
      form.WriteLine("    FOREIGNKEYCONSTRAINT");
      ForeignKeyConstraint f = con as ForeignKeyConstraint;
      form.WriteLine("    Related Table: {0}",
        f.RelatedTable.TableName);
      DumpColumns("Columns", f.Columns, "    ");
      DumpColumns("Related Columns", f.RelatedColumns,
                     "    ");
      form.WriteLine("      Delete Rule:     {0}",
        f.DeleteRule);
      form.WriteLine("      Update Rule:     {0}",
        f.UpdateRule);
      form.WriteLine("      AcceptRejectRule: {0}",
        f.AcceptRejectRule);
    }
    else
    {
      form.WriteLine("    UNKNOWN TYPE");
    }
  }
}
```

```
private void DumpColumns(string title,
  DataColumn[] cols,
  string indent)
{
  Console.WriteLine("{0}{1}",indent, title);
  foreach (DataColumn col in cols)
  {
    Console.WriteLine("{0} Column:{1}", indent,
col.ColumnName);
  }
}
```

Running this sample yields:

```
Table: Customers
  Name: Constraint1
    UNIQUECONSTRAINT
    Is on Primary Key: True
      Columns
        Column: CustomerID
Table: Invoices
  Name: Constraint1
    UNIQUECONSTRAINT
    Is on Primary Key: True
      Columns
        Column: InvoiceID
  Name: Customers_Invoices
    FOREIGNKEYCONSTRAINT
    Related Table: Customers
      Columns
        Column: CustomerID
      Related Columns
        Column: CustomerID
    Delete Rule:      Cascade
    Update Rule:      Cascade
    AcceptRejectRule: None
Table: InvoiceItems
  Name: Constraint1
    UNIQUECONSTRAINT
    Is on Primary Key: True
      Columns
        Column: InvoiceItemID
  Name: Invoices_InvoiceItems
    FOREIGNKEYCONSTRAINT
    Related Table: Invoices
```

```
Columns
   Column: InvoiceID
Related Columns
   Column: InvoiceID
Delete Rule:        Cascade
Update Rule:        Cascade
AcceptRejectRule: None
```

You can see from this that because of the three primary keys we set on each of the tables, each contains a `UniqueConstraint` for their primary key. In addition, there are two `ForeignKeyConstraints`. The constraints are the relations between the `Customer` and `Invoice` tables as well as between the `Invoice` and `InvoiceItem` tables.

You can probably guess that because the `UniqueConstraint` class has the `IsOnPrimaryKey` property that you can create your own `UniqueConstraints` that may not be for the primary key. Every column in your database that is marked unique should have a constraint of this type, as shown in Listing 5.20.

Listing 5.20: *Creating Multiple Column UniqueConstraints*

```
. . .

// Create a UniqueConstraint to make sure all
// LastName/FirstName combos are unique

// Create an array of columns with LastName/FirstName
DataColumn[] uniqueCols = new DataColumn[]
   { customerTable.Columns["LastName"],
     customerTable.Columns["FirstName"] };

// Create the unique constraint
customerTable.Constraints.Add("UniqueNamesPlease",
                              uniqueCols, false);
```

The job of the `UniqueConstraint` is quite simple; therefore, the class is quite simple as well. It contains an array of columns that the constraint affects and a Boolean to say whether the constraint applies to a primary key.

The `ForeignKeyConstraint`, on the other hand, is more complex. The purpose of this constraint is to hold a set of rules that dictates what happens to child tables on changes to related rows in the parent table. For example, if the `Customer` table is the parent table, the `Invoice` table is the child. Should the DataSet automatically cascade the delete so that all the customer's rows in the `Invoice` table are also deleted? The `ForeignKey-Constraint` is where you make these decisions.

The `ForeignKeyConstraint` class contains two arrays of Data-Columns. The first array (`Columns`) is for the columns that are part of the current table. The second array (`RelatedColumns`) is composed of the columns from the related table. We should now be done setting up our DataSet so that it can do the consistency checks.

5.3.4.5   *Triggers (DataSet Events)*

Most database engines allow you to set up actions to be taken when data is changed, added, or deleted. For example, when a new customer is added to a new database, a trigger may be set up to insert that new user into a lookup table for all users. In the DataSet, you can register to be notified (and allow code to be run) whenever certain types of operations happen in each DataTable. The supported events are:

- `RowChanging`: Fired before any change to a row in the DataTable
- `RowChanged`: Fired after the change to a row in the DataTable
- `ColumnChanging`: Fired before the data in a column is changed
- `ColumnChanged`: Fired after the data in a column is changed
- `RowDeleting`: Fired before a row is deleted in the DataTable
- `RowDeleted`: Fired after a row is deleted in the DataTable

Conspicuous by its absence is an event for adding a row. In fact, it is there because ADO.NET treats any change to the `Rows` property (including adding a new row) as a change for the `RowChanged` and `RowChanging` events. The `RowChanging`, `RowChanged`, `RowDeleting`, and `RowDeleted` events all send a reference to the row affected and a `DataRowChange-EventArgs` object. The event `args` object exposes a `DataRowAction` enumeration that specifies what happened to the row. The possible values are:

- `Add`: The row was added to the DataTable.
- `Change`: The row has been modified.

- **Commit**: Any changes to the row have been committed.
- **Delete**: The row was deleted.
- **Nothing**: The row was not modified.
- **Rollback**: The most recent changes to the row have been rolled back.

From this `DataRowAction`, we can determine exactly what has been changed in the row. Because a `DataRowChangeEventArgs` object is used for all row events, you might expect that the `RowChanging` and `Row-Changed` events will fire if you delete the row as well. This is not true; only the `RowDeleting` and `RowDeleted` events will fire.

When monitoring a row for changes, you might want to discover exactly what has changed. That is what the `ColumnChanging` and `Column-Changed` events are for. They are fired with both the row that changed and the column that changed in that row.

To set up a trigger, you add a new handler for the type of event you want notification from (see Listing 5.21).

Listing 5.21: *DataSet Events*

```
...

// Create a DataAdapter for each of the tables we're filling
SqlDataAdapter daCustomers = new SqlDataAdapter(
                              "SELECT * FROM CUSTOMER;",
                              conn);

// Create your blank DataSet
DataSet dataSet = new DataSet();

// Fill the DataSet with each DataAdapter
daCustomers.Fill(dataSet, "Customers");

// Add a new handler to catch events for changes
// (For row and column, this is like a trigger)
dataSet.Tables[0].RowChanged += new
        DataRowChangeEventHandler(RowIsChanged);
dataSet.Tables[0].ColumnChanged += new
        DataColumnChangeEventHandler(ColumnIsChanged);

// Change a row to see the event fired
dataSet.Tables[0].Rows[0]["LastName"] = "FooBar";
```

. . .

```
// RowChanged event handler
public void RowIsChanged(object sender,
                          DataRowChangeEventArgs e)
{
  Console.WriteLine("After Row changed:" +
                  " Action {0}, " +
                  " Row Value: {1}",
                  e.Action,
                  e.Row["LastName"] );
}

// ColumnChanged event handler
public void ColumnIsChanged(object sender,
                          DataColumnChangeEventArgs e)
{
  Console.WriteLine("After Column Changed:" +
                " LastName={0};
                " Column={1};
                " original LastName={2}",
                e.Row["LastName"],
                e.Column.ColumnName,
                e.Row["LastName", DataRowVersion.Original] );
}
```

In this example, we can see that we are adding new handlers (`DataRow-EventHandler` and `DataColumnEventHandler`) to the delegates of the DataTable. When these events occur, we are notified. The change events will be fired on inserts and updates, but not deletes.

The different change events serve two different purposes. The `Data-RowChanging` and `DataRowChanged` events are used when you need to handle just the fact that a row was changed. The `DataColumnChanging` and `DataColumnChanged` events are used to handle the fact that specific columns changed within a row. The event arguments sent with each of these events serves these different purposes. DataRow events send you the entire row that changed. In contrast, the DataColumn events send you the column.

5.3.5 Column Schema

In addition to table schema, we will need to define what data can be stored within our table. The DataTable is made up of rows of data. Each row of data has a collection of data that is segmented by columns. We can specify the schema for these columns to control the rules for what data can be stored in our table. Within the DataTable, ADO.NET relies on the `Columns` collection (`DataColumnCollection`) to hold the set of rules that dictates what can be stored within the rows. Each DataColumn represents a single column in the DataTable. Therefore, the DataColumn specifies rules such as the following:

- **DataType**: Type of data that can be stored in this column
- **ColumnName**: The name of the column
- **MaxLength**: The size of the data in the column
- **DefaultValue**: The value assigned to a column when one is not specified
- **ReadOnly**: Determines whether a particular column can be changed
- **AllowNull**: Determines whether a column supports holding `DbNull` as a value
- **Unique**: Determines whether the values in the column must be unique throughout the DataTable

Whenever you create a new DataSet from a database or XML file, you get a minimum of column schema. The standard information included in the schema contains the basic information required to do the DataSet's job. Listing 5.22 is an example that interrogates the schema of a new DataSet:

Listing 5.22: *Column Schema*

```
. . .

// Create a DataAdapter for each of the tables we're filling
SqlDataAdapter daCustomers = new
                SqlDataAdapter("SELECT * FROM CUSTOMER;",
                conn);

// Create your blank DataSet
DataSet dataSet = new DataSet();

// Fill the DataSet with each DataAdapter
daCustomers.Fill(dataSet, "Customers");
```

```
// Grab our DataTable for simplicity
DataTable customersTable = dataSet.Tables["Customers"];

// Dump the column schema
foreach (DataColumn col in Authors.Columns)
{
  Console.WriteLine("{0}",              col.ColumnName    );
  Console.WriteLine(" Mapping:\t{0}",    col.ColumnMapping );
  Console.WriteLine(" Type:\t\t{0}",     col.DataType.Name );
  Console.WriteLine(" Default:\t{0}",    col.DefaultValue  );
  Console.WriteLine(" ReadOnly?:\t{0}", col.ReadOnly      );
  Console.WriteLine(" Unique?:\t{0}",    col.Unique        );
  Console.WriteLine(" Max Length:\t{0}",col.MaxLength      );
}
```

This piece of code generates the following results:

```
CustomerID
  Type:       Guid
  Default:
  ReadOnly?:  False
  Unique?:        False
  Max Length: -1
  Allow Null: True
FirstName
  Type:       String
  Default:
  ReadOnly?:  False
  Unique?:        False
  Max Length: -1
  Allow Null: True
LastName
  Type:       String
  Default:
  ReadOnly?:  False
  Unique?:    False
  Max Length: -1
  Allow Null: True
MiddleName
  Type:       String
  Default:
  ReadOnly?:  False
  Unique?:        False
  Max Length: -1
  Allow Null: True
```

```
State
  Type:       String
  Default:
  ReadOnly?:  False
  Unique?:    False
  Max Length: -1
  Allow Null: True

  . . .
```

Because the DataSet was generated straight from the database query, there was no way for ADO.NET to determine what the complete schema should be. The managed providers that come directly from Microsoft all determine a table's schema based on the schema information provided by the DataReader (which is used to fill the DataTables as well). The results tell us that it figured out the type correctly, but the rest of the schema information is not set because of a lack of information available to the DataSet and DataAdapter. In this case, we want to make some schema changes to make the DataSet more robust. We want to make sure that the Customer ID is read-only so that nobody accidentally changes the keys. We also want to set the maximum length of some of the strings to the maximum capacity of our database schema. Listing 5.23 is an expanded version that includes this improved column schema:

Listing 5.23: *Extended Column Schema*

```
. . .

// Create a DataAdapter for each of the tables we're filling
SqlDataAdapter daCustomers = new
  SqlDataAdapter("SELECT * FROM CUSTOMER;",
  conn);

// Create your blank DataSet
DataSet dataSet = new DataSet();

// Fill the DataSet with each DataAdapter
daCustomers.Fill(dataSet, "Customers");

// Grab our DataTable for simplicity
DataTable customersTable = dataSet.Tables["Customers"];
```

```
// Improve the schema
customersTable.Columns["CustomerID"].ReadOnly = true;
customersTable.Columns["CustomerID"].Unique = true;
customersTable.Columns["LastName"].MaxLength = 50;
customersTable.Columns["LastName"].AllowDBNull = false;
customersTable.Columns["FirstName"].MaxLength = 50;
customersTable.Columns["FirstName"].AllowDBNull = false;
customersTable.Columns["MiddleName"].MaxLength = 50;
customersTable.Columns["State"].DefaultValue = "MA";
customersTable.Columns["State"].MaxLength = 2;

// Dump the column schema
foreach (DataColumn col in customersTable.Columns)
{
  form.WriteLine("{0}",                col.ColumnName    );
  form.WriteLine("  Type:\t\t{0}",     col.DataType.Name );
  form.WriteLine("  Default:\t{0}",    col.DefaultValue  );
  form.WriteLine("  ReadOnly?:\t{0}",  col.ReadOnly      );
  form.WriteLine("  Unique?:\t{0}",    col.Unique        );
  form.WriteLine("  Max Length:\t{0}", col.MaxLength     );
  form.WriteLine("  Allow Null:\t{0}", col.AllowDBNull   );
}
```

This example generates:

```
CustomerID
  Type:       Guid
  Default:
  ReadOnly?:  True
  Unique?:    True
  Max Length: -1
  Allow Null: True
FirstName
  Type:       String
  Default:
  ReadOnly?:  False
  Unique?:    False
  Max Length: 50
  Allow Null: False
LastName
  Type:       String
  Default:
  ReadOnly?:  False
  Unique?:    False
  Max Length: 50
  Allow Null: False
```

```
MiddleName
   Type:       String
   Default:
   ReadOnly?:  False
   Unique?:    False
   Max Length: 50
   Allow Null: True
State
   Type:       String
   Default:    MA
   ReadOnly?:  False
   Unique?:    False
   Max Length: 2
   Allow Null: True
```

. . .

What we accomplished here was an expansion of the power of data validation to the DataSet. Creating the schema in the database guarantees consistency, but by strengthening our schema in the DataSet we can catch data problems earlier, instead of trying to reconcile them after the database chokes on our data. In this way, using the schema in the DataSet is crucial to making your job easier.

5.3.5.1 *Using* `AutoIncrement` *Columns*

If you read the "Primary Key Strategies" section (5.3.4.2) and decided to use an `AutoIncrement` column, despite the challenges to its use, the code to set up an `AutoIncrement` column is trivial, as shown in Listing 5.24.

Listing 5.24: *Using AutoIncrement Columns*

```
// Create your blank DataSet
DataSet dataSet = new DataSet();

// Create our DataTable
DataTable dataTable = dataSet.Tables.Add("AutoInc");

// Create a new integer column
// (AutoIncrement columns *must* be of type integer
DataColumn autoIncColumn =
               dataTable.Columns.Add("TheKey", typeof(int));
```

```
// Set the column to be an AutoIncremented column
autoIncColumn.AutoIncrement = true;

// Specify the xeed (or starting number)
autoIncColumn.AutoIncrementSeed = 1;

// Specify the xtep
// (or the amount to increment from the seed for every
// new entry in the column)
autoIncColumn.AutoIncrementStep = 1;
```

When creating an `AutoIncrement` column, your DataColumn must be an integer (`int`) type, otherwise an exception will be thrown when you set the `AutoIncrement` property to `true`.

5.3.5.2 *Using Expression Columns*

There are two standard approaches to using calculated columns in ADO.NET. The first is to do the calculation when you retrieve the data using the SQL query. For example:

```
SELECT Description,
       Vendor,
       Price,
       Quantity,
       Discount,
       ((Price - (Price * Discount))* Quantity) as LineTotal
  FROM InvoiceItem
  JOIN Product on InvoiceItem.ProductID = Product.ProductID
```

The other approach is to have an expression column. The benefit of an expression column is that you can use the calculation on newly inserted data, not just data retrieved from the database (see Listing 5.25).

Listing 5.25: *Using Expression Columns*

```
. . .

// Create a DataAdapter for each of the tables we're filling
string sql = @"SELECT Description, Vendor, Price,
                  Quantity, Discount
            FROM InvoiceItem
            JOIN Product on
                InvoiceItem.ProductID = Product.ProductID";
```

```
SqlDataAdapter daItems = new SqlDataAdapter(sql, conn);

// Create your blank DataSet
DataSet dataSet = new DataSet();

// Fill the DataSet with each DataAdapter
daItems.Fill(dataSet, "Items");

// Create an Expression column
DataColumn exColumn = new DataColumn("LineTotal");
exColumn.DataType = typeof(float);
exColumn.Expression =
                "((Price - (Price * Discount)) * Quantity)";

// Add the column to the data
dataSet.Tables["Items"].Columns.Add(exColumn);
```

The syntax for expression columns is different than that used for C# or VB .NET. In addition to mathematical calculations (as shown above), the expression syntax supports simple aggregation or concatenation:

```
// Concatenation
exColumn.Expression = "LastName + ', ' + Firstname";

// Aggregation
exColumn.Expression = "Avg(Price)";
```

Of significance is the ability to aggregate information down relationships. To navigate through a parent relationship, use `Parent`:

```
// Parent relationship
exColumn.Expression = "Max(Parent.Cost)";
```

To navigate through a child relationship, use `Child`:

```
// Child relationship
exColumn.Expression = "Avg(Child.Price)";
```

If you have more than one child relationship set up for a table, you need to qualify the child relationship by name:

```
// Specific child relationship
exColumn.Expression =
                "Avg(Child(InvoiceItem2Product).Price)";
```

Normally, the navigability of relationships in this way is done for aggregation only. There are cases where you might want to include a related field as part of an expression column. The only way to really do this is to fake an aggregation by using `Max`:

```
// Get the extension Price in an invoice
exColumn.Expression = "Quantity * Max(Child.Price))";
```

For a complete reference to the syntax, consult the `DataColumn.Expression` documentation.[3]

5.4 Conclusion

Hopefully, this chapter has shown you the real power of the DataSet's ability to describe an in-memory database. By leveraging the raw power of the DataSet schema, you can realize the potential performance increases of client (or middle-tier) validation of data. The power of the databases to maintain their own internal consistency is wonderful, but it comes at a cost of waiting until the data actually makes it to the database. By leveraging the DataSet's schema, you can find consistency issues and resolve them without using expensive network resources.

---

3. See msdn.microsoft.com/library/en-us/cpref/html/
   frlrfSystemDataDataColumnClassExpressionTopic.asp.

■ 6 ■
Typed DataSets

IN CHAPTER 5, I extolled the virtues of setting up your DataSets like in-memory databases. Unfortunately, I asked you to write quite a bit of code to do all the work. I was only teasing you. This chapter will show you how to use Typed DataSets to make that job a lot easier, while at the same time creating type-safety at compilation time.

6.1 What Are Typed DataSets?

Typed DataSets are a different animal than most of what we have discussed so far. They are not a set of classes in the framework, but instead, they are a set of generated classes that inherit directly from the DataSet family of classes. Figure 6.1 contains the class diagram from Chapter 5, which shows how the elements of the DataSet are related.

In contrast, the Typed DataSet derives from these classes. The class diagram looks like that shown in Figure 6.2.

But why are they called Typed DataSets? In Chapter 5 we saw that we could create DataColumns for our DataTables to specify what type of data could be stored in each column. This enforces runtime type-safety, but on most occasions we would like to know that our DataSets are type-safe when we write the code. Typed DataSets generate classes that expose each object in a DataSet in a type-safe manner. With a DataSet, our code would look like Listing 6.1.

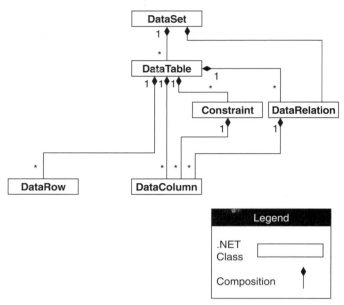

Figure 6.1: *The structure of a DataSet*

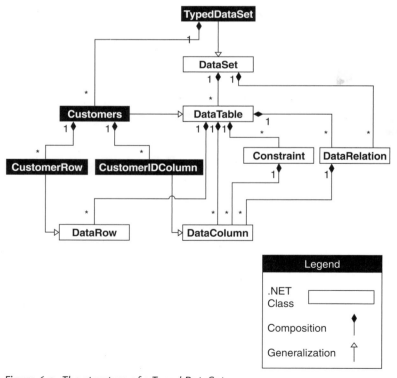

Figure 6.2: *The structure of a Typed DataSet*

Listing 6.1: *Using a DataSet*

```
. . .

// Create a DataAdapter for each of the tables we're filling
SqlDataAdapter daCustomers =
        new SqlDataAdapter("SELECT * FROM CUSTOMER;", conn);

// Create the Invoice DataAdapter
SqlDataAdapter daInvoices =
        new SqlDataAdapter("SELECT * FROM INVOICE", conn);

// Create your blank DataSet
DataSet dataSet = new DataSet();

// Fill the DataSet with each DataAdapter
daCustomers.Fill(dataSet, "Customers");
daInvoices.Fill(dataSet, "Invoices");

// Show the customer name
Console.WriteLine(dataSet.Tables["Customers"].
                        Rows[0]["FirstName"].ToString());
Console.WriteLine(dataSet.Tables["Customers"].
                        Rows[0]["LastName"].ToString());
Console.WriteLine(dataSet.Tables["Customers"].
                        Rows[0]["HomePhone"].ToString());

// Change an invoice number with a string
// this shouldn't work because InvoiceNumber
// expects an integer
dataSet.Tables["Invoices"].
                        Rows[0]["InvoiceNumber"] = "15234";
```

We need to use indexers with the DataSet to get each piece of the hierarchy until we finally get down to the row level. At any point you can misspell any name and get an error when this code is executed. In addition, the last line of the example shows us attempting to set the invoice number using a string. The DataSet knows that this column can only hold integers so we will get a runtime error enforcing that rule. In Listing 6.2, we do the same thing with a Typed DataSet.

Listing 6.2: *Using a Typed DataSet*

```
// Create a DataAdapter for each of the tables we're filling
SqlDataAdapter daCustomers =
        new SqlDataAdapter("SELECT * FROM CUSTOMER;", conn);

// Create the invoice DataAdapter
SqlDataAdapter daInvoices =
        new SqlDataAdapter("SELECT * FROM INVOICE", conn);

// Create your blank DataSet
CustomerTDS dataSet = new CustomerTDS();

// Fill the DataSet with each DataAdapter
daCustomers.Fill(dataSet, "Customers");
daInvoices.Fill(dataSet, "Invoices");

// Show the customer name
Console.WriteLine(dataSet.Customer[0].FirstName);
Console.WriteLine(dataSet.Customer[0].LastName);
Console.WriteLine(dataSet.Customer[0].HomePhone);
Console.WriteLine(DataSet.Customer[0].FullName);

// This will not compile because InvoiceNumber expects
// an integer
dataSet.Invoice[0].InvoiceNumber = "12345";
```

There are a few things to notice in this example. First, we create our Typed DataSet much like we created a DataSet in the first example—the difference is that the schema already exists in our Typed DataSet. Second, even though this is a Typed DataSet, the CustomerTDS class directly derives from the DataSet class. Therefore, when we call the DataAdapters to fill our DataSet, it will accept our Typed DataSet. In fact, the Typed DataSet is a DataSet . . . a specialized DataSet. Next, you should notice that the syntax to get at tables and fields is much more straightforward with Typed DataSets. Each DataTable is now referenced with a property of CustomerTDS. Likewise, each field is a property of a row. Not only is this syntax more straightforward, but you will get compiler errors if you misspell any of the elements. Lastly, when we try to set our invoice number with a string we also get a compiler error, because our generated class knows that invoice numbers are integers.

In addition to normal columns, you can set up expression columns in our Typed DataSets to make sure that expressions can be returned in a type-safe manner. For instance, in the above example, we can retrieve the `FullName` property from `Customer`. `FullName` is just an expression field that puts our customer's first and last names together in a convenient form. Because it is part of the Typed DataSet, this expression is returned as a string.

Lastly, as we will see in this chapter, using Typed DataSets as the basis for data object or business object layers is a powerful tool. By deriving directly from Typed DataSets we can eliminate much of the tedium of writing these layers, while at the same time achieving the type-safety we want.

6.2 Generating Typed DataSets

Now that you understand what Typed DataSets are all about, let's create our own. Typed DataSets can be generated in two ways: from within Visual Studio .NET or with the XSD.exe command-line tool. I will start with the Visual Studio .NET solution.

6.2.1 Using Visual Studio .NET to Create a Typed DataSet

This section will walk you through creating a Typed DataSet in Visual Studio. NET. To get started, please create a new Console C# project, as shown in Figure 6.3. Next, in the Solution Explorer add a new item, as shown in Figure 6.4.

From the Data folder in the Local Project Items, select a new DataSet and name it ADONET.xsd, as shown in Figure 6.5. If you add an XML Schema file instead (they both are .XSD files), the Typed DataSet will not generate. Make sure it is a DataSet. When you finish, the IDE will look something like what is shown in Figure 6.6.

You probably have noticed already that the Typed DataSet has an extension of .xsd. This is because the source of a Typed DataSet is an XML Schema Document. What the IDE asks you to do is to create a new .XSD file that represents the schema of the DataSet. This will include the schema information we discussed in Chapter 5. The XSD can include table and column names as well as keys, relationships, and constraints.

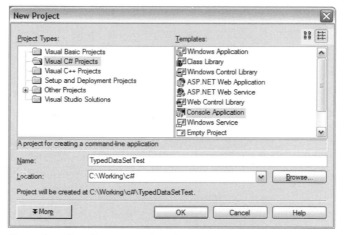

Figure 6.3: *Creating a new C# project*

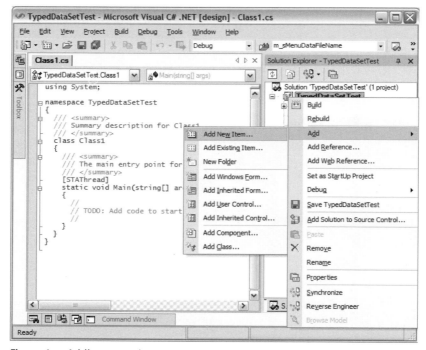

Figure 6.4: *Adding a new item*

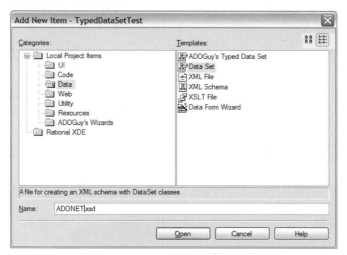

Figure 6.5: *Adding a DataSet*

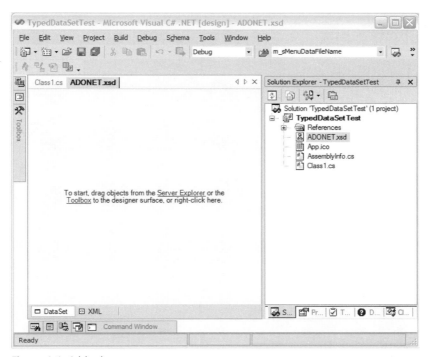

Figure 6.6: *A blank canvas*

Now that you have a new Typed DataSet added to your project, you can use either the Server Explorer to add tables to the DataSet or the Toolbox to add elements to the DataSet. Using the Server Explorer to add tables is shown in Figure 6.7.

After you have the Server Explorer open to an existing database, you can simply drag and drop the tables you want onto the .XSD file, to produce something that looks like Figure 6.8.

At this point, the new Typed DataSet will include two tables, but the tables remain unrelated. Unfortunately Visual Studio .NET does not try to discern all the schema information that may be contained in the database. In order to set the schema information, you will need to add it to the XSD.

We will start by adding a relationship between the `Customer` and `Invoice` tables. To do this, drag a new Relation from the Toolbox onto the `Customer` table, as shown in Figure 6.9. Once you do that, the Edit Relation dialog box appears, as shown in Figure 6.10.

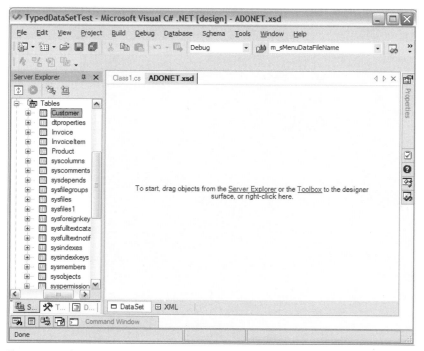

Figure 6.7: *The Server Explorer*

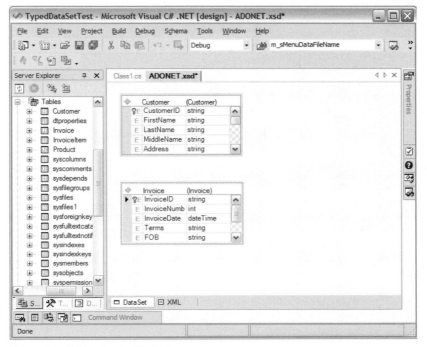

Figure 6.8: *Tables in the .XSD file*

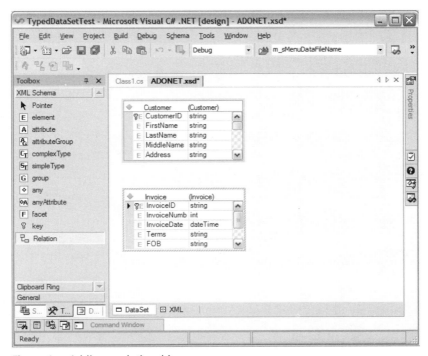

Figure 6.9: *Adding a relationship*

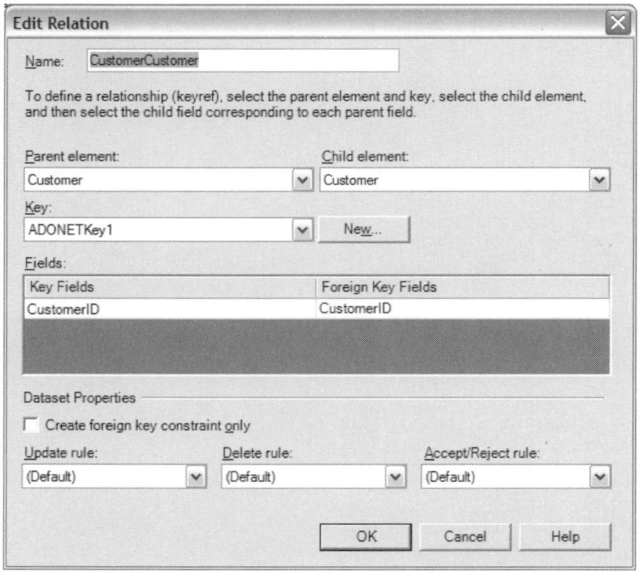

Figure 6.10: *The Edit Relation dialog box*

The Edit Relation dialog box is where you will provide the specifics of the relationship. You will need to change the child element to the child table (in this case `Invoice`). Usually the dialog box will correctly select the foreign key field(s). If necessary, you can change the way that the Update rule, Delete rule, and Accept/Reject rule settings affect cascading changes to the DataSet. After you make these changes you should see something similar to what is shown in Figure 6.11.

After you click OK, you will see the Relation, as shown in Figure 6.12.

Now that we have our tables and the relationship set up, let's add an expression column to our `Customer` table. To add an expression column, go to the bottom of the `Customer` table and add a new row. Name it `Full-Name` and look at the properties for the column. Set the expression of the column to:

```
LastName + ', ' + FirstName
```

Once you have done this, it should look like that shown in Figure 6.13.

Lastly, we need to add a unique constraint on `Home Phone` to make sure all of our customers' home phone numbers are unique. In the Typed

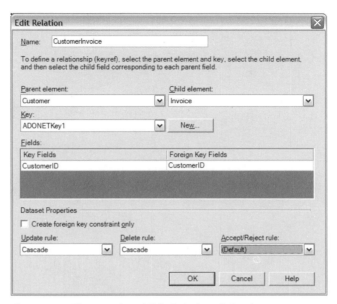

Figure 6.11: *The completed Edit Relation dialog box*

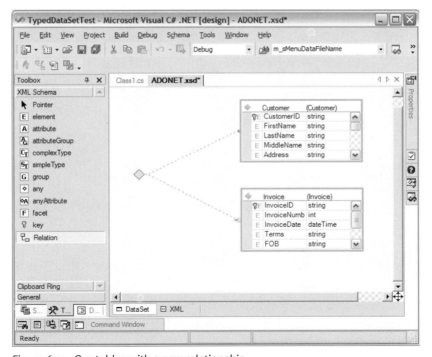

Figure 6.12: *Our tables with a new relationship*

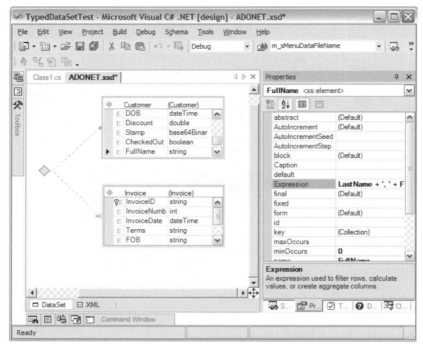

Figure 6.13: *Adding an expression column*

DataSet vernacular, you will need to add a key to that column. Select the column, right-click on it, and select Add Key, as shown in Figure 6.14. This will launch the Edit Key dialog box, shown in Figure 6.15.

If you do nothing but name the key and click OK, you've created a unique constraint. There may be cases in which you want to support having a multi-column unique key. To do this you would add fields to the key in the dialog box, as shown in Figure 6.16.

This unique constraint will force the DataSet to make sure that all Home-Phone and BusinessPhone combinations are unique. Congratulations, you now have your Typed DataSet defined.

Before we can see the code that Visual Studio .NET will generate, we need to build the project. After you build the project, your new Typed DataSet will be available for use.

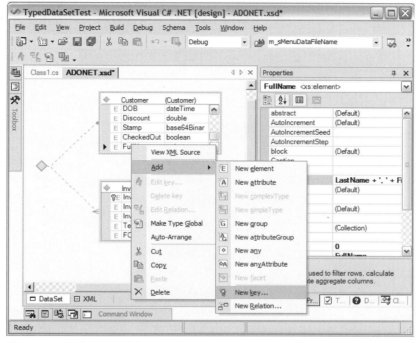

Figure 6.14: *Selecting Add Key*

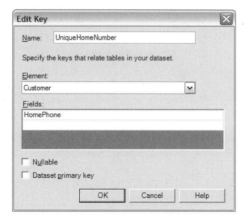

Figure 6.15: *Naming the key*

Figure 6.16: *Supporting a multi-column unique key*

6.2.2   Using XSD.exe to Create a Typed DataSet

Much like creating the class from Visual Studio .NET, Typed DataSets can also be created directly from an XML Schema Document (XSD) using the command-line XSD.exe tool that is included in the .NET Framework SDK. If you are not using Visual Studio .NET or just like your tools to be command-line tools, XSD.exe is for you. If you are using Visual Studio .NET, its built-in support for Typed DataSets is much easier than the tool and produces the same classes.

This tool is used to generate code from XML Schema Documents—both classes derived from the .NET XML classes and those derived from the DataSet family of classes. Before we can start, we will need an XSD document. We can use the DataSet to create one of these for us, as in Listing 6.3.

Listing 6.3: *Creating an XSD from a DataSet*

```
. . .

// Create a DataAdapter for each of the tables we're filling
SqlDataAdapter daCustomers =
        new SqlDataAdapter("SELECT * FROM CUSTOMER", conn);

// Create your blank DataSet
DataSet dataSet = new DataSet();
```

```
            // Fill the DataSet with each DataAdapter
            daCustomers.Fill(dataSet, "Customers");

            // Grab our DataTable for simplicity
            DataTable customersTable = dataSet.Tables["Customers"];

            // Improve the schema
            customersTable.Columns["CustomerID"].ReadOnly = true;
            customersTable.Columns["CustomerID"].Unique = true;
            customersTable.Columns["LastName"].MaxLength = 50;
            customersTable.Columns["LastName"].AllowDBNull = false;
            customersTable.Columns["FirstName"].MaxLength = 50;
            customersTable.Columns["FirstName"].AllowDBNull = false;
            customersTable.Columns["MiddleName"].MaxLength = 50;
            customersTable.Columns["State"].DefaultValue = "MA";
            customersTable.Columns["State"].MaxLength = 2;
            customersTable.Columns["HomePhone"].Unique = true;

            // Write out our XSD file to use to generate our
            // typed DataSet
            dataSet.WriteXmlSchema(@"c:\CustomerDS.xsd");
```

Once we run this code, we will have a CustomersDS.xsd file to use with XSD.exe. To generate the class, simply go to the command line and use the XSD.exe tool, as shown in Figure 6.17.

The most interesting options are:

- /d specifies to create a schema class that is of type DataSet. For Typed DataSet you will always specify this flag.
- /l specifies the language in which to generate the classes—CS is C#, VB is VB .NET and JS is Jscript .NET.
- /n specifies the namespace to create our class in. This flag is optional.

Figure 6.17: *Running the XSD.exe tool from the command line*

- /o specifies the output directory. If used, the output directory must already exist; the tool will not create it. If this is not specified, the classes will be created in the current directory.

Now you have your class file to include in your project.

6.2.3 Customizing the Generated Code with Annotations

ADO.NET allows you to control some aspects of the generated code by annotating the XSD that you use to generate the Typed DataSets. You can do this by annotating your XSD with several special attributes. All of these attributes are prefixed with the namespace of `codegen`. These attributes are:

- **typedName**: Specifies the name of an object.
- **typedPlural**: Specifies the name of the collection of objects.
- **typedParent**: Specifies the name of the parent relationship.
- **typedChildren**: Specifies the name of the child relationship.
- **nullValue**: Specifies how to handle a `DBNull` value for a particular row value. When you use this annotation, there are several possible values for the `nullValue` attribute:
  - **Replacement Value**: The value to return instead of a null (for example, `codegen:nullValue=""` will return an empty string instead of a null for a string field).
  - **_throw**: Throws an exception when the value is accessed and is null (for example, `codegen:nullValue=_throw`). If the user would use the `IsNull` properties as part of the Typed DataSet to determine whether the field is null before trying to retrieve it. This is the default behavior if not annotated.
  - **_null**: Returns a null reference from the field. If a value type is encountered an exception is thrown.
  - **_empty**: Returns a reference created with an empty constructor. For strings, it returns `String.Empty`. For value types, an exception is thrown.

These must be added directly to the .XSD file. If you are using Visual Studio .NET, you must go to the XML view of your XSD to add these annotations. These annotations are added to an XSD like so:

```xml
<?xml version="1.0" encoding="utf-8" ?>
<xs:schema id="AnnotatedTDS"
      targetNamespace="http://tempuri.org/AnnotatedTDS"
      elementFormDefault="qualified"
      attributeFormDefault="qualified"
      xmlns="http://tempuri.org/AnnotatedTDS"
      xmlns:mstns="http://tempuri.org/AnnotatedTDS"
      xmlns:xs="http://www.w3.org/2001/XMLSchema"
      xmlns:msdata="urn:schemas-microsoft-com:xml-msdata"
      xmlns:codegen="urn:schemas-microsoft-com:xml-msprop" >
  <xs:element name="AnnotatedTDS" msdata:IsDataSet="true">
    <xs:complexType>
      <xs:choice maxOccurs="unbounded">
        <xs:element name="Customer"
                  codegen:typedName="OurCustomer"
                  codegen:typedPlural="OurCustomers">
...
            <xs:element name="MiddleName" type="xs:string"
                      minOccurs="0"
                      codegen:nullValue="_empty" />
...
        </xs:element>
        <xs:element name="Invoice"
                  codegen:typedName="TheirInvoice"
                  codegen:typedPlural="TheirInvoices">
...
            <xs:element name="Terms" type="xs:string"
                      minOccurs="0"
                      codegen:nullValue="Net 30" />
...
        </xs:element>
      </xs:choice>
    </xs:complexType>
    <xs:keyref name="CustomerInvoice"
              refer="ADONETKey1"
              msdata:AcceptRejectRule="Cascade"
              msdata:DeleteRule="Cascade"
              msdata:UpdateRule="Cascade"
              codegen:typedChildren="Invoices"
              codegen:typedParent="Customer">
      <xs:selector xpath=".//mstns:Invoice" />
      <xs:field xpath="mstns:CustomerID" />
    </xs:keyref>
...
  </xs:element>
</xs:schema>
```

Let's walk through this XSD and see where we have put the annotations.

1. The first thing we needed to do was to add the namespace reference to the schema header. This simply tells the XSD that we have a namespace defined and to allow the attributes.

2. Next, we make some changes to the Customer Element. `typedName` changes the name of the Typed DataRow in the DataTable to `OurCustomer`. When you ask for an individual row from the DataTable, it will return you an instance of the `OurCustomer` class instead of the default of `Customer`. `typedPlural` changes the name of the property on the DataSet that returns the specific DataTable. When retrieving the `Customer` DataTable, you would call the `OurCustomers` property.

3. Next, we added the `codegen:nullValue="_empty"` to the `MiddleName` element. This annotated our XSD so that a `DBNull` in the middle name element should be treated as an empty string in our generated Typed DataSet.

4. Next, we changed the `Invoice` element just like we did the `Customer` element. We renamed the Typed DataRow to `TheirInvoice` and the property that returns it to `TheirInvoices`.

5. Last, we changed the names of each end of our relationship by annotating the `keydef` tag with `typedChildren` and `typedParent`. This changes how each side of the relationship is named. The `Customer` class will have a method called `Invoices` (instead of `GetInvoiceTable`) to navigate down the relationship and the `Invoice` class will have a method called `Customer` (instead of `GetCustomerTable`) to navigate up the relationship.

6.3   Using Typed DataSets

In most cases, you can use your Typed DataSet everywhere you would normally use a DataSet. Your Typed DataSet directly derives from DataSet so all the DataSet-related classes and methods will work. One of the distinct advantages of using a Typed DataSet is that elements of the DataSet are strongly typed and strongly named. The use of the new class is a little different than our old DataSet examples, as shown in Listing 6.4.

Listing 6.4: *Using a Typed DataSet*

```
...

// Create the Customer DataAdapter
SqlDataAdapter customerAdapter =
        new SqlDataAdapter("SELECT * FROM CUSTOMER", conn);

// Create the Invoice DataAdapter
SqlDataAdapter invoiceAdapter =
        new SqlDataAdapter("SELECT * FROM INVOICE", conn);

// Create the DataSet
CustomerTDS typedDS = new CustomerIDS();

// Use the DataAdapters to fill the DataSet
customerAdapter.Fill(typedDS, "Customer");
invoiceAdapter.Fill(typedDS, "Invoice");

// Show the address and # of invoices for each customer
foreach(CustomerTDS.CustomerRow custRow in typedDS.Customer)
{
  Console.WriteLine(custRow.FullName);
  Console.WriteLine(custRow.Address);
  Console.WriteLine("{0}, {1}  {2}",
                    custRow.City,
                    custRow.State,
                    custRow.Zip);
  Console.WriteLine("{0} (hm)",
                    custRow.IsHomePhoneNull() ?"" :
                    custRow.HomePhone);
  Console.WriteLine("{0} (bus)",
                    custRow.IsBusinessPhoneNull() ? "" :
                    custRow.BusinessPhone);
  Console.WriteLine("Invoices: " +
          custRow.GetChildRows("CustomerInvoice").Length);
  Console.WriteLine("");
}
```

When filling the Typed DataSet with data, you can deal with the new class just like a DataSet (because it derives directly from it). Once we fill it, we can use the typed accessors to get at rows and columns in a more direct way than with an untyped DataSet.

Because we allowed our `HomePhone` and `BusinessPhone` columns to be null, we need to check to see whether they are null before accessing them. If you do not do this, you will get a `TypedDataSetException` thrown unless you have used annotations to modify the generated code.

6.4 Simplification of Business Object Layers

I have spent more of my adult life writing business object layers than any other work I have done. The work always involved several tasks:

- Mapping our relational model to a hierarchical model.
- Reading and writing those objects to and from the database.
- Adding business logic to handle our business needs for the data.

Mapping the relational model to the hierarchical model and the database manipulation code were the most tedious aspects of this work. Luckily, by using Typed DataSets you can eliminate the need to write this code yourself. When you create a Typed DataSet with multiple tables and relationships, you already have your relational-to-object mapping. By viewing a single row in a single table as the top of an object graph, you can navigate the relationships to get a tree of items. This is similar to what was done when business object layers were written with database joins across multiple tables to get an object graph in a database result. In the DataSet and Typed DataSet, the difference is that if you navigate the relationships, you are navigating to only the related rows in the related table. In this way, the Typed DataSet relieves you from writing the relational-to-object mapping, because it is inherent in the way the DataSet works.

The next job of the database programmer in this situation is usually to write the database manipulation code. Because ADO.NET has abstracted the DataSet from the database manipulation code (primarily in the managed providers), you will not have to write much code to make the database manipulation work. You may still have to write the stored procedures to handle the CRUD (Create, Read, Update, Delete) operations to the database and tie those stored procedures to the DataAdapter (see Chapter 8 for more information on how this is done), but in the larger picture ADO.NET does a lot of the heavy lifting.

That leaves only the business logic or rules to write, which in my experience is usually the easiest of the code to write. What is this business logic exactly? In some systems, business logic is as simple as data validation, whereas in other systems it is as complicated as integrating various systems to keep them in sync. Business logic is really any logic that needs to be added to the raw data in the database. So in this model where we are using Typed DataSets to get around writing business logic layers, where do we put our business logic? I recommend deriving from your generated Typed DataSets to put this logic in place.

6.4.1 Hooking Up Your Business Logic

The code generated from the .XSD file is still just a class, so you can inherit from it very simply—but how do you hook up your business logic? There are two approaches, and both are appropriate in the right circumstances. Both approaches begin by inheriting directly from the generated Typed DataSet.

6.4.1.1 *Event-Driven DataSet*

In the case where you do not have much business logic, you can decide to derive from the Typed DataSet and register for event notification to do your business logic. Within the DataSet, you register for notification from many different events, but the ones that make the most sense for most business logic are the `RowChanging` and `RowChanged` events. Listing 6.5 is an example of that solution.

Listing 6.5: *Capturing Events from a Typed DataSet*

```
public class CustomersObject : CustomerTDS
{
  public CustomersObject() : base()
  {
    Register();
  }

  protected CustomersObject(SerializationInfo info,
                            StreamingContext context) :
    base(info, context)
  {
    Register();
  }
```

```csharp
private void Register()
{
  Invoice.InvoiceRowChanging +=
        new InvoiceRowChangeEventHandler(InvoiceChanging);
}

private void InvoiceChanging(object source,
                             InvoiceRowChangeEvent args)
{
  if (args.Action == DataRowAction.Add ||
      args.Action == DataRowAction.Change)
  {
    if (args.Row.InvoiceDate > DateTime.Today)
    {
      throw new Exception("Cannot Create Invoices" +
                          "in the Future");
    }
  }
}
}
```

We create a new class that derives from our Typed DataSet (CustomerTDS) and create two constructors. The first of these is for normal construction, and the other is for XML deserialization. The constructor that is
used for deserialization must be implemented or there will be no support
for XML serialization. Other than calling the base class's constructors, the
only other thing we do here is call our new Register method, which is
used to register for the events we are interested in. In this case, we have registered for the InvoiceRowChangingEvent. This is fired before the change
to the row actually takes place. In our handler method (InvoiceChang-
ing), we check to see whether the changed row was added or changed. If
either of these actions occurred, we make sure the invoice date does not
occur in the future. If it does, we throw an exception. We would use our
new Typed DataSet as in Listing 6.6.

Listing 6.6: *Testing Our Event-driven Typed DataSet Business Logic*

. . .

```csharp
// Create a DataAdapter for each of the tables we're filling
SqlDataAdapter daCustomers =
        new SqlDataAdapter("SELECT * FROM CUSTOMER;", conn);
```

```
// Create the invoice DataAdapter
SqlDataAdapter daInvoices =
        new SqlDataAdapter("SELECT * FROM INVOICE", conn);

// Create an instance of our inherited Typed DataSet
CustomersObject dataset = new CustomersObject();

// Use the DataAdapters to fill the DataSet
daCustomers.Fill(dataset, "Customer");
daInvoices.Fill(dataset, "Invoice");

// This will throw an exception because we're creating
// an invoice date in the future
CustomerTDS.InvoiceRow invoice;
Invoice = dataset.Invoice.AddInvoiceRow(Guid.NewGuid(),
                    DateTime.Now + new TimeSpan(4,0,0,0),
                    "",
                    "",
                    "",
                    dataset.Customer[0]);
```

The use of our derived Typed DataSet is identical to how the original Typed DataSet is used. But because we have registered for events, we will be notified during certain types of operations to implement our business logic. In this case, when we add a new invoice, we are creating it with an invoice date four days in the future so the event will throw an exception to let the user know he did something wrong.

6.4.1.2 *Deriving from Typed DataSets*

The other approach is not only to derive from the Typed DataSet, but also to derive from the Typed DataTable and Typed DataRow classes. This allows us to override any behavior to implement our business logic. We do not have to derive from each and every DataTable or DataRow, just the ones that need specific business logic. If we are going to need to derive from the DataRow, we will need to derive from its parent DataTable.

For this example, we want to put some logic into the Invoice table to check for credit before we allow a new invoice to be added to the table. Ultimately, we want our logic to look something like Listing 6.7.

Listing 6.7: *AddInvoiceRow Method*

```
public void AddInvoiceRow(InheritedInvoiceRow row)
{
  if (DoesCustomerHaveCredit())
  {
    base.AddInvoiceRow(row);
  }
  else
  {
    throw new Exception(
                "Customer Invoice cannot be created, " +
                "no credit available");
  }
}
```

To get to the point where we can make this change, we will have to start by inheriting from the Typed DataTable, as shown in Listing 6.8.

Listing 6.8: *Inheriting from a Typed DataSet*

```
public class InheritedTDS : FixedCustomerTDS
{

...

  public class InheritedInvoiceDataTable : InvoiceDataTable
  {
    internal InheritedInvoiceDataTable() : base()
    {
    }

    internal InheritedInvoiceDataTable(DataTable table) :
      base(table)
    {
    }

  ...

  }

...

}
```

Inheriting from the Typed DataTable requires that we support two constructors again. This time, the second constructor takes a DataTable. This second constructor is used for XML serialization as well. Creating the `InheritedInvoiceDataTable` was easy; the hard part is getting the Typed DataSet to use this class for its `InvoiceDataTable`. The generated code makes it hard on us because it is creating the entire schema (including our DataTable) during the base class's construction. This means that in order to replace the old DataTable with our inherited class we need to re-create much of the schema that is in the constructor. To get around this we could edit the generated code in a few small ways. First we could add a new virtual method that is called during construction to build the Data-Table we want to replace, as shown in Listing 6.9.

Listing 6.9: *Adding a Create Table Method*

```
// This is the generated class
public class FixedCustomerTDS : DataSet
{

. . .

  protected virtual InvoiceDataTable
          CreateInvoiceDataTable(DataTable table)
  {
    if (table == null) return new InvoiceDataTable();
    else return new InvoiceDataTable(table);
  }

. . .

}
```

This method will return a Typed DataTable object. This is important because when we inherit from the Typed DataSet, we will need to override this method and return the same Typed DataTable. It ensures that our inherited DataTable actually does inherit from their Typed DataTable. The generated code will have code that depends on the DataTable being typed and by writing the method this way, we will guarantee not to break the generated code.

Next, we need to override this method when we inherit from the Typed DataSet. Because the method is virtual (or overridable in VB .NET), the

Typed DataSet will call our version of this method when it constructs the DataTables. To hook this up to our Typed DataSet, we will need to inherit from the Typed DataSet and override the creation method, as shown in Listing 6.10.

Listing 6.10: *Calling the Create Table Method*

```
public class InheritedTDS : FixedCustomerTDS
{
  public InheritedTDS() : base()
  {
  }

  protected InheritedTDS(SerializationInfo info,
                         StreamingContext context)
    : base(info, context)
  {
  }

  protected override InvoiceDataTable
               CreateInvoiceDataTable(DataTable table)
  {
    if (table == null)
    {
      return new InheritedInvoiceDataTable()
                                  as InvoiceDataTable;
    }
    else
    {
      return new InheritedInvoiceDataTable(table)
                                  as InvoiceDataTable;
    }
  }

...

}
```

This should look very much like the method in the base class, except that it creates our derived DataTable, but returns it as an instance of the base DataTable.

Next, we need to modify the generated code to replace all calls to construction of our DataTable to use this method (see Listing 6.11).

Listing 6.11: *Changing Default Behavior of the Typed DataSet*

```
// This is the generated class
public class FixedCustomerTDS : DataSet
{

...

  private void InitClass()
  {

    ...

    /* Originally
    this.tableInvoice = new InvoiceDataTable();
    */

    // New
    this.tableInvoice = CreateInvoiceDataTable(null);

    ...

  }

...

  protected FixedCustomerTDS(SerializationInfo info,
                            StreamingContext context)
  {

    ...

    /* Originally
    this.Tables.Add(
        new InvoiceDataTable(ds.Tables["Invoice"]));
    */

    // New
    this.Tables.Add(
        CreateInvoiceDataTable(ds.Tables["Invoice"]));

    ...

  }

...

}
```

We need to replace two different styles of construction. Each happens a couple times per Typed DataSet. The first style is `new NameDataTable()`. We want to replace this with `CreateNameDataTable()`. The second style is `new NameDataTable(SomeDataTable)`. We want to replace this with `CreateNameDataTable(SomeDataTable)`. In the above example, both styles are shown as they originally looked and as they looked after we changed them.

The last piece that will help make our derived Typed DataSet useful is to create a new property to hide the base class's DataTable property, as shown in Listing 6.12.

Listing 6.12: *Hiding the DataTable Property*

```
public class InheritedTDS : FixedCustomerTDS
{

. . .

  public new InheritedInvoiceDataTable Invoice
  {
    get
    {
      return (InheritedInvoiceDataTable)base.Invoice;
    }
  }

. . .

}
```

By creating a new `Invoice` property, we are not only hiding the base class's `Invoice` property, but also making sure all code that references the `Invoice` property is dealing with our derived version of the DataTable.

With all of this in place, we can put some business logic into our inherited DataTable, as shown in Listing 6.13.

Listing 6.13: *Adding Our Business Logic to the Derived Class*

```
public class InheritedTDS : FixedCustomerTDS
{

. . .
```

```
public class InheritedInvoiceDataTable : InvoiceDataTable
{

...

    public void AddInvoiceRow(InheritedInvoiceRow row)
    {
      if (DoesCustomerHaveCredit())
      {
        base.AddInvoiceRow(row);
      }
      else
      {
        throw new Exception(
                "Customer Invoice cannot be created, " +
                "no credit available");
      }
    }

...

    }

...

}
```

Now, when a user attempts to call the DataTable and add a new invoice for a customer, we will make sure that the customer can have a new invoice; otherwise, we can throw an exception. This should allow us to put business logic at the table level, but that may not be enough. We might want to control some different behavior at the row level. To ensure that none of our users create invoices that are accidentally dated in the future, we want the following business object added to the DataRow's Invoice-Date property (see Listing 6.14).

Listing 6.14: *Protecting the Invoice Date*

```
public new DateTime InvoiceDate
{
  get
  {
    return base.InvoiceDate;
  }
```

```
    set
    {
      if (value > DateTime.Today)
      {
        return new StrongTypingException("Invoice Date" +
                                    "cannot be in the" +
                                    "future", null);
      }
      else
      {
        base.InvoiceDate = value;
      }
    }
  }
}
```

To accomplish this, Listing 6.15 shows how we need to derive from the Typed DataRow as well.

Listing 6.15: *Enabling Deriving from the DataRow*

```
public class InheritedTDS : FixedCustomerTDS
{

...

  public class InheritedInvoiceRow : InvoiceRow
  {

    public InheritedInvoiceRow(DataRowBuilder builder) :
    base(builder)
    {
    }

  ...

  }

...

}
```

In the case of deriving from the Typed DataRow, the only constructor that is required is to support one that takes a `DataRowBuilder`. This constructor is used by the `DataTable.NewRowFromBuilder()` method. This method is called by the DataTable when a user asks for a new row for the DataTable. The base class calls the method to create rows that are type-safe. To make this work, Listing 6.16 shows how we need to override the `New-RowFromBuilder()` and `GetRowType()` methods in our DataTable.

Listing 6.16: *Allowing Creation of New Derived DataRows*

```
public class InheritedTDS : FixedCustomerTDS
{

...

  public class InheritedInvoiceDataTable : InvoiceDataTable
  {

  ...

    protected override DataRow
                    NewRowFromBuilder(DataRowBuilder builder)
    {
      return new InheritedInvoiceRow(builder);
    }

    protected override System.Type GetRowType()
    {
      return typeof(InheritedInvoiceRow);
    }

  ...

  }

...

}
```

This ensures that all new rows created from this DataTable will be of our derived type (such as `InheritedInvoiceRow`). We need our DataTable to be handing out our new DataRows to users instead of the base class's implementation. To do this, we create a couple of new methods, as shown in Listing 6.17.

Listing 6.17: *Overriding DataRow Creation*

```
public class InheritedTDS : FixedCustomerTDS
{

...

  public class InheritedInvoiceDataTable : InvoiceDataTable
  {

    ...

    public new InheritedInvoiceRow this[int index]
    {
      get
      {
        return ((InheritedInvoiceRow)(this.Rows[index]));
      }
    }

    public new InheritedInvoiceRow
                AddInvoiceRow(Guid InvoiceID,
                              DateTime InvoiceDate,
                              string Terms,
                              string FOB,
                              string PO,
                              CustomerRow
                      parentCustomerRowByCustomerInvoice)
    {
      ...
    }

    public new InheritedInvoiceRow NewInvoiceRow()
    {
      ...
    }

  ...

  }

...

}
```

We first create a new indexer to return our new DataRow class to support returning our new DataRow, instead of the base class's indexer, which returns the base class. Next, we create new `AddInvoiceRow()` and `NewInvoiceRow()` methods (created in the Typed DataSet) to return our new DataRow class as well. Now our derived class should be type-safe and completely inherited.

Now that all the right plumbing is there, we can put our business logic in our DataRow class, as shown in Listing 6.18.

Listing 6.18: *Adding Our Business Logic*

```
public class InheritedTDS : FixedCustomerTDS
{

...

  public class InheritedInvoiceRow : InvoiceRow
  {

    ...

    public new DateTime InvoiceDate
    {
      get
      {
        return base.InvoiceDate;
      }
      set
      {
        if (value > DateTime.Today)
        {
          throw new StrongTypingException(
                    "Invoice Date Cannot be in the future",
                    null);
        }
        else
        {
          base.InvoiceDate = value;
        }
      }
    }

    ...
```

```
          }

    . . .

    }
```

In this business logic, we wanted to check to make sure that whenever an invoice date is set, it is not set in the future. Putting this logic into the property makes sure users cannot set the invoice date incorrectly, but since the DataRow is ultimately the base class, we will need to make sure that users cannot set our invoice date by using the indexer (which would skip calling our property). One way we can do this is by overriding the indexer to make it read-only (see Listing 6.19).

Listing 6.19: *Protecting Our Business Logic*

```
public class InheritedTDS : FixedCustomerTDS
{

  . . .

  public class InheritedInvoiceRow : InvoiceRow
  {

    . . .

    // Only allow read by the indexer
    public new object this[int index]
    {
      get
      {
        return base[index];
      }
    }
    . . .

  }

  . . .

}
```

By overriding the indexer, users will have to use the properties to set the individual values. This way we do not have to duplicate our business logic or route the calls through our properties.

In our example, I derived from the invoice DataTable and the invoice DataRow. Our Typed DataSet also has type-safe classes for the customer's DataTable and DataRow. We did not derive from these because we did not need to add any business logic. So you can see that when you inherit from a Typed DataSet you do not need to derive from every DataTable, only the ones you want to add business logic into.

In this section we were able to derive from the Typed DataSet by manually editing the generated code. Because the generated code could change, it is generally a bad idea to edit it. To allow you to inherit without editing the generated code, Chris Sells and I have made a Visual Studio Add-in that will replace the standard Typed DataSet generator to make these changes for you in the generated code. You can download this code at my Web site (www.adoguy.com/book/AGDataSetGenerator).

6.5 Conclusion

We can probably agree that type-safety is good and that by generating Typed DataSets we can reduce mistakes and misuse of our database. You have also learned how to generate Typed DataSets in Visual Studio .NET and from the command line, as well as how to customize the generation by using annotations.

Typed DataSets allow us to employ a new programming paradigm where we specialize generated classes to put business logic into our ADO.NET code. The code that Microsoft generates is problematic for using this paradigm, but we can get around this with a tool that is available on my Web site.

■7■
Working with DataSets

Aftter Chapters 5 and 6, we should have some solid DataSets created. Now, what do we do with them? We need to rip off the covers
and peek inside the data. The data inside the DataSets not only contains the
information we need to maintain our disconnected cache of the database
data, but it also presents a powerful facility that should change the way we
look at database data. By setting up relations, we can navigate up and
down them to see our databases as the hierarchical data they most often
are. Let's get started.

7.1 Changing the Data

Ultimately, the main reason for DataSets to exist is to store and manipulate
your data. Whether you are reading from a database or creating a DataSet
on the fly, all DataSets will store data.

DataRows are the basic storage for all data within the DataSet. At the
heart of it, the DataRow contains an array of values that represent a single
row in a DataTable. DataRows are held in the DataTable with the `Rows()`
property, which is a collection of `DataRow` objects (using the `DataRowCol-`
`lection` class). The DataRow is unlike traditional field collections in that
it contains more information than just the current value for each column in
the row. The DataRow contains the following information:

- The current value of each column in the row
- The original value of each column in the row, if the column has changed
- The state of the row (that is, added, deleted, modified, unchanged, and so on)
- The connection to walk to parent or child rows (for relations)

DataSet or DataReader?

When I talk with working developers, the question I hear most often is: Which is the right approach? The answer depends on your problem domain. The DataReader is a forward-only fire hose for data. It is often the perfect solution for reporting on data in the database. But forcing a design to use it may involve writing your own DataSet-like container for data if you need to use the data after you read a single row.

The DataSet, on the other hand, is a great way to hold data from the database, but filling it comes with a performance penalty. If you need to manipulate your data and save it back to the database, the DataSet is really the only game in town. Using the DataSet to simply report on data (like on a Web page, for instance) usually is the wrong approach. I say "usually" because there are always exceptions to this rule.

Let's look at a specific domain problem: an e-commerce site. Assuming we have a large number of salable items, I would use DataReaders to show the user the products they are looking for and a DataSet for the shopping basket. When you list products by caching all the items in your catalog, you usually lose efficiency when the cache is too large. I usually like to let the database handle the caching of recently used items. It does a better job in most cases. But a smaller DataSet to contain the user's information and shopping basket could be cached in the Web session so that we can limit the number of database reads and writes. If the visitor never ends up buying anything, their shopping basket could simply disappear (and never get persisted) when his or her session dies.

Just remember this caveat: If you need it cached, use a DataSet; if you need it once, use a DataReader.

7.1.1   Adding Rows

Adding new rows to the DataTable is fairly painless. You can either create an array of values to add to the row collection as a row, or you can ask the DataTable to create a new row for you, as shown in Listing 7.1.

Listing 7.1: *Adding DataRows*

```
. . .

// Get object reference of the table for simplified use
DataTable dataTable = dataSet.Tables[0];

// Add a row by creating a new DataRow
DataRow newRow = dataTable.NewRow();
newRow["CustomerID"] = Guid.NewGuid();
newRow["LastName"] = "Millwood";
newRow["FirstName"] = "Kevin";
dataTable.Rows.Add(newRow); // <- Important!

// Add a row by appending an item array (of objects)
object[] newValues = new object[dataTable.Columns.Count];
newValues[0] = Guid.NewGuid();
newValues[1] = "Damian";
newValues[2] = "Moss";
dataTable.Rows.Add(newValues); // <- Important!
```

The `DataRowCollection.Add()` method supports both methods of adding a new row. So, why use one over the other? I suggest that you use the `DataTable.NewRow()` method to create a new row, because you can fill it and be assured that the data you store is the same as the column dictates. The reason this is a more sound approach is that the values in the new DataRow are associated with the schema of the DataTable, so you cannot add values to the row that are inconsistent with the column schema. In addition, the different types of lookups for the row elements will make your code more readable. The first way of adding the new DataRow is a lot more understandable because we can see that column zero is the customer's ID, column one is the customer's first name, and column two is the customer's last name.

It is important to remember that `DataTable.NewRow()` does not add the row to the DataTable. You must make the subsequent call to `Data-Table.Rows.Add()` to add the new row.

There is no requirement that your new row always be added at the end. If you want to add a new row somewhere in the middle of the collection, this can be done with the `DataTable.Rows.InsertAt()` method, as demonstrated in Listing 7.2.

Listing 7.2: *Inserting DataRows*

```
. . .


// Add a row by creating a new DataRow
DataRow insertedRow = dataTable.NewRow();
insertedRow["CustomerID"] = Guid.NewGuid();
insertedRow["LastName"] = "Marquis";
insertedRow["FirstName"] = "Jason";
dataTable.Rows.InsertAt(insertedRow, 1);
```

7.1.2 Deleting Rows

When using disconnected data, deleting rows from the collection has a special requirement: The row needs to continue to exist until the DataSet updates the data store, but we do not need to know about it right away. There are three methodologies for deleting rows:

• Use `DataTable.Rows.Remove()` to remove a row based on its Data-Row instance.
• Use `DataTable.Rows.RemoveAt()` to remove a row based on its ordinal number.
• Use `DataRow.Delete()` to ask the row to remove itself.

With all three methods we can delete (or remove) specific rows. It is important that you understand how the row's ordinal number is affected when you delete. If you add and delete a row before the changes are accepted by the DataTable, the system will actually delete the item from the collection. If you delete an item that exists outside the DataTable, the row is preserved, but is marked as deleted—we need the information stored in the row in order to update the data store with the fact that it has been deleted. Because of this fact, using row ordinal numbers is dangerous because the number may change every time you add or delete items. Listing 7.3 shows how to delete rows.

Listing 7.3: *Deleting DataRows*

```
...

// Get object reference of the table for simplified use
DataTable dataTable = dataSet.Tables[0];

// Add a row by creating a new DataRow
DataRow newRow = dataTable.NewRow();
newRow["CustomerID"] = Guid.NewGuid();
newRow["LastName"] = "Millwood";
newRow["FirstName"] = "Kevin";
dataTable.Rows.Add(newRow); // <- Important!

// Now let's delete it
dataTable.Rows.Remove(newRow);

// Get the first row
DataRow row = dataSet.Tables[0].Rows[0];

// Delete it!
row.Delete();

// Now let's delete Row 2 by ordinal number
dataTable.Rows.RemoveAt(2);
```

7.1.3 Reading and Writing DataRow Values

Simple reporting of data within the DataSet can be done by walking through the DataRows of a specific DataTable, as shown in Listing 7.4.

Listing 7.4: *Reading DataRow Values*

```
...

// Get object reference of the Table for simplified use
DataTable dataTable = dataSet.Tables[0];

// Write the name of each customer to the console
Console.WriteLine("Customer List");
Console.WriteLine("=============");
foreach (DataRow row in dataTable.Rows)
{
  Console.WriteLine("{0}, {1}", row["LastName"],
                                row["FirstName"]);
}
```

This example shows how to dump a simple list of data from a single table. The key here is that we are getting each DataRow from the table in this DataSet. The DataRow class supports the syntax of a string-based indexer (or `Item` property in VB .NET) to retrieve the column of that particular row (for example, `row["LastName"]`). In addition, the DataRow's indexer also supports by ordinal number or by the DataColumn that represents that column in the DataTable, as Listing 7.5 demonstrates.

Listing 7.5: *DataRow Indexers*

```
. . .

// Write the name of each customer to the
// console using the column name
Console.WriteLine("Customer List");
Console.WriteLine("=============");
foreach (DataRow row in dataTable.Rows)
{
   Console.WriteLine("{0}, {1}", row["LastName"],
                                  row["FirstName"]);
}

// Write the name of each customer to the
// console using the column ordinal number
Console.WriteLine("Customer List");
Console.WriteLine("=============");
foreach (DataRow row in dataTable.Rows)
{
   Console.WriteLine("{0}, {1}", row[1], row[2]);
}

// Get object references to the DataColumns
DataColumn lastNameColumn = dataTable.Columns["LastName"];
DataColumn firstNameColumn = dataTable.Columns["FirstName"];

// Write the name of each customer to the
// console using the column ordinal number
Console.WriteLine("Customer List");
Console.WriteLine("=============");
foreach (DataRow row in dataTable.Rows)
{
   Console.WriteLine("{0}, {1}", row[lastNameColumn],
                                  row[firstNameColumn]);
}
```

The DataRow index returns a value of a column as a `System.Object` instance. This value knows its type (like all .NET types). You can cast it or write it out without casting, as needed. In addition to this type information, you also have access to the DataTable's `Column` collection, which contains the schema information about what types it expects in each column. In Chapter 5 we discussed how the DataColumn is the container for simple schema information about a particular column. By interrogating the Data-Column you can make runtime decisions about how to deal with the data (or lack of data) in the column. In most cases this is inefficient, but if you are dealing with amorphous data, this facility can be very powerful. Listing 7.6 gives an example of this.

Listing 7.6: *Interrogating DataColumns*

```
...

// Write the name of each customer to the
// console using the column name
Console.WriteLine("Customer List");
Console.WriteLine("=============");
foreach (DataRow row in dataTable.Rows)
{
  Console.WriteLine("{0}, {1}:", row["LastName"],
                                 row["FirstName"]);
  for (int x = 0; x < row.ItemArray.GetLength(0); ++x)
  {
    object obj = row.ItemArray[x];
    if (obj.GetType() == typeof(Guid))
    {
      Console.WriteLine("  {0} : {1} *Should be readonly*",
                        obj.GetType().Name,
                        obj);
    }
    else if (obj.GetType() == typeof(DBNull))
    {
      Console.WriteLine("  {0} : ColumnType: {1}",
                        obj.GetType().Name,
                        dataTable.Columns[x].DataType.Name);
    }
    else
    {
      Console.WriteLine("  {0} : {1}",
                        obj.GetType().Name,
                        obj);
    }
  }
}
```

In this example we tested the object's underlying type to see if it was a Guid. When we find a Guid, we tell the user that the type really should be read-only (especially if this data was retrieved directly from the database). We also test for a type of DBNull, which is a special type used for values that are null in the database. In the case of detecting a DBNull value, the only place to get the type that the database is expecting is to look at the DataColumn for that column. In this example, we simply alert the user to the underlying column type.

An alternative to checking for the DBNull type of a value is to ask the row if the column is null. When calling the DataRow.IsNull() function, you can use the same overloads that exist for the indexer (name, ordinal, or DataColumn). For example:

```
if (row.IsNull("LastName")) ...
if (row.IsNull(1)) ...
if (row.IsNull(lastNameColumn)) ...
```

Reading data is one thing, but we must be able to manipulate the data in our DataSet as well. As you would expect, the DataTable, DataRow-Collection, and DataRow classes support the basic CRUD (Create, Read, Update, and Delete) operations.

By using the DataRow's indexer you also can set new or updated values to the row. Be careful when you set new values because the DataRow will throw an InvalidCastException if the object you set is in conflict with the DataColumn's DataType. The value does not have to be specifically the type defined in the DataColumn, but it must be convertible. See Listing 7.7 for an example.

Listing 7.7: *Adding Convertible Values*

```
...

// Get object reference of the first row for simplified use
DataRow row = dataSet.Tables[0].Rows[0];

// Set some valid values
row["LastName"] = "Millwood";
row["FirstName"] = "Kevin";
```

```
// Set a Double
row["Discount"] = .15;

// Set a Date
// (succeeds since this converts
// to a DateTime easily)
row["DOB"] = "04/24/1969";

// This would fail because the date is bad
row["DOB"] = "04/31/1969";

// Set a bad type
// (Fails because this string is incompatible
// with the float)
// ".15" would work, though, because it is convertible
// to a float
row["Discount"] = "15%";
```

In this example, the last two value changes will throw exceptions because the conversions fail. There is not a type check as such, but more like a `Convert.ChangeType()` call. In most cases, the DataRow will attempt to do the conversion for you. This may be problematic because implicit conversions may not do the conversion you are expecting. In most code, I would suggest explicitly converting/casting to the preferred type. This is often less error-prone than trusting that the conversion you want is happening behind the scenes.

7.1.3.1 *Batch Changes to a Row*

There are times when you will want to make changes in parallel to a specific DataRow. Usually this is done when a single piece of the change will invalidate a constraint or if you want the ability to cancel the change before committing it. For example, we will assume that you have a table with a constraint that one of two columns must not be null, but in addition, both of the columns cannot be filled in. If you tried to code around the constraints, you would start pulling your hair out to find intermediate states where the row was still valid in the eyes of the constraints. To fix this, the DataRow exposes the `BeginEdit`, `EndEdit`, and `CancelEdit` methods. Once you call `BeginEdit()`, the changes are not actually saved to the DataRow until the `EndEdit()` occurs. If you decide that the change is a mistake, you can call

CancelEdit, which will return the row to its initial state before BeginEdit was called. During the span of the edit, no constraints will be enforced and no notifications of changed values will be fired. See Listing 7.8 for an example of batch changes to a row.

Listing 7.8: *Batch Changes to a DataRow*

```
. . .

// Get object reference of the first row for simplified use
DataRow row = dataSet.Tables[0].Rows[0];

// Start the edit
row.BeginEdit();

// Set some valid values
row["LastName"] = "Millwood";
row["FirstName"] = "Kevin";

// Set a Double
row["Discount"] = .15;

// End the edit
row.EndEdit();

// Start the edit again
row.BeginEdit();

// Set a Date
// (succeeds since this converts
// to a DateTime easily)
row["DOB"] = "04/24/1969";

// We want to revert, so we call CancelEdit()
row.CancelEdit();
```

7.1.3.2 *Bulk Loading Data into DataTables*

As with needing to suspend notifications and constraints during the editing of a particular row, you may find it useful to turn off these facilities when loading lots of information into a DataTable. The DataTable class allows for this by supplying the BeginLoadData() and EndLoadData() methods. In addition to notifications and constraints being suspended during the data loading, indexes are also not being maintained, which will make the loading of this data very fast. The DataTable expects you to use the `LoadData()` method to actually add or change rows. See Listing 7.9 for an example.

Listing 7.9: *Bulk Loading into a DataTable*

```
. . .

// Get object reference of the first row for simplified use
DataTable dataTable = dataSet.Tables[0];

// Start the DataLoad
// (disabling constraints, notifications,
// and indexes)
dataTable.BeginLoadData();

// Create a row
object[] row = new object[dataTable.Columns.Count];
row[0] = Guid.NewGuid();
row[1] = "Kevin";
row[2] = "Millwood";

// Add it,
// but don't tell the row that it's been
// updated in the data store
dataTable.LoadDataRow(row, false);

// Create a row
row = new object[dataTable.Columns.Count];
row[0] = System.Object.Empty;
row[1] = "Damian";
row[2] = "Moss";

// Add it,
// and tell it to mark the row as already
// updated in the data stored
dataTable.LoadDataRow(row, true);

// Finish the loading
// (turning back on constraints, notifications,
// and indexes)
dataTable.EndLoadData();
```

In this example, we can see how to add a row at a time with the `Load-DataRow()` method. The signature of this method is much like adding a new row with an array of objects. If a column in the DataRow is autogenerated or if you want the default value to be used, you would pass `System.Object.Empty` as the value.

The second parameter of the `LoadDataRow()` method refers to the action to be taken after the `LoadDataRow()` is called. If this parameter is true, `DataTable.AcceptChanges()` will be called. In effect, this will tell the DataTable that all additions and changes in the DataTable are accepted as permanent changes. This has no effect on the database itself; it is only telling the DataTable to treat these changes as accepted. Because `DataTable.AcceptChanges()` is called, all changes in the DataTable (not just the DataRow you added) will be accepted. If you specify false as the second parameter of `LoadDataRow()`, the DataRow will be added as an insertion and may be inserted into the database when you next update the database.

7.1.4   Row Version

In many older data access layers, all editing of data rows took place in our class and at the database at the same time. Because ADO.NET is disconnected, none of our changes take place at the database server until we explicitly ask it to update itself from the DataSet. These changes are not propagated immediately, so we need to have some data in our DataSet that specifies what data has changed. At first, you might assume that there is a simple `IsDirty` flag on each row or on each value in a row. That flag would be unsuitable, though, because we may need to roll back our changes or know about the original version of an individual row in order to do concurrency checking when we update the database. To support all this metadata required for each value, the DataRow keeps up to two copies of each value in a DataRow as well as a flag to determine its state (somewhat like a complex `IsDirty` flag).

While you are editing a particular row, the row keeps two versions of the data that belongs to the row: the original value and (if a new value has been assigned) the proposed value. The usual lifecycle of the row is as shown in Figure 7.1.

What this diagram shows is that when you edit a value in a DataRow, it is marked as changed until either `AcceptChanges()` or `RejectChanges()` is called. These methods tell the DataRow to do one of two things:

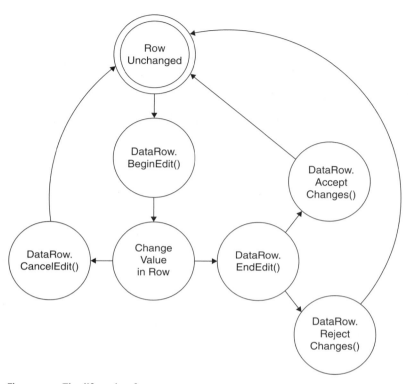

Figure 7.1: *The lifecycle of a row*

- **AcceptChanges**: Change the proposed value to the original value, getting rid of the original value. Mark the DataRow as unchanged.
- **RejectChanges**: Get rid of the proposed value and mark the row as unchanged again.

Certainly, you could call these methods yourself, but they are really used by the DataAdapter to change each DataRow as it is updated to the database. The important piece of information to understand is that if your DataRow has changes that have not been accepted or rejected, you still have access to either of those versions.

To retrieve a particular version of the data, the DataRow class uses the DataRowVersion enumeration to specify which version you want. The enumerations are:

- **Current**: This is the current value of the column. This will be the proposed value after a change has been made, or the same as the original value after `AcceptChanges` has been called.
- **Default**: This is not a value state, but a holder that will point to the right state based on the state of the entire row.
- **Original**: The value of the column in the row when the row was created, or after the last time `AcceptChanges()` was called.
- **Proposed**: The changed value of the column before `AcceptChanges()` is called. This will become available after you edit a row.

When you need to retrieve a specific version of the row's data, you will need to specify the `DataRowVersion` in the itemizer of the DataRow:

```
string oldString = row["FirstName",
                       DataRowVersion.Original];
string newString = row["FirstName",
                       DataRowVersion.Proposed];
```

You can test whether a DataRow has these extra versions of the data by calling the `DataRow.HasVersion()` method. This is useful if you need a certain version that is included in the DataRow. By retrieving `DataRow-Version.Default`, you will always get the most relevant version, depending on your DataRow's status. In fact, you will get the `DataRowVersion.Default` version if you do not specify a version.

7.1.5 Row State

Whenever you make any change to a row (including adding or deleting it), the DataRow class records the current state of the row. This information is used to craft the updates to the data stores. Listing 7.10 has an example of this.

Listing 7.10: *Interrogating Row State*

```
...

// Get object reference of the table for simplified use
DataTable dataTable = dataSet.Tables[0];

// Add a row
DataRow newRow = dataTable.NewRow();
```

```
newRow["CustomerID"] = Guid.NewGuid();
newRow["LastName"] = "Millwood";
newRow["FirstName"] = "Kevin";
dataTable.Rows.Add(newRow);

// Report the state
Console.WriteLine("New Row State:\t\t{0}", newRow.RowState);

// Get the first row
DataRow deleteRow = dataSet.Tables[0].Rows[0];

// Delete it!
deleteRow.Delete();

// Report the State
Console.WriteLine("Deleted Row State:\t\t{0}",
                    deleteRow.RowState);

// Get another row
DataRow changeRow = dataSet.Tables[0].Rows[1];

// Change a value
changeRow["DOB"] = "04/24/1969";

// Report the State
Console.WriteLine("Changed Row State:\t{0}",
                    changeRow.RowState);

// Get yet another row
DataRow unchangedRow = dataSet.Tables[0].Rows[2];

// Report the State
Console.WriteLine("Unchanged Row State:\t{0}",
                    unchangedRow.RowState);
```

The output of this example is:

```
New Row State:          Added
Deleted Row State:      Deleted
Changed Row State:      Modified
Unchanged Row State:    Unchanged
```

In this example we can see that the RowState is changing to reflect the current state that the row has been left in. After the data store has been updated, the states will be reset to `RowState.Unchanged`. Please see Chapter 8 for more information on how the database is updated.

7.2   Navigating the DataSet

Navigating through the data in your DataSet provides much more than just iterating over the rows in a table. ADO.NET provides powerful facilities for navigating through your data.

7.2.1   Using Relations to Navigate

Welcome to the real power of the DataSet. Navigable relations provide the capability to view your relational data as a hierarchical object graph. Unlike relations in database schema, you can navigate relations between DataTables. In database schema, ordinarily you join data between tables at the same point of linkage that the relations use (such as foreign keys). When you join two tables in the database, you are returned a result that can contain duplicate data in which a single row is related to multiple child rows. In ADO.NET it is different—each table stays on its own, but the DataSet allows you to navigate at the row level to the related rows between the tables.

In Figure 7.2, we can see how the relations between the `Customer`, `Invoice`, `InvoiceItem`, and `Product` tables are constituted. We can navigate up and down each of these relations. In order to walk up and down the relation chain, you start with a DataRow. The DataRow supports navigating both down to child rows and up to parent rows. See Listing 7.11 for an example.

Listing 7.11: *Navigating Relations*

```
...

// Walk through the customers and
// show all the invoices
foreach (DataRow custRow in
        dataSet.Tables["Customers"].Rows)
{
  // Write out customer name
  Console.WriteLine("{0}, {1}", custRow["LastName"],
                                custRow["FirstName"]);
```

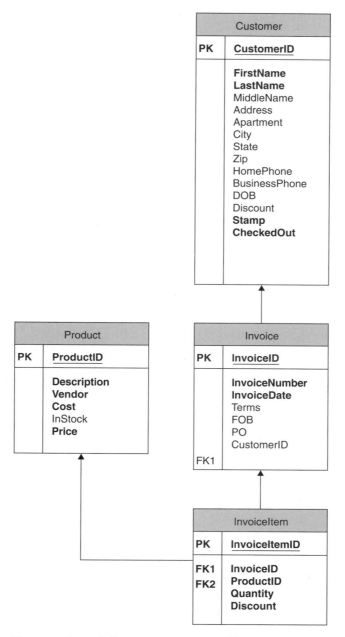

Figure 7.2: *The relations among our four tables*

```
// List invoices
DataRow[] invoiceRows =
                custRow.GetChildRows("Customer_Invoice");
foreach(DataRow invRow in invoiceRows)
{
  string invoiceDate =
    ((DateTime)invRow["InvoiceDate"]).ToShortDateString();
  Console.WriteLine("  {0} : {1}",
                    invRow["InvoiceNumber"],
                    invoiceDate);
  Decimal grandTotal = 0;

  // Write out invoice items
  DataRow[] itemRows =
                invRow.GetChildRows("Invoice_Item");
  foreach (DataRow itemRow in itemRows)
  {
    DataRow productRow =
                itemRow.GetChildRows("Item_Product")[0];
    int quantity = ((int)itemRow["Quantity"]);
    Decimal total = ((Decimal)productRow["Price"]) *
                    quantity;
    grandTotal += total;
    Console.WriteLine("    {0} {1} @ {2:C} ea",
                      productRow["Description"],
                      quantity,
                      total);
  }
  Console.WriteLine("    Total: {0:C}", grandTotal);
}

}
```

This code produces this output:

```
Maddux, Greg
  100 : 3/21/2002
    Basketball 2 @ $29.00 ea
    Baseball Mitt 3 @ $89.97 ea
    Total: $327.91
  101 : 3/31/2002
    Baseball Bat, Slugger 1 @ $19.99 ea
    Total: $19.99
Glavine, Tom
  102 : 3/24/2002
```

```
      Baseball Mitt 1 @ $29.99 ea
      Total: $29.99
  Smoltz, John
    103 : 3/27/2002
      Baseball Bat, Slugger 1 @ $19.99 ea
      Total: $19.99
    104 : 4/1/2002
      Baseball 1 @ $1.75 ea
      Total: $1.75
```

As you can see, we are getting only the rows that are directly related. We are exclusively using GetChildRows() to retrieve the array of DataRows that are linked through the relation to the child table. In the last use of GetChildRows(), we have specific knowledge that one (and only one) row in the Product table corresponds to the information about the product, so we get the first row. If we were going to write this in production code, we would have code to make sure that the returned DataRow arrays did not return nulls (which would happen if the child table did not contain any matching rows).

For parent rows, the DataRow class provides two virtually identical calls: GetParentRows() and GetParentRow(). The only difference between these calls is that the former returns an array of DataRows, and the latter returns a single row (or the first row).

7.2.2 DataViews

The DataView class is used to provide for data binding to Window Forms controls and Web Controls in ASP.NET. (These are discussed in Chapter 10.) Here I will show you how to use a DataView to search, sort, or filter a DataTable. Each DataTable has a built-in DataView. The default DataView is called DataTable.DefaultView(), but you can create as many Data-Views as you like. This is useful when you want to show the same data, filtered or sorted in a different way. See Listing 7.12 for an example.

Listing 7.12: *The Default DataView*

```
...

// Get object reference of the table for simplified use
DataTable dataTable = dataSet.Tables[0];
```

```
// Get a count of the rows in the default view
Console.WriteLine("DefaultView Count: {0}",
                  dataTable.DefaultView.Count);

// Create a new DataView
DataView sortedView = new DataView(dataTable);
sortedView.Sort = "LastName";
```

In this example we have two different views (the default view and sortedView). They do not affect the underlying data; they just have a different point of view into the data.

7.2.2.1 *Sorting with a DataView*

The DataView supports sorting by way of the DataView.Sort property. The Sort property is a string that describes the sorting criteria. To make the DataView sort, simply set the Sort property to the name of one or many columns with either ASC or DESC to determine whether the sort should be ascending or descending. In practice, ascending is the default behavior, so you do not need to specify it. See Listing 7.13 as an example.

Listing 7.13: *Sorting a DataView*

```
. . .

// Get object reference of the table for simplified use
DataTable dataTable = dataSet.Tables[0];

// Sort by the LastName, Ascending order by default
dataTable.DefaultView.Sort = "LastName";

// Sort by the LastName, Descending order
dataTable.DefaultView.Sort = "LastName DESC";

// Sort by the LastName (Ascending),
// and secondarily by FirstName (Descending)
dataTable.DefaultView.Sort = "LastName, FirstName DESC";
```

7.2.2.2 *Filtering with a DataView*

You can filter a DataView by setting the DataView.RowFilter(). The RowFilter property of the DataView takes a string that is evaluated at runtime to filter out rows that do not match the `RowFilter`. As an example, see Listing 7.14.

Listing 7.14: *Filtering with a DataView*

```
. . .

// Get object reference of the table for simplified use
DataTable dataTable = dataSet.Tables[0];

// Set a filter to only see Rawlings items
dataTable.DefaultView.RowFilter = "Vendor = 'Rawlings'";

// Check count
Console.WriteLine("Rawlings Products: {0}",
                  dataTable.DefaultView.Count);
```

The syntax of this string is identical to the syntax of the `DataColumn.Expression` property.[1] This syntax is a client-side query language—you can think of it as disconnected data querying. Here are some common forms of the `RowFilter`:

Text Filters:
```
dataTable.DefaultView.RowFilter = "FirstName = 'John'";
```

Simple text comparisons take the form of an exact match. Be careful if you are used to using the C# equality operator (==); the equality operator in this syntax is a single equal character (=). In addition, the inequality operator (<>) is different from the C# inequality operator (!=).

Date Filters:
```
dataView.RowFilter = "BirthDate = #04/24/1969#";
```

Dates can be used in filtering, but you must surround them with hash signs (#) to signify them as dates.

---

1. In the initial release of Visual Studio.NET, the MSDN link was msdn.microsoft.com/library/en-us/cpref/html/frlrfSystemDataDataColumnClassExpressionTopic.asp.

Comparison Operators:
```
dataView.RowFilter = "Cost > 24.99";
```

Comparison operators (<, >, <=, and >=) are completely supported.

Compound Expressions:
```
dataView.RowFilter = "(Cost <= 24.99) AND (Cost > 50.00)";
```

Boolean concatenation (AND, OR, and NOT) and parenthetical grouping are supported for compound expressions.

Wildcard Expressions:
```
dataView.RowFilter = "Company LIKE 'Microsoft*'";
```

For text comparisons, wildcard matching is supported with the LIKE syntax. Both the asterisk (*) and the percent sign (%) are identically supported as wildcard symbols. So, in this example, we would get all companies that started with "Microsoft", no matter how many characters are after the first nine.

Parent Relations:
```
dataView.RowFilter = "Parent.Birthdate < #01/01/1978#";
```

You can reference data in the parent relation of the rows you are filtering with the Parent syntax.

Child Relations:
```
dataView.RowFilter = "Child.InvDate >= #01/01/2001#";
dataView.RowFilter = "Child(Cust2Inv).InvDate >= " +
                     "#01/01/1969#";
```

You can reference data in the relations of the rows you are filtering with the simple Child syntax if there is only one child relation in the row; otherwise, you must use the name of the child relation to define which child relation to use.

7.2.2.3 *Filtering on* RowState *in a DataView*

The DataView supports a different method for filtering on the state of the rows in the DataTable, as shown in Listing 7.15.

Listing 7.15: *Filtering a DataView on RowState*

```
. . .

// Get object reference of the table for simplified use
DataTable dataTable = dataSet.Tables[0];

// Set a filter to see the original data
// (in modified rows, the original values
//  will be shown)
dataTable.DefaultView.RowStateFilter =
                          DataViewRowState.OriginalRows;
```

To filter on RowState, you need to use the DataViewRowState enumeration. This enumeration supports filtering rows out by the RowState of the row as well as showing different versions of the row's data. Here is a quick explanation of all the values in the enumeration:

- **CurrentRows**: Shows the current row data based on the DataRowState of the row. All rows should be shown with the exception of the deleted rows. This is the default.
- **Added**: Only shows rows added since the last time DataTable.AcceptChanges() was called.
- **Deleted**: Only shows rows deleted since the last time DataTable.AcceptChanges() was called.
- **ModifiedCurrent**: Shows the current version of any modified rows. Rows are marked as modified when any value in a row is changed. This value will tell the DataView to show only rows that have been modified since the last time that DataTable.AcceptChanges() was called.
- **ModifiedOriginal**: Shows the original version of any modified rows. Rows are marked as modified when any value in a row is changed. This value will tell the DataView to show only rows that have been modified since the last time that DataTable.AcceptChanges() was called.
- **None**: No rows are shown.
- **OriginalRows**: Shows all rows in their original form. This includes unchanged, modified, new, and deleted rows.
- **Unchanged**: Shows only the rows that remain unchanged since the last time that DataTable.AcceptChanges() was called.

7.3 Searching the DataSet

Unfortunately the DataSet does not support a full SQL Query engine. Eventually you will need to search through your DataTables for data based on some criteria. ADO.NET supports doing a simple search within a DataTable to return the rows that match. In addition, you can use a DataView to do indexed based searches.

7.3.1 Searching with DataTable.Select

When searching a DataTable for specific criteria, you simply use the `Data-Table.Select()` method to find one or more rows that match your criteria. This criteria is made up of an expression that signifies what you are searching for. The syntax of this expression is the same syntax as the `Data-Column.Expression` property takes. The result of the `DataTable.Select()` method is an array of DataRows that match the criteria. The array has a length of zero if the criteria is not met. An example of how to call select can be seen in Listing 7.16.

Listing 7.16: *Searching a DataTable with Select( )*

```
...

// Get object reference of the table for simplified use
DataTable dataTable = dataSet.Tables[0];

// Find the DataRows that have Wilson as its vendor
DataRow[] rows = dataTable.Select("Vendor = 'Wilson'");
Console.WriteLine("Simple Select Search:");

// Show them all
foreach (DataRow row in rows)
{
  Console.WriteLine("  Item: {0} - Vendor: {1}",
                    row["ProductID"],
                    row["Vendor"]);
}

// Find DataRows that match our compound expression
DataRow[] compoundRows = dataTable.Select("Vendor =
                        'Wilson' " + "AND Price > 20.00");
Console.WriteLine("Compound Select Search:");
```

```
// Show them all
foreach (DataRow row in compoundRows)
{
  Console.WriteLine("  Item: {0} - Vendor: "+
                    "{1} - Price: {2}",
                    row["ProductID"],
                    row["Vendor"],
                    row["Price"]);
}
```

When working with DataSets with related DataTables, the DataRow array that is returned is still related. This is very useful for searching a DataTable within a relational DataSet to get a subset of the DataSet that matches a specific query. Listing 7.17 shows how this would work. This example uses DataSet merging, which is discussed in Section 7.4.

Listing 7.17: Creating a Subset DataSet Using Select and Merge

```
...

// Search for Customers whose addresses are in Georgia
DataRow[] gaCusts =
        dataSet.Tables["Customers"].Select("State = 'GA'");

// Create a new DataSet
DataSet newDataSet = new DataSet();

// Copy the schema from the old DataSet to a stream
MemoryStream strm = new MemoryStream();
dataSet.WriteXmlSchema(strm);

// Reset the Stream so we can read it
strm.Position = 0;

// Read in the schema to the new DataSet
newDataSet.ReadXmlSchema(strm);

// Copy the Rows into the new DataSet
newDataSet.Merge(gaCusts);
```

7.3.2   Searching with a DataView

A DataView can be used to do searches against a DataTable by using the `RowFilter` property. Often, setting a `RowFilter` will be functionally equivalent to a search. By using the `RowFilter` property, you can find rows in the DataTable that match criteria. This methodology is functionally similar to using DataTable.Select(), but may be a better fit if you are already using DataViews. This eliminates any data copies and gives you a working rectangular piece of data to work with that is more useful than simply an array of DataRows.

In contrast, the `Find` and `FindRows` methods of the DataView are meant to find a row (or rows) that match a specific key. In order to perform a search in the DataView, you must set the `DataView.Sort` property with a key (or keys) that you want to search against. Then you can call the `DataView.Find()` or `DataView.FindRows()` method. The `DataView.Find()` method returns an integer that specifies the ordinal number of the row in the DataView (not in the DataTable). The `DataView.FindRows()` method returns an array of `DataRowView` objects that represent the rows that matched the query. For an example, see Listing 7.18.

Listing 7.18: *Searching with a DataView*

```
. . .

// Get object reference of the table for simplified use
DataTable dataTable = dataSet.Tables[0];

// Set a sort order
dataTable.DefaultView.Sort = "Vendor";

// Find the Wilson product
int found = dataTable.DefaultView.Find("Wilson");
Console.WriteLine("Vendor: {0}",
                    dataTable.DefaultView[found]["Vendor"]);

// Find all Rawlings products
DataRowView[] rows =
                dataTable.DefaultView.FindRows("Rawlings");
Console.WriteLine("Rawlings count: {0}", rows.Length);

// Set a compound sort order
dataTable.DefaultView.Sort = "Vendor, Price DESC";
```

```
// Find the compound criteria product
object[] criteria = new object[] {"Wilson", 29.99};
found = dataTable.DefaultView.Find(criteria);
Console.WriteLine("Compound Vendor Search: {0}",
                 dataTable.DefaultView[found]["Vendor"]);
```

The last criteria type in the example shows a compound key. With a sort that includes two keys, our search needs to be an array of keys. Both `DataView.Find()` and `DataView.FindRows()` accept this syntax for composite keys.

7.4 **Merging DataSets**

Now that we are working with DataSets and their contents, we find the need to merge two DataSets together. Your application may be responsible for analyzing data that is made up of multiple DataSets. In order to relate tables from different DataSets, you will need to get them all into a single DataSet. In addition, you may be updating remote DataSets through a Web Service or other remote communication., in which case you might need to merge the changes that the remote DataSet sent in to your local DataSet. To allow this, ADO.NET supports merging DataSets in the following ways:

• Copy contents of DataSets with the same schema to join all the rows in each DataSet.
• Update the state of records from one DataSet into another DataSet, again with the same schema.
• Merge two DataSets with dissimilar schema to get a DataSet with all the DataTables from both DataSets.

The `DataSet.Merge()` method takes care of handling all these merge scenarios by using overloads that take different parameters. When calling `Merge`, be aware that the data sent to the `Merge` method will be merged into the DataSet being called. In the process of a merge, the schema is merged first, then the data.

These three merge scenarios can be seen in these examples:

```
// Merge two DataSets together
targetDataSet.Merge(sourceDataSet);

// Merge two DataSets together
targetDataSet.Merge(sourceDataSet.Tables["Products"]);
```

In these examples, we are merging the source DataSet and the product DataTable into the target DataSet. The default behavior of these overloads is to add schema if the DataTable is missing in the main DataSet.

```
// Merge changes from one DataSet into another where they
// both have similar schema
targetDataSet.Merge(sourceDataSet.GetChanges());

// Merge changes from one DataSet into another where they
// both have similar schema
targetDataSet.Merge(
          sourceDataSet.Tables["Products"].GetChanges());
```

These examples show how you would merge just the changes of the source DataSet into the target DataSet.

```
// Merge two DataSets, setting row state to Unchanged
targetDataSet.Merge(sourceDataSet, false);

// Merge two DataSets, preserving the row state and versions
targetDataSet.Merge(sourceDataSet, true);
```

These overloads support specifying whether you want to preserve the changes in the source DataSet's rows (the row state and versions) when merged. When true is specified for the second parameter, it merges rows and preserves the row state and the different versions of each of the values in a row. Calling this method overload with false is identical to not specifying the parameter at all.

```
// Merge two DataSets with dissimilar schema
targetDataSet.Merge(sourceDataSet,
               false,
               MissingSchemaAction.Add);
```

```
// Merge two DataSets with similar schema
// (but want to specify to throw an error if the schemas are
//  different)
targetDataSet.Merge(sourceDataSet,
               false,
               MissingSchemaAction.Error);
```

Finally, these overloads support specifying what to do when there is a schema missing from the target DataSet. The first version of this call is functionally identical to calling `DataSet.Merge(DataSet)` because sending false and `MissingSchemaAction.Add` is the default behavior. On the other hand, the second version shows that we expect the schemas of the DataSets to be identical and that we want an error (exception) to be thrown if they are not.

7.5 Conclusion

The facilities for manipulating and navigating the data contained in the DataSet provide functionality that makes the DataSet more than just an in-memory database. The simplified way of changing rows coupled with the strength of the DataRow that contains historical data make the creating, reading, updating, and deleting of the DataSet data that much more powerful. In addition, the ability to navigate through the relations between DataTables provides a mechanism that never really existed in older Microsoft data access layers. Finally, even though it lacks a real SQL engine to provide powerful searching, ADO.NET allows us to filter, sort, and search DataTables with `DataTable.Select()`, and when it is used in conjunction with the DataView, ADO.NET provides for everything we need in a majority of cases.

■ 8 ■
Updating the Database

U P   T O   T H I S   P O I N T, the news of disconnected data has been mostly good. We can keep a local cache of the database, make the changes locally, and access the data without using a connection to the database. Unfortunately, all of this comes at a cost.

8.1   The Trouble with Disconnected Data

The hardest part of using disconnected data is handling the synchronization of your copies of the DataSet and the data in the database. Simply saving your data back to the database is fairly trivial in ADO.NET. The real issue with this updating is handling concurrency.

Back in the old connected days, we would deal with concurrency by having the database handle it. We would specify the type of concurrency we wanted to support, and the database would do the heavy lifting of making sure that rows were locked while we had them. When we would do a database operation, we would specify the type of database locking we wanted the database to use.

The `Isolationlevel` parameter of the `IDbTransaction` interface (supported by the `SqlTransaction`, `OleDbTransaction`, `OdbcTransaction`, and `OracleTransaction` classes) will manage how concurrency will work during a transaction. Although we can use transactions to help with our concurrency, a transaction is tied to a connection. In the disconnected world of ADO.NET this does not work. We cannot start a transaction (and connection) and keep it open the entire time we want to use our DataSet.

For example, assume we are writing a typical e-commerce Web application. We retrieve a user from our database to have the user confirm their mailing and shipping address. In the majority of these cases users do not change anything, but occasionally they do. If we use a transaction and connection to lock the record while we wait for the user to confirm the addresses, we would be locking out other users of the record (like our shipping department). Because our application is Web-based, it's possible that the user just closed their browser and we are waiting for some timeout to happen to release the record. This just does not work well. We need to deal with the concurrency issues outside the database; however, this does not mean that we cannot enlist the database to help us manage concurrency.

8.2   Concurrency in ADO.NET

We need to figure out what kind of concurrency our specific need dictates. There are three types of concurrency that ADO.NET can help you implement:

- **Optimistic concurrency**: Everyone has access to the data that the DataSet contains in the database, but access is prohibited while any one person is writing to the database. This is the most common concurrency model in ADO.NET.
- **Pessimistic concurrency**: Nobody is allowed access to the data that the DataSet contains in the database while you have a copy (have a lock on the data).
- **Destructive concurrency**: Everyone has access to the data that the DataSet contains in the database, but the last one to write the updated row always succeeds. This is effectively no concurrency control. Microsoft refers to this concurrency model as "Last in Wins Concurrency."

To find out what type of concurrency you need, you will need to understand your use of the database data. There is a big trade-off between limiting the access to data and maintaining consistency of that data.

ADO.NET supports optimistic concurrency with the use of the `CommandBuilder` class. Within this chapter I will show you how to use

`CommandBuilders` to get optimistic concurrency as well as how to roll your own optimistic, pessimistic, and destructive concurrencies.

8.2.1 How DataAdapters Update the DataSet

Before we learn how concurrency works in ADO.NET, we must have an understanding of what DataAdapters are doing when you call `Update`. DataAdapters are capable of updating only a single DataTable, so your DataSet should have a one-to-one ratio of DataTables to DataAdapters. When you call `DataAdapter.Update()`, the DataAdapter takes the table and gets a list of changed rows. For each row it executes the specified command object. For example, if the row is new, it calls `InsertCommand`; if the row is changed, it calls `UpdateCommand`; and if the row has been deleted, it calls `DeleteCommand`. DataAdapter makes a roundtrip for every command. The DataAdapter does not support batching.

For DataAdapters to best do their job, you should keep them for the life of the DataSet. When you fill your DataSet, stash the DataAdapters away and re-use them to update the database. For an example, see Listing 8.1.

Listing 8.1: *Using Multiple DataAdapters*

```
// Create and open the Connection
SqlConnection conn = new SqlConnection(
                            "server=localhost;" +
                            "database=ADONET;" +
                            "Integrated Security=true;");

// Create the DataAdapters
SqlDataAdapter customerAdapter =
        new SqlDataAdapter("SELECT * FROM CUSTOMER", conn);
SqlDataAdapter invoiceAdapter =
        new SqlDataAdapter("SELECT * FROM INVOICE", conn);

// Create the DataSet
DataSet dataSet = new DataSet();

// Use the DataAdapters to fill the DataSet
customerAdapter.Fill(dataSet, "Customers");
invoiceAdapter.Fill(dataSet, "Invoices");

// Make some changes
...
```

```
// Update the DataSet
// (each Table separately)
invoiceAdapter.Update(dataSet, "Invoices");
customerAdapter.Update(dataSet, "Customers");
```

8.2.2 Implementing Optimistic Concurrency

The ultimate goal of optimistic concurrency is to not overwrite newer updates to the database. For example, let's say you have a customer management system and you have retrieved a particular customer. At the same time, a customer service representative has retrieved that customer to deal with a support issue and changes some of the user's demographic information. If your code attempts to make a different change after the customer service change went into effect, do you want your change to possibly overwrite the customer service change? How do you resolve the discrepancy? Optimistic concurrency dictates that you can only change the customer record if the customer has not changed since you retrieved it. In this case your change would not happen and you would be alerted that your change did not occur.

With disconnected data we can get optimistic concurrency by ensuring that our records are identical to when we retrieved them from the database. Luckily for us ADO.NET can do this in an automated way using the CommandBuilder class. Listing 8.2 is an example of optimistic concurrency in action.

Listing 8.2: *Optimistic Concurrency Using a CommandBuilder*

```
...

// Grab the DataTable for convenience
DataTable custTable = dataSet.Tables["Customers"];

// Add a new customer
DataRow newRow = custTable.NewRow();
newRow.BeginEdit();
newRow["CustomerID"] = Guid.NewGuid();
newRow["LastName"] = "Remlinger";
newRow["FirstName"] = "Mike";
newRow["Address"] = "10 Aaron Way";
newRow["City"] = "Atlanta";
newRow["State"] = "GA";
```

```
newRow["Zip"] = "30307";
newRow["HomePhone"] = "(404) 543-8765";
newRow.EndEdit();
custTable.Rows.Add(newRow);

// Add a new customer
newRow = custTable.NewRow();
newRow.BeginEdit();
newRow["CustomerID"] = Guid.NewGuid();
newRow["LastName"] = "Jones";
newRow["FirstName"] = "Chipper";
newRow["Address"] = "10 Aaron Way";
newRow["City"] = "Atlanta";
newRow["State"] = "GA";
newRow["Zip"] = "30307";
newRow["HomePhone"] = "(404) 543-8768";
newRow.EndEdit();
custTable.Rows.Add(newRow);

// Change a customer
DataRow oldRow = custTable.Rows[0];
oldRow["Address"] = "53 Peachtree Center";
oldRow["Zip"] = "30342";

// Delete a customer
DataRow delRow = custTable.Rows[1];
delRow.Delete();

// Create a CommandBuilder to generate the
// inserts/updates/deletes
SqlCommandBuilder bldr = new SqlCommandBuilder(dataAdapter);

// Update the database
dataAdapter.Update(custTable);
```

Most of this code should be familiar by now. First we create a simple
DataSet. We then create a new row in the Customer table, change an exist-
ing customer, and finally delete a customer. When we call the Data-
Adapter.Update() method, it goes through the custTable DataTable
and inserts the new record, deletes the deleted row, and performs an
update to the changed row. We never set up the INSERT, UPDATE, or
DELETE commands in the DataAdapter, because we let the Command-
Builder create the commands as we need them.

The `Update` method of DataAdapter classes has a number of overloads. In this example we send in a DataTable. This is the most common case, but you may also send in an array of DataRows or a complete DataSet. The caveat of using the DataSet overload of `Update` is that it expects that the DataSet contains a DataTable named "Table". Naïvely, you could assume that calling `DataAdapter.Update()` with the DataSet will update the entire DataSet, but it will only update a DataTable within the DataSet called "Table". Alternatively, you can call the `Update` method with the DataSet and the name of the table you want to update.

8.2.2.1 *Row Identification in Optimistic Concurrency*

Disconnected optimistic concurrency depends on having a way to identify whether a row in the database has changed since we fetched it from the database. There are several ways to handle this identification, as shown in Table 8.1.

TABLE 8.1 Row Identification Methods in Optimistic Concurrency

Method	Description
Timestamp	This involves creating a column that is used specifically for concurrency checking. Typically a timestamp or datetime field is updated on insert and every update. This is only possible if you have control over the schema of the database you are working with.
Comparison	This is the approach that the CommandBuilder uses. It makes sure that every value in the row is identical to what it was when it was fetched.
Checksum	This is a more complicated version of the timestamp. A checksum is made of all the fields in a row, and comparison is made between the original as it was fetched and what is in the database. This requires more sophisticated code to do the actual checksumming. Checksum is a bit more efficient than the comparison approach because you do not have to transport the entire row for validation on every update. However, some of the efficiency is lost in doing the checksum calculations.

8.2.2.2 ***About the CommandBuilder***

The CommandBuilder class is responsible for generating queries on the fly as the DataAdapter needs them. For this to work we must create the CommandBuilder and pass the DataAdapter in the constructor. Once the CommandBuilder knows about the DataAdapter, it uses the information in the `DataAdapter.SelectCommand` property to discern the columns in the DataTable so that it can generate command objects for inserts, updates, and deletes as needed. If you use a CommandBuilder and your DataAdapter already contains some of the commands (like `UPDATE` and `DELETE`), the CommandBuilder will build only the commands that are missing. It does this by registering with the DataAdapter's `RowUpdating` event so that when the DataAdapter attempts to update an individual row, it creates the commands required. In order to know how to generate the SQL statements, the CommandBuilder registers with the `DataAdapter.RowUpdating()` event. Each managed provider contains its own implementation of the CommandBuilder class (`SqlCommandBuilder`, `OleDbCommandBuilder`, `OdbcCommandBuilder`, and `OracleCommandBuilder`). There are a few caveats to make sure the CommandBuilder can do its job:

- `DataAdapter.SelectCommand` must contain a valid command that was used to fill the DataTable that is being updated. It uses the SQL in the `SELECT` command to figure out how to write the insert, update, and delete queries.
- The DataTable that will be updated in the DataSet must contain either a column with all unique values or a `PrimaryKey` set for the DataTable. Otherwise, the CommandBuilder cannot determine how to identify a record in the database. For example, without these unique values, the `WHERE` clause of the `UPDATE` and `DELETE` commands is impossible to discern.
- If any changes to the schema of the DataTable have been made since it was filled by the `DataAdapter.SelectCommand`, you should call `CommandBuilder.RefreshSchema()` before calling `DataAdapter.Update()`. Otherwise, the CommandBuilder will not be able to tie a column in the DataTable with information discerned from `SelectCommand`.
- The CommandBuilder creates the command objects as needed on the fly. The command objects do not live long after the update is completed. This

means that the lifespan of the CommandBuilder needs to overlap the `DataAdapter.Update()` command.

• For the CommandBuilder to update within a transaction, make sure that a transaction on the connection object is attached to `SelectCommand`. It will inherit any transaction that exists there.

• The CommandBuilder generates commands based on the raw column metadata of the table. Therefore, it will update the database without regard for relationships, constraints, or other tables in the DataSet.

As long as all of these needs are satisfied, the CommandBuilder will dutifully create your UPDATE, INSERT, and DELETE commands.

The CommandBuilder generates SQL code that handles optimistic concurrency by making sure that each and every column in the updated and deleted rows is identical to the original data for that row. This is the methodology for dealing with disconnected optimistic concurrency—we simply assure ourselves that no one has touched the row since we retrieved it. This generated code will be similar for each of the managed providers, with some subtle changes (for example, question marks instead of named parameters for the OLE DB Managed Provider). Here in Listings 8.3, 8.4, and 8.5 are what the parameterized queries created with the Command-Builder look like for our example above:

Listing 8.3: UPDATE *Query*

```
UPDATE CUSTOMER SET Address = @p1 , Zip = @p2
WHERE ( (CustomerID = @p3) AND
    ((FirstName IS NULL AND @p4 IS NULL) OR
     (FirstName = @p5)) AND
    ((LastName IS NULL AND @p6 IS NULL) OR
     (LastName = @p7)) AND
    ((MiddleName IS NULL AND @p8 IS NULL) OR
     (MiddleName = @p9)) AND
    ((Address IS NULL AND @p10 IS NULL) OR
     (Address = @p11)) AND
    ((Apartment IS NULL AND @p12 IS NULL) OR
     (Apartment = @p13)) AND
    ((City IS NULL AND @p14 IS NULL) OR (City = @p15)) AND
    ((State IS NULL AND @p16 IS NULL) OR (State = @p17)) AND
    ((Zip IS NULL AND @p18 IS NULL) OR (Zip = @p19)) AND
    ((HomePhone IS NULL AND @p20 IS NULL) OR
```

```
        (HomePhone = @p21)) AND
    ((BusinessPhone IS NULL AND @p22 IS NULL) OR
     (BusinessPhone = @p23)) AND
    ((DOB IS NULL AND @p24 IS NULL) OR (DOB = @p25)) AND
    ((Discount IS NULL AND @p26 IS NULL) OR
     (Discount = @p27)) AND
    ((CheckedOut IS NULL AND @p28 IS NULL) OR
     (CheckedOut = @p29)) )
```

Listing 8.4: DELETE *Query*

```
DELETE FROM CUSTOMER WHERE ( (CustomerID = @p3) AND
    ((FirstName IS NULL AND @p4 IS NULL) OR
     (FirstName = @p5)) AND
    ((LastName IS NULL AND @p6 IS NULL) OR
     (LastName = @p7)) AND
    ((MiddleName IS NULL AND @p8 IS NULL) OR
     (MiddleName = @p9)) AND
    ((Address IS NULL AND @p10 IS NULL) OR
     (Address = @p11)) AND
    ((Apartment IS NULL AND @p12 IS NULL) OR
     (Apartment = @p13)) AND
    ((City IS NULL AND @p14 IS NULL) OR (City = @p15)) AND
    ((State IS NULL AND @p16 IS NULL) OR (State = @p17)) AND
    ((Zip IS NULL AND @p18 IS NULL) OR (Zip = @p19)) AND
    ((HomePhone IS NULL AND @p20 IS NULL) OR
     (HomePhone = @p21)) AND
    ((BusinessPhone IS NULL AND @p22 IS NULL) OR
     (BusinessPhone = @p23)) AND
    ((DOB IS NULL AND @p24 IS NULL) OR (DOB = @p25)) AND
    ((Discount IS NULL AND @p26 IS NULL) OR
     (Discount = @p27)) AND
    ((CheckedOut IS NULL AND @p28 IS NULL) OR
     (CheckedOut = @p29)) )
```

Listing 8.5: INSERT *Query*

```
INSERT INTO CUSTOMER( CustomerID , FirstName , LastName ,
                      MiddleName , Address , Apartment ,
                      City , State , Zip , HomePhone ,
                      BusinessPhone , DOB , Discount )
VALUES ( @p1 , @p2 , @p3 , @p4 , @p5 , @p6 , @p7 , @p8 ,
         @p9 , @p10 , @p11 , @p12 , @p13 )
```

The CommandBuilder-generated SQL statements are very robust, but are not very efficient because SQL code is much larger than it needs to be, which will increase compilation on the server and make the size of the data sent to the database larger than necessary. In addition, the Command-Builder is generating them as needed at runtime, which will have some impact on the speed of updates. The statements are regenerated for every update that is called. In most cases you will know more about the database, which will allow you to be more efficient, as we will see in the next section. In the best case, I would suggest using stored procedures for each of the operations. This will improve performance by having the query plans and code precompiled on the server.

8.2.2.3 *Improving on the CommandBuilder Commands*

If you are dealing with amorphous data or if fast development is preferable to performance, the CommandBuilder is the way to go. If this is not the case, however, I would suggest building your own INSERT, UPDATE, and DELETE command objects for the DataAdapter.

In most cases where you are writing to database servers (SQL Server, Oracle, DB2, and so on), you can achieve a performance increase by wrapping all the INSERT, UPDATE, and DELETE commands into stored procedures. For clarity, I will write the native SQL code and leave it as an exercise for you to make stored procedures for your particular database vendor.

8.2.2.3.1 Writing DataAdapter Commands with Parameters. Before we can write our own commands, we must understand how the Data-Adapter's Command objects use their parameters to figure out what data to try to update. The DataAdapter's Command objects contain commands to insert, update, and delete the database. These commands have a set of parameters that represent each column in the database. In this way, the DataAdapter uses the parameters as the connection point between the DataRow and the database. The properties of the Parameter classes (OleDbParameter, SqlParameter, OracleParameter, and OdbcParameter) that are important to this stage of the game are:

- **SourceColumn**: The name of the column in the DataTable that this parameter maps to.
- **SourceVersion**: The `DataRowVersion` of the data stored in the Data-Row to map this parameter to. Back in Chapter 7 we discussed how different versions of the data are kept in the DataRow. With the `SourceVersion`, you can map the original version of a column to a parameter. In this way you might map the original version of a column to one parameter, and the modified version to another parameter.
- **Direction**: I discussed this parameter in Chapter 3. It has special impact here because, if the parameter is `Output` or `InputOutput` and is mapped to a `SourceColumn`, it will retrieve the value of the parameter and put it in the column of the DataRow.

When we create our own commands to do the updates, we must craft `Command` objects that are tied to the DataTable they are to update. The first two parameter properties (`SourceColumn` and `SourceVersion`) tie the parameter to a particular column. `SourceVersion` is meant to determine which version of the data in the row to tie to. In general, tie to `DataRow-Version.Current` for parameters that will be used to actually change values in the database, and to `DataRowVersion.Original` for values that will be used in the WHERE clause of the SQL statement to determine row identity.

The `Direction` property is `Input` by default, but you may want to change it if you have parameters that need to be discerned from the database. A good example of this is row identity for inserted rows. You can craft your INSERT statement to make the primary key column be an output parameter, so you can have the SQL statement or stored procedure set this parameter after the new row is inserted. See Section 8.3.3 for more information on how this works.

8.2.2.3.2 **The INSERT Command.** The INSERT command created by the CommandBuilder is actually pretty efficient. But because we may want to get rid of the CommandBuilder completely, we will need to create all our own commands, as shown in Listing 8.6.

Listing 8.6: *Adding an InsertCommand to a DataAdapter*

```
...

// Build the INSERT command
string insQry =
insQry = @"INSERT INTO CUSTOMER(
            CustomerID, FirstName,  LastName,
            MiddleName, Address, Apartment,
            City, State, Zip, HomePhone,
            BusinessPhone, DOB, Discount)
          VALUES ( @CustomerID, @FirstName,
            @LastName, @MiddleName, @Address,
            @Apartment, @City, @State, @Zip,
            @HomePhone, @BusinessPhone, @DOB,
            @Discount )";

SqlCommand insCmd = conn.CreateCommand();
insCmd.CommandText = insQry;

// Get a reference of the collection for simplification
SqlParameterCollection insParams = insCmd.Parameters;

// Build the Parameters
insParams.Add("@CustomerID", SqlDbType.UniqueIdentifier, 0,
            "CustomerID");
insParams.Add("@FirstName", SqlDbType.NVarChar, 50,
            "FirstName");
insParams.Add("@MiddleName", SqlDbType.NVarChar, 50,
            "MiddleName");
insParams["@MiddleName"].IsNullable = true;
insParams.Add("@LastName", SqlDbType.NVarChar, 50,
            "LastName");
insParams["@LastName"].IsNullable = true;
insParams.Add("@Address", SqlDbType.NVarChar, 50,
            "Address");
insParams["@Address"].IsNullable = true;
insParams.Add("@Apartment", SqlDbType.NVarChar, 50,
            "Apartment");
insParams["@Apartment"].IsNullable = true;
insParams.Add("@City", SqlDbType.NVarChar, 50, "City");
insParams["@City"].IsNullable = true;
insParams.Add("@State", SqlDbType.NChar, 2, "State");
insParams["@State"].IsNullable = true;
insParams.Add("@Zip", SqlDbType.NVarChar, 10, "Zip");
insParams["@Zip"].IsNullable = true;
```

```
insParams.Add("@HomePhone", SqlDbType.NVarChar, 14,
        "HomePhone");
insParams["@HomePhone"].IsNullable = true;
insParams.Add("@BusinessPhone", SqlDbType.NVarChar, 14,
        "BusinessPhone");
insParams["@BusinessPhone"].IsNullable = true;
insParams.Add("@DOB", SqlDbType.DateTime, 0, "DOB");
insParams["@DOB"].IsNullable = true;
insParams.Add("@Discount", SqlDbType.Float, 8, "Discount");
insParams["@Discount"].IsNullable = true;

// Assign the INSERT command to the DataAdapter
dataAdapter.InsertCommand = insCmd;
```

The INSERT command that the CommandBuilder created for us was pretty much identical to what we needed. Listing 8.6 shows the actual code to duplicate the INSERT command that it created.

The interesting part of this code is the SqlParametersCollection. Add() method's use of the name of the field that we want to retrieve data from. It uses this fourth parameter of the method to determine which Sql-Parameter is mapped to which column in each row. During the Data-Adapter.Update() method, this command is called once for each changed row.

8.2.2.3.3 The DELETE Command.
The CommandBuilder created a complex DELETE command that used the fact that all the changed fields had not changed as proof that we could delete the record. In this example, I am using a SQL Server Timestamp field. Most databases have something like this field. The purpose of this field is to be updated with a new timestamp every time the row is updated, so we can use this value as our guarantee that the row has not changed since we retrieved it. Because we are using Timestamp instead of the fact that each value has not changed, our DELETE command has only two parameters. See Listing 8.7 as an example.

Listing 8.7: *Adding a DeleteCommand to a DataAdapter*

```
...

// Build the DELETE command
string delQry
```

```
delQry = @"DELETE FROM CUSTOMER
            WHERE CustomerID = @CustomerID AND
              Stamp = @Stamp";

SqlCommand delCmd = conn.CreateCommand();
delCmd.CommandText = delQry;

// Get a reference of the collection for simplification
SqlParameterCollection delParams = delCmd.Parameters;

// Build the parameters
delParams.Add("@CustomerID", SqlDbType.UniqueIdentifier, 0,
            "CustomerID");
delParams.Add("@Stamp", SqlDbType.Timestamp, 0, "Stamp");
delParams["@Stamp"].SourceVersion = DataRowVersion.Original;

// Assign the DELETE command to the DataAdapter
dataAdapter.DeleteCommand = delCmd;

...
```

The really interesting part of this example is that we are telling the Stamp parameter to retrieve its data for the command from the original version of the row. This means that even if someone changes the Stamp value, we are always comparing against the original that we retrieved.

8.2.2.3.4 The UPDATE Command.

The UPDATE command that the CommandBuilder created requires that you send both the changed values and all original values of the row to make sure that the row has not changed since it was fetched. To make this more efficient, I have chosen to use the Stamp field (which contains a Timestamp). The difficulty here is that when we update the database, we need to get the new timestamp so that the next time we update we have the newest timestamp for the row. Luckily, ADO.NET allows us to do it all in one roundtrip to the database by performing the insert and then querying for the new value in the Stamp field. This is shown in Listing 8.8.

Listing 8.8: *Adding an UpdateCommand to a DataAdapter*

```
...

// Build the UPDATE command
string updQry =
updQry = @"UPDATE CUSTOMER SET
            CustomerID = @CustomerID,
            FirstName = @FirstName,
            LastName = @LastName,
            MiddleName = @MiddleName,
            Address = @Address,
            Apartment = @Apartment,
            City = @City,
            State = @State, Zip = @Zip,
            HomePhone = @HomePhone,
            BusinessPhone = @BusinessPhone,
            DOB = @DOB,
            Discount = @Discount
        WHERE Stamp = @Stamp AND CustomerID =
                        @CustomerID
        SELECT @Stamp = Stamp FROM CUSTOMER
        WHERE CustomerID = @CustomerID";

SqlCommand updCmd = conn.CreateCommand();
updCmd.CommandText = updQry;

// Get a reference of the collection for simplification
SqlParameterCollection updParams = updCmd.Parameters;

// Build the parameters
updParams.Add("@CustomerID", SqlDbType.UniqueIdentifier, 0,
            "CustomerID");
updParams.Add("@FirstName", SqlDbType.NVarChar, 50,
            "FirstName");
updParams.Add("@MiddleName", SqlDbType.NVarChar, 50,
            "MiddleName");
updParams["@MiddleName"].IsNullable = true;
updParams.Add("@LastName", SqlDbType.NVarChar, 50,
            "LastName");
updParams["@LastName"].IsNullable = true;
updParams.Add("@Address", SqlDbType.NVarChar, 50,
            "Address");
updParams["@Address"].IsNullable = true;
updParams.Add("@Apartment", SqlDbType.NVarChar, 50,
            "Apartment");
```

```
updParams["@Apartment"].IsNullable = true;
updParams.Add("@City", SqlDbType.NVarChar, 50, "City");
updParams["@City"].IsNullable = true;
updParams.Add("@State", SqlDbType.NChar, 2, "State");
updParams["@State"].IsNullable = true;
updParams.Add("@Zip", SqlDbType.NVarChar, 10, "Zip");
updParams["@Zip"].IsNullable = true;
updParams.Add("@HomePhone", SqlDbType.NVarChar, 14,
            "HomePhone");
updParams["@HomePhone"].IsNullable = true;
updParams.Add("@BusinessPhone", SqlDbType.NVarChar, 14,
            "BusinessPhone");
updParams["@BusinessPhone"].IsNullable = true;
updParams.Add("@DOB", SqlDbType.DateTime, 0, "DOB");
updParams["@DOB"].IsNullable = true;
updParams.Add("@Discount", SqlDbType.Float, 8, "Discount");
updParams["@Discount"].IsNullable = true;
updParams.Add("@Stamp", SqlDbType.Timestamp, 0, "Stamp");
updParams["@Stamp"].SourceVersion = DataRowVersion.Original;
updParams["@Stamp"].Direction =
                        ParameterDirection.InputOutput;

// Assign the INSERT command to the DataAdapter
dataAdapter.UpdateCommand = updCmd;
```

In this command, we are not only specifying that we want the original
`DataRowVersion`, but also that the `ParameterDirection` is `InputOutput`. This tells ADO.NET to take the parameter when we get back from the
database and automatically put it in the `Stamp` column of the row. We need
this new version of the `Stamp` so that when we make a change to the row
again and call `DataAdapter.Update()`, we will have a valid `Stamp` (from
the database) to perform the concurrency check.

Putting it all together, we get a fairly lengthy setup of the Data-
Adapter's commands, but it does work in just the way you want, as in Listing 8.9.

Listing 8.9: *Putting It All Together*

```
// Create and open the connection
SqlConnection conn = new SqlConnection(
  "server=localhost;" +
  "database=ADONET;" +
  "Integrated Security=true;");
```

```csharp
// Create the DataAdapter
SqlDataAdapter dataAdapter =
        new SqlDataAdapter("SELECT * FROM CUSTOMER", conn);

// Build the INSERT command
string insQry =
insQry = @"INSERT INTO CUSTOMER(
            CustomerID, FirstName,  LastName,
            MiddleName, Address, Apartment,
            City, State, Zip, HomePhone,
            BusinessPhone, DOB, Discount)
          VALUES ( @CustomerID, @FirstName,
            @LastName, @MiddleName, @Address,
            @Apartment, @City, @State, @Zip,
            @HomePhone, @BusinessPhone, @DOB,
            @Discount )";

SqlCommand insCmd = conn.CreateCommand();
insCmd.CommandText = insQry;

// Get a reference of the collection for simplification
SqlParameterCollection insParams = insCmd.Parameters;

// Build the parameters
insParams.Add("@CustomerID", SqlDbType.UniqueIdentifier, 0,
            "CustomerID");
insParams.Add("@FirstName", SqlDbType.NVarChar, 50,
            "FirstName");
insParams.Add("@MiddleName", SqlDbType.NVarChar, 50,
            "MiddleName");
insParams["@MiddleName"].IsNullable = true;
insParams.Add("@LastName", SqlDbType.NVarChar, 50,
            "LastName");
insParams["@LastName"].IsNullable = true;
insParams.Add("@Address", SqlDbType.NVarChar, 50,
            "Address");
insParams["@Address"].IsNullable = true;
insParams.Add("@Apartment", SqlDbType.NVarChar, 50,
            "Apartment");
insParams["@Apartment"].IsNullable = true;
insParams.Add("@City", SqlDbType.NVarChar, 50, "City");
insParams["@City"].IsNullable = true;
insParams.Add("@State", SqlDbType.NChar, 2, "State");
insParams["@State"].IsNullable = true;
insParams.Add("@Zip", SqlDbType.NVarChar, 10, "Zip");
insParams["@Zip"].IsNullable = true;
```

```
insParams.Add("@HomePhone", SqlDbType.NVarChar, 14,
            "HomePhone");
insParams["@HomePhone"].IsNullable = true;
insParams.Add("@BusinessPhone", SqlDbType.NVarChar, 14,
            "BusinessPhone");
insParams["@BusinessPhone"].IsNullable = true;
insParams.Add("@DOB", SqlDbType.DateTime, 0, "DOB");
insParams["@DOB"].IsNullable = true;
insParams.Add("@Discount", SqlDbType.Float, 8, "Discount");
insParams["@Discount"].IsNullable = true;

// Assign the INSERT command to the DataAdapter
dataAdapter.InsertCommand = insCmd;

// Build the DELETE command
string delQry
delQry = @"DELETE FROM CUSTOMER
        WHERE CustomerID = @CustomerID AND
          Stamp = @Stamp";

SqlCommand delCmd = conn.CreateCommand();
delCmd.CommandText = delQry;

// Get a reference of the collection for simplification
SqlParameterCollection delParams = delCmd.Parameters;

// Build the parameters
delParams.Add("@CustomerID", SqlDbType.UniqueIdentifier, 0,
            "CustomerID");
delParams.Add("@Stamp", SqlDbType.Timestamp, 0, "Stamp");

// Assign the DELETE command to the DataAdapter
dataAdapter.DeleteCommand = delCmd;

// Build the UPDATE command
string updQry =
updQry = @"UPDATE CUSTOMER SET
          CustomerID = @CustomerID,
          FirstName = @FirstName,
          LastName = @LastName,
          MiddleName = @MiddleName,
          Address = @Address,
          Apartment = @Apartment,
          City = @City,
          State = @State, Zip = @Zip,
          HomePhone = @HomePhone,
```

```
                BusinessPhone = @BusinessPhone,
                DOB = @DOB,
                Discount = @Discount
            WHERE Stamp = @Stamp AND CustomerID = @CustomerID
            SELECT @Stamp = Stamp FROM CUSTOMER
            WHERE CustomerID = @CustomerID";

SqlCommand updCmd = conn.CreateCommand();
updCmd.CommandText = updQry;


// Get a reference of the collection for simplification
SqlParameterCollection updParams = updCmd.Parameters;

// Build the parameters
updParams.Add("@CustomerID", SqlDbType.UniqueIdentifier, 0,
            "CustomerID");
updParams.Add("@FirstName", SqlDbType.NVarChar, 50,
            "FirstName");
updParams.Add("@MiddleName", SqlDbType.NVarChar, 50,
            "MiddleName");
updParams["@MiddleName"].IsNullable = true;
updParams.Add("@LastName", SqlDbType.NVarChar, 50,
            "LastName");
updParams["@LastName"].IsNullable = true;
updParams.Add("@Address", SqlDbType.NVarChar, 50,
            "Address");
updParams["@Address"].IsNullable = true;
updParams.Add("@Apartment", SqlDbType.NVarChar, 50,
            "Apartment");
updParams["@Apartment"].IsNullable = true;
updParams.Add("@City", SqlDbType.NVarChar, 50, "City");
updParams["@City"].IsNullable = true;
updParams.Add("@State", SqlDbType.NChar, 2, "State");
updParams["@State"].IsNullable = true;
updParams.Add("@Zip", SqlDbType.NVarChar, 10, "Zip");
updParams["@Zip"].IsNullable = true;
updParams.Add("@HomePhone", SqlDbType.NVarChar, 14,
            "HomePhone");
updParams["@HomePhone"].IsNullable = true;
updParams.Add("@BusinessPhone", SqlDbType.NVarChar, 14,
            "BusinessPhone");
updParams["@BusinessPhone"].IsNullable = true;
updParams.Add("@DOB", SqlDbType.DateTime, 0, "DOB");
updParams["@DOB"].IsNullable = true;
updParams.Add("@Discount", SqlDbType.Float, 8, "Discount");
updParams["@Discount"].IsNullable = true;
```

```
updParams.Add("@Stamp", SqlDbType.Timestamp, 0, "Stamp");
updParams["@Stamp"].SourceVersion = DataRowVersion.Original;
updParams["@Stamp"].Direction =
ParameterDirection.InputOutput;

// Assign the INSERT command to the DataAdapter
dataAdapter.UpdateCommand = updCmd;

// Create the DataSet
DataSet dataSet = new DataSet();

// Use the DataAdapter to fill the DataSet
dataAdapter.Fill(dataSet, "Customers");

// Grab the DataTable for convenience
DataTable custTable = dataSet.Tables["Customers"];

// Add a new customer
DataRow newRow = custTable.NewRow();
newRow.BeginEdit();
newRow["CustomerID"] = Guid.NewGuid();
newRow["LastName"] = "Remlinger";
newRow["FirstName"] = "Mike";
newRow["Address"] = "10 Aaron Way";
newRow["City"] = "Atlanta";
newRow["State"] = "GA";
newRow["Zip"] = "30307";
newRow["HomePhone"] = "(404) 543-8765";
newRow.EndEdit();
custTable.Rows.Add(newRow);

// Delete a customer
DataRow delRow = custTable.Rows[1];
delRow.Delete();

// Change a customer
DataRow oldRow = custTable.Rows[0];
oldRow["MiddleName"] = "Andrew";

try
{
  // Update the database
  dataAdapter.Update(custTable);
  Console.Write("Successfully Updated the Database");
}
catch (SqlException ex)
```

```
{
  // Failed
  Console.WriteLine(ex.Message);
}
```

That is a lot of code to set these up. You are probably asking yourself why you would not just use the CommandBuilder. In many cases you can and should. But if performance is the most important requirement in a project, crafting your own commands can provide performance gains. It's simply a design-time decision.

8.2.2.4 *Handling Concurrency Violations*

Sometimes bad things happen to bad databases. You may find yourself in a situation in which the optimistic concurrency correctly determines that you are trying to change a row that has been changed since you fetched it. You need to handle these concurrency violations or roll back the changes to the DataSet. Let's see how this works.

During the process of updating the database, the DataAdapter checks to see how many rows were affected on each execution of an insert, update, or delete. If the result is zero (usually because the WHERE clause did not find a row that matched the changed row when it was initially fetched), the DataAdapter throws a DBConcurrencyException. It is important to know that whenever one of these queries returns a zero for rows affected, this exception is thrown. Usually it is at fault, but it may not be. Now, let's create a concurrency violation (shown in Listing 8.10) so you know how it looks to handle one.

Listing 8.10: *Handling DBConcurrencyException*

```
// Grab the DataTable for convenience
DataTable custTable = dataSet.Tables["Customers"];

// Change a customer
DataRow oldRow = custTable.Rows[0];
oldRow["MiddleName"] = "Andrew";

// Fake a change in the database
SqlCommand changeCmd = conn.CreateCommand();
changeCmd.CommandText = "UPDATE Customer SET Zip = '{0}'" +
                        " WHERE CustomerID = '{1}'";
```

```
// Insert the ID into the CommandText
// and increment the Zip by one to make this
// repeatable
changeCmd.CommandText =
            string.Format(changeCmd.CommandText,
                        Convert.ToInt32(oldRow["Zip"]) + 1,
                        oldRow["CustomerID"]);

// Execute the change in the database
conn.Open();
changeCmd.ExecuteNonQuery();
conn.Close();

// Create a command-builder to generate the
// inserts/updates/deletes
SqlCommandBuilder bldr = new SqlCommandBuilder(dataAdapter);

try
{
  dataAdapter.Update(custTable);
}
catch (DBConcurrencyException ex)
{
  // Found a concurrency issue, report it only
  Console.WriteLine("Concurrency Violation: {0}",
                    ex.Message);
  if (custTable.HasErrors)
  {
    foreach (DataRow row in custTable.GetErrors())
    {
     Console.WriteLine("  Violation Row: (CustomerID: {0})",
                       row["CustomerID"]);
    }
  }
}
```

In this example, we are causing a change in the database by changing it before we try to update the DataTable, which will cause a concurrency violation. This violation causes the DBConcurrencyException to be thrown after the update is complete. In our case, we are going to fail immediately and an exception is thrown. We can now walk through the DataTable to see which row(s) were involved in the concurrency violation. You can see from this code that the violation caused both the DataTable and each row affected to contain an error. In this example we are not really managing the change, we are just reporting it. Because the DataTable now contains errors, we can use that information to actually resolve the issue and ask the DataAdapter to update the DataTable again.

In the default behavior, the DataAdapter attempts to update every changed row and when a concurrency violation happens, it throws the exception and stops trying to update the database. It does not roll back the rows that already successfully updated.

This may not be the behavior you want. If you change the `Data-Adapter.ContinueUpdateOnError` property to true (false is the default), the DataAdapter will attempt an update on every row and mark the ones that have concurrency errors. It will continue to try to update every row after the error(s). When we finish the update, we will have to manually check the `DataTable.HasErrors` property to see whether any failures occurred. If there are errors, each row will have its `RowError` property filled with information about the failure. If there are no errors, we can safely assume that all rows without errors successfully updated the database.

How you would handle these concurrency violations really depends on the type of project you are working on. It is up to you to decide how to go about handling them. There are a few different approaches to handling these violations:

• Present the concurrency failure and tell the user that the data is stale and any changes will be lost. At that point you can refresh from the database and have the user re-enter changes if he or she wants.

• Present the option of overwriting the data; however, this option is not always possible or recommended.

• If appropriate for the data, you can do column-level collision. This means that you need to look at the current record in the database and decide if the particular column has changed. If it has not, you can make a change for just that column. The problem here comes when you need to write code to make sure that some columns are all changed together or not at all (such as `Address`, `City`, `State`, and `Zip`).

Deciding the right approach for handling concurrency is really a domain-specific problem. Listing 8.11 shows an example of dealing with the concurrency violation with row-level collision.

Listing 8.11: *Using Row-Level Collision to Handle Concurrency Violations*

```
. . .

// Found a concurrency issue
if (custTable.HasErrors)
{
  foreach (DataRow row in custTable.GetErrors())
  {
    // We can only resolve UPDATE errors
    if (row.RowState == DataRowState.Modified)
    {
      //////////////////////////////////////////
      // Make a new UpdateCommand
      // We should build a new UPDATE command
      // to deal with our specific issue

      // Save the old command (if there is one)
      SqlCommand oldUpdateCmd = null;
      if (dataAdapter.UpdateCommand != null)
      {
        oldUpdateCmd = dataAdapter.UpdateCommand;
      }

      // Create a new command
      SqlCommand updCmd = conn.CreateCommand();

      // Go through the changed rows and create a new
      // SQL statement
      string updateSQL = "UPDATE CUSTOMER SET ";
      string whereSQL = "WHERE ";
      SqlParameterCollection updParams = updCmd.Parameters;
      for (int x = 0; x < row.ItemArray.Length; ++x)
      {
        if (row[x, DataRowVersion.Original] !=
                        row[x, DataRowVersion.Current])
        {
          // Add the parameter
          DataColumn col = custTable.Columns[x];
          updParams.Add("@" + col.ColumnName, null);
          updParams["@" + col.ColumnName].SourceColumn =
                        col.ColumnName;
```

```
        updParams.Add("@old" + col.ColumnName, null);
        updParams["@old" + col.ColumnName].SourceColumn =
                        col.ColumnName;
        updParams["@old" + col.ColumnName].SourceVersion =
                        DataRowVersion.Original;

        // Update the SQL statements
        updateSQL += string.Format("{0} = @{0} , ",
                                col.ColumnName);
        whereSQL += string.Format("(({0} = @old{0}) OR " +
                                "({0} IS NULL)) AND ",
                                col.ColumnName);
    }
}

// Fix up the string and concatenate them
if (updateSQL.Substring(updateSQL.Length - 2) ==
                    ", " &&
    whereSQL.Substring(whereSQL.Length - 4) == "AND ")
{
    updateSQL =
            updateSQL.Substring(0, updateSQL.Length - 2);
    whereSQL += " CustomerID = @CustomerID";

    // Add the CustomerID parameter
    updParams.Add("@CustomerID",
                SqlDbType.UniqueIdentifier,
                0, "CustomerID");

    // Set the command SQL
    updCmd.CommandText = updateSQL + whereSQL;

    // Set the UpdateCommand
    dataAdapter.UpdateCommand = updCmd;

    // Make an array of the one row and
    // ask the DataAdapter to update it
    DataRow[] arrayDRs = {row};
    try
    {
        dataAdapter.Update(arrayDRs);
        Console.WriteLine("Database Updated! " +
                    "(After Row Level Collision Testing");
    }
    catch (DBConcurrencyException nestedEx)
    {
        Console.WriteLine("Concurrency Violation: {0}",
                    nestedEx.Message);
```

```
                    Console.WriteLine("  Row: State={0}, ID={1}",
                                      row["CustomerID"],
                                      row.RowState);
            }
            catch (SqlException sqlex)
            {
              Console.WriteLine("SQL Exception: {0}",
                                sqlex.Message);
              Console.WriteLine("  Row: State={0}, ID={1}",
                                row["CustomerID"],
                                row.RowState);
            }

          }
          else
          {
            Console.WriteLine("Concurrency Violation: {0}",
                              ex.Message);
            Console.WriteLine("  Row: State={0}, ID={1}",
                              row["CustomerID"],
                              row.RowState);
          }

          // Reset the UpdateCommand
          dataAdapter.UpdateCommand = oldUpdateCmd;
        }
        else
        {

          // Can't handle other types so report them
          Console.WriteLine("Concurrency Violation: {0}",
                            ex.Message);
          Console.WriteLine("  Row: State={0}, ID={1}",
                            row["CustomerID"],
                            row.RowState);
        }
      }
    }
```

In this (admittedly long-winded) example, we are handling the concurrency error by retrying to update each row if the columns that we are intent on changing have not been updated. The more interesting part of the code is where we are composing the SQL statement based on the dirty columns of each row. Because we are constructing the SQL statements based on the changed elements of a single row, we are using `DataAdapter.Update()` with a single row at a time.

This is just an example of what could be done to handle concurrency violations. The important part of the example is to show you how much control you can have over the concurrency issues.

8.2.3 Implementing Pessimistic Concurrency

Pessimistic concurrency is really just row locking. If you get a row from the database, you must lock it to prevent anyone else from getting at the data in that row. Pessimistic concurrency works well if you have a check-out/check-in methodology. In order to use this concurrency model, we must have a way to limit access to the database rows while we have the data "checked out." Because the database cannot lock the rows while we are disconnected, we must craft our own solution.

For example, we need to craft some SQL that will attempt to check out a specific customer from the database. Most of the magic of pessimistic concurrency occurs in the SQL statements (or hopefully in a stored procedure). We should make sure that the customer is not already checked out, and if not we mark it as checked out and get the customer from the database. All of this happens in a transaction so that we do not get into a state where customers are checked out, but never gotten.

At the end of our change, we will do the reverse to check in the customer. We update the customer and change the checked-out flag to zero (or false). There is no transaction on this call because the change is atomic (all changes happen in one operation in the database). At the end we reset the DataSet because we do not have the customer checked out; therefore, we cannot continue to change this customer. Listing 8.12 shows what the code looks like.

Listing 8.12: *Pessimistic Concurrency*

```
. . .

// T-SQL To get an individual customer
// (In a perfect world this should be
//  a stored procedure)
// CustID was passed in as an identifier to the customer
```

```
string getSQL;
getSQL = @"/* Make Transactional */
           BEGIN TRAN

           DECLARE @isCheckedOut bit
           DECLARE @CustID varchar(38)
           SELECT @CustID = '{0}';

           /* Check to make sure it
              isn't already checked out */
           SELECT @isCheckedOut = CheckedOut
             FROM Customer
             WHERE CustomerID = @CustID

           IF @isCheckedOut = 1
           BEGIN
             RAISERROR ('Customer already checked out',16,1)
             ROLLBACK TRAN
             RETURN
           END

           /* Check it out */
           UPDATE Customer SET CheckedOut = 1
             WHERE CustomerID = @CustID

           /* Get the Customer */
           SELECT CustomerID, FirstName, LastName,
                  MiddleName, Address, Apartment,
                  City, State, Zip, HomePhone,
                  BusinessPhone, DOB, Discount,
                  Stamp
             FROM Customer
             WHERE CustomerID = @CustID

           /* Since we got this far,
              commit the transaction */
           COMMIT TRAN";

// Format the Query to include the Guid
// for the customerID
getSQL = string.Format(getSQL, custID);

// Create the DataAdapter
SqlDataAdapter dataAdapter = new SqlDataAdapter(getSQL,
                                                conn);
```

```csharp
// Create the DataSet
DataSet dataSet = new DataSet();

// Use the DataAdapter to fill the DataSet
try
{
  dataAdapter.Fill(dataSet, "Customers");
}
catch (SqlException ex)
{
  Console.WriteLine("SqlException: {0}", ex.Message);
  return;
}

// Grab the DataTable for convinence
DataTable custTable = dataSet.Tables[0];

// Update the Customer with the new address
DataRow customer = custTable.Rows[0];
customer["Address"] = "55 Peachtree Center";
customer["Zip"] = "30312";

// Create the Update Query
// In a perfect world, this should be a
// Stored Procedure
string updQry;
updQry = @"UPDATE CUSTOMER SET
             CustomerID = @CustomerID,
             FirstName = @FirstName,
             LastName = @LastName,
             MiddleName = @MiddleName,
             Address = @Address,
             Apartment = @Apartment,
             City = @City,
             State = @State, Zip = @Zip,
             HomePhone = @HomePhone,
             BusinessPhone = @BusinessPhone,
             DOB = @DOB,
             Discount = @Discount,
             CheckedOut = 0
          WHERE Stamp = @Stamp AND
             CustomerID = @CustomerID
          AND CheckedOut = 1";

SqlCommand updCmd = conn.CreateCommand();
updCmd.CommandText = updQry;
```

```csharp
    // Get a reference of the collection for simplification
    SqlParameterCollection updParams = updCmd.Parameters;

    // Build the Parameters
    updParams.Add("@CustomerID", SqlDbType.UniqueIdentifier,
                0, "CustomerID");
    updParams.Add("@FirstName", SqlDbType.NVarChar, 50,
                "FirstName");
    updParams.Add("@MiddleName", SqlDbType.NVarChar, 50,
                "MiddleName");
    updParams["@MiddleName"].IsNullable = true;
    updParams.Add("@LastName", SqlDbType.NVarChar, 50,
                "LastName");
    updParams["@LastName"].IsNullable = true;
    updParams.Add("@Address", SqlDbType.NVarChar, 50,
                "Address");
    updParams["@Address"].IsNullable = true;
    updParams.Add("@Apartment", SqlDbType.NVarChar, 50,
                "Apartment");
    updParams["@Apartment"].IsNullable = true;
    updParams.Add("@City", SqlDbType.NVarChar, 50, "City");
    updParams["@City"].IsNullable = true;
    updParams.Add("@State", SqlDbType.NChar, 2, "State");
    updParams["@State"].IsNullable = true;
    updParams.Add("@Zip", SqlDbType.NVarChar, 10, "Zip");
    updParams["@Zip"].IsNullable = true;
    updParams.Add("@HomePhone", SqlDbType.NVarChar, 14,
                "HomePhone");
    updParams["@HomePhone"].IsNullable = true;
    updParams.Add("@BusinessPhone", SqlDbType.NVarChar, 14,
                "BusinessPhone");
    updParams["@BusinessPhone"].IsNullable = true;
    updParams.Add("@DOB", SqlDbType.DateTime, 0, "DOB");
    updParams["@DOB"].IsNullable = true;
    updParams.Add("@Discount", SqlDbType.Float, 8,
                "Discount");
    updParams["@Discount"].IsNullable = true;

    // Set the Adapters Update Command
    dataAdapter.UpdateCommand = updCmd;

    // Update the Database
    try
    {
      dataAdapter.Update(custTable);
      Console.WriteLine("Finished updating the database");
    }
```

```
catch (SqlException ex)
{
  Console.WriteLine("SqlException: {0}", ex.Message);
}

// Clear the DataSet
dataSet.Reset();
```

In the case where you really need disconnected pessimistic concurrency, the check-in/check-out pattern should help you implement it.

8.2.4 Implementing Destructive Concurrency

I am being a bit tongue-in-cheek by including destructive concurrency. In fact, destructive concurrency is really no concurrency checking at all. The last writer always wins. There are cases where this is the most appropriate case. Unfortunately, if you want to use the CommandBuilder, it has no support for destructive concurrency; we need to implement this concurrency model ourselves, as shown in Listing 8.13.

Listing 8.13: *Destructive Concurrency*

```
...

// Create the DataAdapter
SqlDataAdapter dataAdapter =
        new SqlDataAdapter("SELECT * FROM CUSTOMER", conn);

// Build the INSERT command
string insQry =
insQry = @"INSERT INTO CUSTOMER(
        CustomerID, FirstName,  LastName,
        MiddleName, Address, Apartment,
        City, State, Zip, HomePhone,
        BusinessPhone, DOB, Discount)
      VALUES ( @CustomerID, @FirstName,
        @LastName, @MiddleName, @Address,
        @Apartment, @City, @State, @Zip,
        @HomePhone, @BusinessPhone, @DOB,
        @Discount )";

SqlCommand insCmd = conn.CreateCommand();
insCmd.CommandText = insQry;
```

```
// Get a reference of the collection for simplification
SqlParameterCollection insParams = insCmd.Parameters;

// Build the parameters
insParams.Add("@CustomerID", SqlDbType.UniqueIdentifier, 0,
            "CustomerID");
insParams.Add("@FirstName", SqlDbType.NVarChar, 50,
            "FirstName");
insParams.Add("@MiddleName", SqlDbType.NVarChar, 50,
            "MiddleName");
insParams["@MiddleName"].IsNullable = true;
insParams.Add("@LastName", SqlDbType.NVarChar, 50,
            "LastName");
insParams["@LastName"].IsNullable = true;
insParams.Add("@Address", SqlDbType.NVarChar, 50,
            "Address");
insParams["@Address"].IsNullable = true;
insParams.Add("@Apartment", SqlDbType.NVarChar, 50,
            "Apartment");
insParams["@Apartment"].IsNullable = true;
insParams.Add("@City", SqlDbType.NVarChar, 50, "City");
insParams["@City"].IsNullable = true;
insParams.Add("@State", SqlDbType.NChar, 2, "State");
insParams["@State"].IsNullable = true;
insParams.Add("@Zip", SqlDbType.NVarChar, 10, "Zip");
insParams["@Zip"].IsNullable = true;
insParams.Add("@HomePhone", SqlDbType.NVarChar, 14,
            "HomePhone");
insParams["@HomePhone"].IsNullable = true;
insParams.Add("@BusinessPhone", SqlDbType.NVarChar, 14,
            "BusinessPhone");
insParams["@BusinessPhone"].IsNullable = true;
insParams.Add("@DOB", SqlDbType.DateTime, 0, "DOB");
insParams["@DOB"].IsNullable = true;
insParams.Add("@Discount", SqlDbType.Float, 8, "Discount");
insParams["@Discount"].IsNullable = true;

// Assign the INSERT command to the DataAdapter
dataAdapter.InsertCommand = insCmd;

// Build the DELETE command
string delQry =
delQry = @"DELETE FROM CUSTOMER
            WHERE CustomerID = @CustomerID";
```

```
SqlCommand delCmd = conn.CreateCommand();
delCmd.CommandText = delQry;

// Get a reference of the collection for simplification
SqlParameterCollection delParams = delCmd.Parameters;

// Build the parameters
delParams.Add("@CustomerID", SqlDbType.UniqueIdentifier, 0,
            "CustomerID");

// Assign the Delete command to the DataAdapter
dataAdapter.DeleteCommand = delCmd;

// Build the UPDATE command
string updQry = "";
updQry += "UPDATE CUSTOMER SET ";
updQry += "  CustomerID = @CustomerID, ";
updQry += "  FirstName = @FirstName, ";
updQry += "  LastName = @LastName, ";
updQry += "  MiddleName = @MiddleName, ";
updQry += "  Address = @Address, ";
updQry += "  Apartment = @Apartment, ";
updQry += "  City = @City, ";
updQry += "  State = @State, Zip = @Zip, ";
updQry += "  HomePhone = @HomePhone, ";
updQry += "  BusinessPhone = @BusinessPhone, ";
updQry += "  DOB = @DOB, ";
updQry += "  Discount = @Discount ";
updQry += "WHERE CustomerID = @CustomerID";

SqlCommand updCmd = conn.CreateCommand();
updCmd.CommandText = updQry;

// Get a reference of the collection for simplification
SqlParameterCollection updParams = updCmd.Parameters;

// Build the parameters
updParams.Add("@CustomerID", SqlDbType.UniqueIdentifier, 0,
            "CustomerID");
updParams.Add("@FirstName", SqlDbType.NVarChar, 50,
            "FirstName");
updParams.Add("@MiddleName", SqlDbType.NVarChar, 50,
            "MiddleName");
updParams["@MiddleName"].IsNullable = true;
updParams.Add("@LastName", SqlDbType.NVarChar, 50,
            "LastName");
```

```
updParams["@LastName"].IsNullable = true;
updParams.Add("@Address", SqlDbType.NVarChar, 50,
            "Address");
updParams["@Address"].IsNullable = true;
updParams.Add("@Apartment", SqlDbType.NVarChar, 50,
            "Apartment");
updParams["@Apartment"].IsNullable = true;
updParams.Add("@City", SqlDbType.NVarChar, 50, "City");
updParams["@City"].IsNullable = true;
updParams.Add("@State", SqlDbType.NChar, 2, "State");
updParams["@State"].IsNullable = true;
updParams.Add("@Zip", SqlDbType.NVarChar, 10, "Zip");
updParams["@Zip"].IsNullable = true;
updParams.Add("@HomePhone", SqlDbType.NVarChar, 14,
            "HomePhone");
updParams["@HomePhone"].IsNullable = true;
updParams.Add("@BusinessPhone", SqlDbType.NVarChar, 14,
            "BusinessPhone");
updParams["@BusinessPhone"].IsNullable = true;
updParams.Add("@DOB", SqlDbType.DateTime, 0, "DOB");
updParams["@DOB"].IsNullable = true;
updParams.Add("@Discount", SqlDbType.Float, 8, "Discount");
updParams["@Discount"].IsNullable = true;

// Assign the INSERT command to the DataAdapter
dataAdapter.UpdateCommand = updCmd;

// Create the DataSet
DataSet dataSet = new DataSet();

// Use the DataAdapter to fill the DataSet
dataAdapter.Fill(dataSet, "Customers");

// Grab the DataTable for convenience
DataTable custTable = dataSet.Tables["Customers"];

// Add a new customer
DataRow newRow = custTable.NewRow();
newRow.BeginEdit();
newRow["CustomerID"] = Guid.NewGuid();
newRow["LastName"] = "Remlinger";
newRow["FirstName"] = "Mike";
newRow["Address"] = "10 Aaron Way";
newRow["City"] = "Atlanta";
newRow["State"] = "GA";
newRow["Zip"] = "30307";
newRow["HomePhone"] = "(404) 543-8765";
```

```
newRow.EndEdit();
custTable.Rows.Add(newRow);

// Delete a customer
DataRow delRow = custTable.Rows[1];
delRow.Delete();

// Change a customer
DataRow oldRow = custTable.Rows[0];
oldRow["MiddleName"] = "Andrew";

try
{
  // Update the database
  dataAdapter.Update(custTable);
  Console.Write("Successfully Updated the Database");
}
catch (SqlException ex)
{
  Console.WriteLine(ex.Message);
}
```

This example is virtually identical to our earlier example of an improved optimistic concurrency, with the exception that we have removed the use of the `Stamp` field to assure that the row has not changed since we fetched it from the database. We are always updating and deleting rows without exception.

8.3 Common Updating Issues

In your day-to-day job you will find other issues when you are trying to update the database with disconnected data. While I do not expect that I can cover every possible issue, I have compiled the most common of these problems and suggestions for how to alleviate them.

8.3.1 Dealing with Multi-table DataSets

In most cases, you will not be working with single-table DataSets. Having a relational model in memory is what the DataSet does well, so expect to use it. But how different is updating a database from a multi-table DataSet versus a single-table DataSet? As shown in Listing 8.14, the biggest difference is that we are using one DataAdapter per table.

Listing 8.14: *Handling Deletes with a Multi-table DataSet*

```
...

// Create the DataAdapters
SqlDataAdapter custDA =
        new SqlDataAdapter("SELECT * FROM CUSTOMER", conn);
SqlDataAdapter invDA =
        new SqlDataAdapter("SELECT * FROM INVOICE", conn);

// Create the DataSet
DataSet dataSet = new DataSet();

// Use the DataAdapter to fill the DataSet
custDA.Fill(dataSet, "Customers");
invDA.Fill(dataSet, "Invoices");

// Grab the DataTable for convenience
DataTable custTable = dataSet.Tables["Customers"];
DataTable invTable = dataSet.Tables["Invoices"];

// Set up the relation
DataColumn custCustIDColumn =
                    custTable.Columns["CustomerID"];
DataColumn invCustIDColumn = invTable.Columns["CustomerID"];
dataSet.Relations.Add("rel", custCustIDColumn,
                        invCustIDColumn, true);

// Add a new customer
DataRow newRow = custTable.NewRow();
newRow.BeginEdit();
newRow["CustomerID"] = Guid.NewGuid();
newRow["LastName"] = "Remlinger";
newRow["FirstName"] = "Mike";
newRow["Address"] = "10 Aaron Way";
newRow["City"] = "Atlanta";
newRow["State"] = "GA";
newRow["Zip"] = "30307";
newRow["HomePhone"] = "(404) 543-8765";
newRow.EndEdit();
custTable.Rows.Add(newRow);

// Change a customer
DataRow oldRow = custTable.Rows[0];
oldRow["Address"] = "53 Peachtree Center";
oldRow["Zip"] = "30342";
```

```
// Change an invoice
DataRow oldInv = oldRow.GetChildRows("rel")[0];
oldInv["Terms"] = "Net 10th";

// Delete a customer
DataRow delRow = custTable.Rows[1];
delRow.Delete();

// Create a CommandBuilder to generate the
// inserts/updates/deletes
SqlCommandBuilder custBldr = new SqlCommandBuilder(custDA);
SqlCommandBuilder invBldr = new SqlCommandBuilder(invDA);

// Update the database
try
{
  // Update the children first because we have only a delete
  invDA.Update(invTable);
  custDA.Update(custTable);
}
catch (SqlException ex)
{
  Console.WriteLine("Sql Error: {0}", ex.Message);
}
```

As you can see, the code is close to the same as with the single-table updates. The difference is we have a DataAdapter and a CommandBuilder per DataTable.

The order of the `DataAdapter.Update()` calls is important. You should have noticed that we updated the child row first. This is because we were doing a delete of a customer and we told the DataRelation we added to cascade the delete. It is important to understand that if you set up your database to cascade the deletes and ask your DataSet to do the same, you may get errors on the update because the DataSet will try to delete the child items that you may have deleted in the database when it deleted the parent row. Updating the DataAdapter in reverse order (child first) will help alleviate this but will cause additional issues when you have added new parent and child rows. When you update the child first, they may have a foreign key constraint on the table that requires that the parent exist before you can add a child row. In this case you will need to do updates, inserts, and deletes separately. Listing 8.15 shows more code associated with it, but it should perform nearly identically.

Listing 8.15: *Handling Inserts with a Multi-table DataSet*

```
...

// Create a CommandBuilder to generate the
// inserts/updates/deletes
SqlCommandBuilder custBldr = new SqlCommandBuilder(custDA);
SqlCommandBuilder invBldr = new SqlCommandBuilder(invDA);

// Update the database
try
{
  // Deletes
  // Using reverse order to delete the children first
  invDA.Update(invTable.GetChanges(DataRowState.Deleted));
  custDA.Update(custTable.GetChanges(DataRowState.Deleted));

  // Inserts and updates
  // Using forward order to insert/update the parents first
  custDA.Update(custTable.GetChanges(DataRowState.Added |
                             DataRowState.Modified));
  invDA.Update(invTable.GetChanges(DataRowState.Added |
                             DataRowState.Modified));
}
catch (SqlException ex)
{
  Console.WriteLine("Sql Error: {0}", ex.Message);
}
```

To control the order of the DataAdapter's `Update` methods, we do the deletes in reverse order and the inserts and updates in forward order. We can do this by sending the `Update` method a DataTable that contains only certain rows. Because the column-level metadata for these returned Data-Tables are the same as for the original tables, the CommandBuilder works effectively.

8.3.2 Using Local Transactions to Update the Database

Our above example does work, but what happens if it fails in the middle of the updates? Will the database be left in an inconsistent state? Not if you use a local transaction to link the updates together. Local transactions allow you to roll back changes on failure at the client site. Listing 8.16 shows an example of how that works.

Listing 8.16: *Using Transactions in Updating the Database*

```
...

// Grab the DataTable for convenience
DataTable custTable = dataSet.Tables["Customers"];
DataTable invTable = dataSet.Tables["Invoices"];

// Set up the relation
DataColumn custCustIDColumn =
                            custTable.Columns["CustomerID"];
DataColumn invCustIDColumn = invTable.Columns["CustomerID"];
dataSet.Relations.Add("rel", custCustIDColumn,
                    invCustIDColumn, true);

// Add a new customer
DataRow newRow = custTable.NewRow();
newRow.BeginEdit();
newRow["CustomerID"] = Guid.NewGuid();
newRow["LastName"] = "Remlinger";
newRow["FirstName"] = "Mike";
newRow["Address"] = "10 Aaron Way";
newRow["City"] = "Atlanta";
newRow["State"] = "GA";
newRow["Zip"] = "30307";
newRow["HomePhone"] = "(404) 543-8765";
newRow.EndEdit();
custTable.Rows.Add(newRow);

// Change a customer
DataRow oldRow = custTable.Rows[0];
oldRow["Address"] = "53 Peachtree Center";
oldRow["Zip"] = "30342";

// Change an invoice
DataRow oldInv = oldRow.GetChildRows("rel")[0];
oldInv["Terms"] = "Net 10th";

// Delete a customer
DataRow delRow = custTable.Rows[1];
delRow.Delete();
```

```csharp
// Create CommandBuilders to generate the
// inserts/updates/deletes
SqlCommandBuilder custBldr = new SqlCommandBuilder(custDA);
SqlCommandBuilder invBldr = new SqlCommandBuilder(invDA);

// Update the database
SqlTransaction tx = null;
try
{
  // We must open the connection to start a transaction
  conn.Open();

  // Add a transaction to the Select command
  // so that the CommandBuilder will propagate it
  // to the other commands
  tx = conn.BeginTransaction(IsolationLevel.Serializable);
  invDA.SelectCommand.Transaction = tx;
  custDA.SelectCommand.Transaction = tx;

  // Deletes
  // Using reverse order to delete the children first
  invDA.Update(invTable.GetChanges(DataRowState.Deleted));
  custDA.Update(custTable.GetChanges(DataRowState.Deleted));
  // Inserts and updates
  // Using forward order to insert/update the parents first
  custDA.Update(custTable.GetChanges(DataRowState.Added |
                            DataRowState.Modified));
  invDA.Update(invTable.GetChanges(DataRowState.Added |
                            DataRowState.Modified));

  // If we've gotten this far, we should be able to
  // commit the transaction
  tx.Commit();
}
catch (SqlException ex)
{
  Console.WriteLine("Sql Error: {0}", ex.Message);

  // Roll back the transaction if an error occurs
  if (tx != null) tx.Rollback();
}
finally
{
  if (conn.State != ConnectionState.Closed)
  {
    conn.Close();
  }
}
```

To wrap the updates into a transaction, we simply ask the connection to start a local transaction; assign the transaction to the `DataAdapter`. `SelectCommand` from each of the DataAdapters; and commit or roll back the transaction as necessary. The trick here is setting the transaction to the `DataAdapter.SelectCommand` (which may seem a bit counterintuitive). Remember, when the CommandBuilder creates the `UPDATE`, `DELETE`, and `INSERT` commands, it mimics the command settings from the `Data-Adapter.SelectCommand`.

8.3.3   Retrieving New Row Identity from SQL Server

There are occasions where the database is responsible for creating the identity value for a new row in a table. In SQL Server this is usually done with an `IDENTITY` field. SQL Server has the `@@IDENTITY` server variable, which will return the last identity field created. To use this facility with ADO.NET, you can do the following (shown in Listing 8.17):

Listing 8.17: *Retrieving Row Identity in SQL Server*

```
. . .

// Create the DataAdapter
SqlDataAdapter dataAdapter =
        new SqlDataAdapter("SELECT * FROM PRODUCT", conn);

// Build the INSERT command
string insQry = "";
insQry += "INSERT INTO PRODUCT( ";
insQry += "  Description, Vendor, Cost, Price) ";
insQry += "VALUES ( @Description, ";
insQry += "  @Vendor, @Cost, @Price) ";
insQry += "\n";
insQry += "SELECT @ProductID = @@IDENTITY";

SqlCommand insCmd = conn.CreateCommand();
insCmd.CommandText = insQry;

// Get a reference of the collection for simplification
SqlParameterCollection insParams = insCmd.Parameters;

// Build the parameters
insParams.Add("@ProductID", SqlDbType.Int, 0, "ProductID");
insParams["@ProductID"].Direction =
                                ParameterDirection.Output;
```

```
insParams.Add("@Description", SqlDbType.NVarChar, 255,
            "Description");
insParams.Add("@Vendor", SqlDbType.NVarChar, 255, "Vendor");
insParams.Add("@Cost", SqlDbType.Money, 0, "Cost");
insParams.Add("@Price", SqlDbType.Money, 0, "Price");

// Assign the INSERT command to the DataAdapter
dataAdapter.InsertCommand = insCmd;

// Create the DataSet
DataSet dataSet = new DataSet();

// Use the DataAdapter to fill the DataSet
dataAdapter.Fill(dataSet, "Products");

// Grab the DataTable for convenience
DataTable prodTable = dataSet.Tables["Products"];

// Add a new customer
DataRow newRow = prodTable.NewRow();
newRow.BeginEdit();
newRow["Description"] = "Home Base Broom";
newRow["Vendor"] = "Smith's Hardware";
newRow["Cost"] = 12.54;
newRow["Price"] = 15.00;
newRow.EndEdit();
prodTable.Rows.Add(newRow);

try
{
  // Update the database
  dataAdapter.Update(prodTable);
  Console.Write("Successfully Updated the Database");
}
catch (SqlException ex)
{
  Console.WriteLine(ex.Message);
}
```

What is important to note here is that we have added an additional SELECT statement in the INSERT command. This call fills the @ProductID parameter with the last created identity. Because the command is going to fill the parameter, we need to specify the parameter as an output parameter. After the insert, the new value has its identity column filled in. You can decide to have the DataTable create these values with AutoIncremented columns (see Chapter 5), but if you want to leave it to the database, this facility will help you.

The only issue with using this facility is that you cannot refer to this new product from another table until you update the database to get its identity. In practice, an AutoIncrement DataColumn may be a better approach. Unfortunately, if any updates to the database happen outside your code, this simply will not work. Please see Chapter 5 for more information on how AutoIncrement columns work.

8.4 Conclusion

As cool and fun as disconnected data has been, we have learned that it comes at a cost. Handling real disconnected concurrency is a challenge, but very straightforward. Deciding which concurrency model matches your project or product is the hardest task in handling the disconnected data. In addition, although the CommandBuilder is a powerful development time-saver, it comes at a cost.

PART III
ADO.NET in Action

9
ADO.NET and XML

I KNOW THAT THERE are differing opinions about the importance of XML in software development. Because of this, Microsoft has created their .NET strategy, which makes XML and Web Services the glue that allows interoperability between companies, regardless of the operating system, storage mechanisms, and philosophies of each company. After all, XML is just data and ADO.NET is the data engine of .NET, so it would seem natural that ADO.NET could manage XML just like database data. To that end, ADO.NET is highly integrated with the .NET XML framework.

9.1 .NET and XML

Microsoft's XML strategy in ADO.NET is two-fold. It wants to provide the same tools for accessing data from XML as it does for database data, but at the same time it wants to have ADO.NET as the piece of code that transforms database data into XML. Both are laudable goals. After all, ADO.NET is a bit of a misleading name because it has no family lineage with ADO. What ADO.NET really ends up being is the data engine for .NET development. From that perspective, XML is just another data format, right?

Back in the ADO/OLE DB days, if you needed to treat some data like database data, you would need to write an OLE DB provider. This was complex and fraught with peril. In .NET, you can write managed providers to access nondatabase data, but with the XML integration, you have the ability to provide access to nondatabase data as XML.

9.2 The DataSet and XML

The DataSet has explicit support for XML. Because the database manipulation and XML integration are both first class citizens of the DataSet, it is clear that it was designed for both uses from the ground up.

9.2.1 Getting DataSet Data into XML

Getting an XML representation of your DataSet data is trivial. Controlling how the XML is represented requires more sophistication. Let's take one of our old samples and save our DataSet out as XML (see Listing 9.1).

Listing 9.1: *Getting the XML Representation of a DataSet*

```
. . .

// Create a DataAdapter for each of the tables we're filling
SqlDataAdapter daCustomers = new
  SqlDataAdapter("SELECT * FROM CUSTOMER;",
                conn);
SqlDataAdapter daInvoices = new
  SqlDataAdapter("SELECT * FROM INVOICE;",
                conn);
SqlDataAdapter daInvoiceItems = new
  SqlDataAdapter("SELECT * FROM INVOICEITEM;",
                conn);

// Create your blank DataSet
DataSet dataSet = new DataSet();

// Fill the DataSet with each DataAdapter
daCustomers.Fill(dataSet, "Customers");
daInvoices.Fill(dataSet, "Invoices");
daInvoiceItems.Fill(dataSet, "InvoiceItems");

// Close the connection
conn.Close();

// Grab our tables for simplicity
DataTable customerTable    = dataSet.Tables["Customers"];
DataTable invoiceTable     = dataSet.Tables["Invoices"];
DataTable invoiceItemTable = dataSet.Tables["InvoiceItems"];
```

```
// Set up PrimaryKeys
customerTable.PrimaryKey = new DataColumn[]
  { customerTable.Columns["CustomerID"] };
invoiceTable.PrimaryKey = new DataColumn[]
  { invoiceTable.Columns["InvoiceID"] };
invoiceItemTable.PrimaryKey = new DataColumn[]
  { invoiceItemTable.Columns["InvoiceItemID"] };

// Set up relations
// Create the first relationship
// (between INVOICE and INVOICEITEM)
// We tell the relation to set up a constraint to make sure
// the Relationship is created on a unique key
dataSet.Relations.Add( "Invoices_InvoiceItems",
  dataSet.Tables["Invoices"].Columns["InvoiceID"],
  dataSet.Tables["InvoiceItems"].Columns["InvoiceID"],
  true);

// Create the first relationship (Between CUSTOMER and
// INVOICE)
// We tell the relation to set up a constraint to make sure
// the Relationship is created on a unique key
dataSet.Relations.Add( "Customers_Invoices",
  dataSet.Tables["Customers"].Columns["CustomerID"],
  dataSet.Tables["Invoices"].Columns["CustomerID"],
  true);

// Write out the XML file
Console.WriteLine(dataSet.GetXml());
```

When we run this, we get the following XML:

```
<NewDataSet>
  <Customers>
    <CustomerID>
      a945884d-d309-4b47-ba42-1aff5cd035cf
    </CustomerID>
    <FirstName>Mike</FirstName>
    <LastName>Remlinger</LastName>
    <Address>10 Aaron Way</Address>
    <City>Atlanta</City>
    <State>GA</State>
    <Zip>30307</Zip>
    <HomePhone>(404) 543-8765</HomePhone>
    <Stamp>AAAAAAAAAIA=</Stamp>
    <CheckedOut>false</CheckedOut>
  </Customers>
```

```
...
  <Invoices>
    <InvoiceID>
       463cdf10-2609-41f3-99a3-05f4cedf9fe2
    </InvoiceID>
    <InvoiceNumber>100</InvoiceNumber>
    <InvoiceDate>
       2002-03-21T00:00:00.0000000-05:00
    </InvoiceDate>
    <Terms>Net 10th</Terms>
    <PO>100042</PO>
    <CustomerID>
       11d59cb7-bf61-4540-9317-4f154d717796
    </CustomerID>
  </Invoices>
...
  <InvoiceItems>
    <InvoiceItemID>
       4150d81c-79cb-458b-a303-047e3cd6dbea
    </InvoiceItemID>
    <InvoiceID>
       5e1e9beb-5915-4513-8d67-0f3e0f6a81d0
    </InvoiceID>
    <ProductID>1</ProductID>
    <Quantity>1</Quantity>
    <Discount>0</Discount>
  </InvoiceItems>
...
</NewDataSet>
```

This XML format is very flat. Each entity type is one level below the top container and each entity is unrelated to any other entity. It does this because the relationships are all in the schema for the tables. When you ask for the XML of the DataSet, all you are getting is the raw data without any schema information supplied.

We can specify that the DataRelations in the DataSet are nested so that the XML serialization will know how to generate the relationships. To do that, add Listing 9.2 to Listing 9.1.

Listing 9.2: *Marking Relations as Nested*

```
...

// Set the relations to be nested
dataSet.Relations["Customers_Invoices"].Nested = true;
dataSet.Relations["Invoices_InvoiceItems"].Nested = true;

// Write the XML file out
Console.WriteLine(dataSet.GetXml());
```

Now the XML we are generating looks like this:

```
<NewDataSet>
  <Customers>
    <CustomerID>
      11d59cb7-bf61-4540-9317-4f154d717796
    </CustomerID>
    <FirstName>Greg</FirstName>
    <LastName>Maddux</LastName>
    <Address>53 Peachtree Center</Address>
    <City>Atlanta</City>
    <State>GA</State>
    <Zip>30342</Zip>
    <HomePhone>404-555-1234</HomePhone>
    <Stamp>AAAAAAAAAH8=</Stamp>
    <CheckedOut>false</CheckedOut>
    <Invoices>
      <InvoiceID>
        463cdf10-2609-41f3-99a3-05f4cedf9fe2
      </InvoiceID>
      <InvoiceNumber>100</InvoiceNumber>
      <InvoiceDate>
        2002-03-21T00:00:00.0000000-05:00
      </InvoiceDate>
      <Terms>Net 10th</Terms>
      <PO>100042</PO>
      <CustomerID>
        11d59cb7-bf61-4540-9317-4f154d717796
      </CustomerID>
      <InvoiceItems>
        <InvoiceItemID>
          c7395127-891d-4ed4-8c37-d4e73bcfdf55
        </InvoiceItemID>
```

```
                    <InvoiceID>
                       463cdf10-2609-41f3-99a3-05f4cedf9fe2
                    </InvoiceID>
                    <ProductID>4</ProductID>
                    <Quantity>2</Quantity>
                    <Discount>4.25</Discount>
                  </InvoiceItems>
                  <InvoiceItems>
                    <InvoiceItemID>
                       b30b585f-5fe7-48fd-b97a-e7a31bad0d72
                    </InvoiceItemID>
                    <InvoiceID>
                       463cdf10-2609-41f3-99a3-05f4cedf9fe2
                    </InvoiceID>
                    <ProductID>2</ProductID>
                    <Quantity>3</Quantity>
                    <Discount>0</Discount>
                  </InvoiceItems>
                </Invoices>
                <Invoices>
                  <InvoiceID>
                     5e1e9beb-5915-4513-8d67-0f3e0f6a81d0
                  </InvoiceID>
                  <InvoiceNumber>101</InvoiceNumber>
                  <InvoiceDate>
                     2002-03-31T00:00:00.0000000-05:00
                  </InvoiceDate>
                  <Terms>Net 30</Terms>
                  <PO>100104</PO>
                  <CustomerID>
                     11d59cb7-bf61-4540-9317-4f154d717796
                  </CustomerID>
                  <InvoiceItems>
                    <InvoiceItemID>
                       4150d81c-79cb-458b-a303-047e3cd6dbea
                    </InvoiceItemID>
                    <InvoiceID>
                       5e1e9beb-5915-4513-8d67-0f3e0f6a81d0
                    </InvoiceID>
                    <ProductID>1</ProductID>
                    <Quantity>1</Quantity>
                    <Discount>0</Discount>
                  </InvoiceItems>
                </Invoices>
              </Customers>
            </NewDataSet>
```

Within each customer is a list of their invoices and within each invoice is a list of their invoice item lines. If you want to store your data hierarchically in the XML, you can set the DataSet to make tables nested as needed.

9.2.1.1 *Controlling the Structure of DataColumns*

In the default case, the DataSet uses sub-elements instead of attributes to hold the column data of each table. Stylistically, you may want to serialize each column in your tables as attributes instead of sub-elements. To make the serialization into XML use attributes on a column, you can change the DataColumns of a DataTable to allow for this (see Listing 9.3).

Listing 9.3: *Specifying DataColumn.MappingType*

```
. . .

// Set all columns to output as attributes
foreach(DataColumn col in customerTable.Columns)
  col.ColumnMapping = MappingType.Attribute;
foreach(DataColumn col in invoiceTable.Columns)
  col.ColumnMapping = MappingType.Attribute;
foreach(DataColumn col in invoiceItemTable.Columns)
  col.ColumnMapping = MappingType.Attribute;

// Write the XML file out
dataSet.WriteXml("test.xml");
```

The test.xml file results in:

```
<?xml version="1.0" standalone="yes"?>
<NewDataSet>
  <Customers CustomerID=
            "11d59cb7-bf61-4540-9317- 4f154d717796"
            FirstName="Greg"
            LastName="Maddux"
            Address="100 Henry Aaron Way"
            City="Atlanta"
            State="GA"
            Zip="30307"
            HomePhone="404-555-1234"
            Stamp="AAAAAAAAGk="
            CheckedOut="false">
    <Invoices InvoiceID=
            "463cdf10-2609-41f3-99a3-05f4cedf9fe2"
```

```
                    InvoiceNumber="100"
                    InvoiceDate=
                        "2002-03-21T00:00:00.0000000-05:00"
                    Terms="Net 30"
                    PO="100042"
                    CustomerID=
                        "11d59cb7-bf61-4540-9317-4f154d717796">
                <InvoiceItems
                    InvoiceItemID=
                        "c7395127-891d-4ed4-8c37-d4e73bcfdf55"
                    InvoiceID="463cdf10-2609-41f3-99a3-05f4cedf9fe2"
                    ProductID="4"
                    Quantity="2"
                    Discount="4.25" />


    ...


        </Invoices>
      </Customers>
    </NewDataSet>
```

In this example we go through all the columns in all the tables and set the `ColumnMapping` to the `MappingType` we need (`Attribute` in this case). `MappingType` supports the following types of mapping:

- **Element:** The resulting XML contains an element for this column nested under a table-level element. This is the default.
- **Attribute:** The resulting XML contains an attribute of the table-level element with this column's data.
- **Hidden:** The column is suppressed from the XML.
- **SimpleContent:** The resulting XML writes the column as text within the table-level element. This cannot be used if any columns are using the `Element` mapping or with nested relationships.

The `MappingType` settings are on a column-by-column basis. You have full control over how each and every column is represented in the resulting XML. We can choose to have some of the columns as attributes and leave the rest as elements, as shown in Listing 9.4.

Listing 9.4: *Specifying Arbitrary Columns as Attributes*

```
. . .

// Set the ID columns to output as attributes
customerTable.Columns["CustomerID"].ColumnMapping =
                                    MappingType.Attribute;
invoiceTable.Columns["InvoiceID"].ColumnMapping =
                                    MappingType.Attribute;

// Write the XML file out
dataSet.WriteXml("test.xml");
```

In this example, the test.xml file becomes:

```
<?xml version="1.0" standalone="yes"?>
<NewDataSet>
  <Customers CustomerID=
                "11d59cb7-bf61-4540-9317-4f154d717796">
    <FirstName>Greg</FirstName>
    <LastName>Maddux</LastName>
    <Address>100 Henry Aaron Way</Address>
    <City>Atlanta</City>
    <State>GA</State>
    <Zip>30307</Zip>
    <HomePhone>404-555-1234</HomePhone>
    <Stamp>AAAAAAAAGk=</Stamp>
    <CheckedOut>false</CheckedOut>
    <Invoices InvoiceID=
                "463cdf10-2609-41f3-99a3-05f4cedf9fe2">
      <InvoiceNumber>100</InvoiceNumber>

. . .

</NewDataSet>
```

The ID fields that we set to be attributes in the example are the only fields that become serialized as attributes; the rest of the fields are serialized as elements.

9.2.2 Saving DataSet Data as XML

The more standard reason for using the XML representation of data is to save or stream it somewhere. The DataSet uses the WriteXml method to handle these types of operations. Writing out the XML to a file is as simple as Listing 9.5.

Listing 9.5: *Saving a DataSet to XML*

```
. . .

// Write it out to a file
dataSet.WriteXml("test.xml");
```

In the last section we discussed how to control the structure of the XML file, but in some circumstances we will also want to control the format of the XML file. To do this we will need to get our hands a bit dirty, as shown in Listing 9.6.

Listing 9.6: *Saving a DataSet to XML with Formatting*

```
using System.Xml;
using System.IO;

. . .

// Create a StringWriter to stream into
StreamWriter writer = new StreamWriter("test.xml");

// Create an XmlTextWriter to use to format the XML
XmlTextWriter xmlWriter = new XmlTextWriter(writer);

// Change some options
xmlWriter.Formatting = Formatting.Indented;
xmlWriter.Indentation = 3;

// Write the XML file out
dataSet.WriteXml(xmlWriter);

// Close the writer
xmlWriter.Close();
```

This allows us to set the indention so our XML looks like this:

```
<NewDataSet>
   <Customers>
      <CustomerID>
         11d59cb7-bf61-4540-9317-4f154d717796
      </CustomerID>
```

```
<FirstName>Greg</FirstName>
<LastName>Maddux</LastName>
<Address>100 Henry Aaron Way</Address>

. . .

    </Customers>
</NewDataSet>
```

It is starting to look exactly the way we want. These changes, in conjunction with the DataColumn formatting, allow us to control the format of the XML output.

So far we have been writing out XML as just the raw data. The `Data-Set.WriteXML()` method supports specifying an `XmlWriteMode` enumeration to allow us to save XML in one of three formats:

- **`IgnoreSchema`:** This is the default behavior. It writes out just the data in the DataSet. If no data is loaded, no file is generated.
- **`WriteSchema`:** Writes out the data in the same way as `IgnoreSchema`, but places the schema information as an inline XSD document.
- **`DiffGram`:** Writes out both the original and the current data in the DataSet. Please see Section 9.2.2.2, "Using `XmlWriteMode.DiffGram` Mode," for more information.

`XmlWriteMode` is used as the second parameter in all of `WriteXml()`'s standard overloads. Listing 9.7 is an example.

Listing 9.7: *Specifying Options While Writing DataSet Data as XML*

```
. . .

// Create a StringWriter to stream into
StreamWriter writer = new StreamWriter("test.xml");

// Write the XML file out
dataSet.WriteXml(xmlWriter, XmlWriteMode.WriteSchema);

// Close the writer
xmlWriter.Close();
```

9.2.2.1   *Using* `XmlWriteMode.WriteSchema` *Mode*

When you write out your DataSet with `WriteSchema`, you will get an almost complete DataSet (including schema about relations, primary keys, and data). But you will not get a copy of both the original and current values of the data—you will receive only the current values. If your goal is to serialize your DataSet and preserve the state of all rows (whether they are changed or not) then you should use a DiffGram (see Section 9.2.2.2 for more information on DiffGrams). If you fill a different DataSet with the resulting XML, all the rows in the newly constructed DataSet will have all clean rows. In this case, this could cause some data to not be updated to the database.

9.2.2.2   *Using* `XmlWriteMode.DiffGram` *Mode*

In contrast to `WriteSchema`, the `DiffGram` is used for getting all the data in the DataSet (both original and current values if they are different). Diff-Grams do not include any schema. The assumption is that you have a DataSet with schema that you will fill with a DiffGram. When you serialize the DataSet into XML using the DiffGram mode, you will notice that you get all the data, not just the changes. If you wanted to create an XML document that contained only the changes, you could call the `DataSet.GetChanges()` method and get a DiffGram from that (see Listing 9.8).

Listing 9.8: *Generating DiffGrams*

```
...

// Change a couple rows
invoiceItemTable.Rows[0]["Quantity"] = 5;

// Create a StringWriter to stream into
StreamWriter writer = new StreamWriter("test.xml");

// Create an XmlTextWriter to use to format the XML
XmlTextWriter xmlWriter = new XmlTextWriter(writer);
xmlWriter.Formatting = Formatting.Indented;

// Get a DataSet of the changes
DataSet dataSetChanges = dataSet.GetChanges();

// Write the XML file out
dataSetChanges.WriteXml(xmlWriter, XmlWriteMode.DiffGram);
```

```
// Close the writer
xmlWriter.Close();
```

For more information on how to use DiffGrams to create a DataSet, see Section 9.2.5.

9.2.3 DataSet Namespaces

Within the DataSet, DataTable and DataColumn properties exist that allow you to specify the namespace and prefix for the XML that will be generated or read. For instance, if you want to generate XML with the namespace of "ADONET", using the prefix "an", you would follow Listing 9.9.

Listing 9.9: *Specifying Namespace for XML within the DataSet*

```
...

// Set up the XML namespace and prefix
dataSet.Namespace = "ADONET";
dataSet.Prefix = "an";

// Create a StringWriter to stream into
StreamWriter writer = new StreamWriter("test.xml");

// Create an XmlTextWriter to use to format the XML
XmlTextWriter xmlWriter = new XmlTextWriter(writer);
xmlWriter.Formatting = Formatting.Indented;

// Write the XML file out
dataSet.WriteXml(xmlWriter);

// Close the writer
xmlWriter.Close();
```

The XML is output so that the DataSet element in the XML has this namespace and prefix. You can add additional namespaces to DataTables and DataColumns if you want to be more specific about which namespace each of these elements uses when generating or reading data into the DataSet.

9.2.4 Filling a DataSet with XML

The DataSet can be created from an XML document by using the `DataSet.ReadXml()` method. This method should be a mirror of the `WriteXml()` method, so we must be sure that any XML documents that we want to use to fill the DataSet will match the data model of the DataSet. That means that the DataSet cannot take any XML document you find out on the Web. Here I have a simple piece of XML:[1]

```xml
<?xml version="1.0" encoding="UTF-8"?>
<configuration>
  <system.net>
    <webRequestModules>
      <add prefix="http"
           type="System.Net.HttpRequestCreator"/>
      <add prefix="https"
           type="System.Net.HttpRequestCreator"/>
      <add prefix="file"
           type="System.Net.FileWebRequestCreator"/>
    </webRequestModules>
    <authenticationModules>
      <add type="System.Net.DigestClient"/>
      <add type="System.Net.NegotiateClient"/>
      <add type="System.Net.KerberosClient"/>
      <add type="System.Net.NtlmClient"/>
      <add type="System.Net.BasicClient"/>
    </authenticationModules>
    <connectionManagement>
      <add address="*" maxconnection="2"/>
    </connectionManagement>
  </system.net>
</configuration>
```

This simple piece of XML causes the DataSet to choke. It complains with this message:

```
The same table (add) cannot be the child table in two nested
relations.
```

---

1. This is a fragment of the machine.config file that installed as part of the .NET Framework installation.

This occurs because the DataSet is expecting that the "add" elements are all of the same type, but in this example they are not the same. The DataSet is attempting to create an Add table, but because the different add elements are contained within different elements, the DataSet cannot create the relationship so it gives up. The only way to get this XML into the DataSet would be to transform it into a schema that is friendlier to the DataSet.

Here is a piece of XML that has its entities more defined:

```
<?xml version="1.0" encoding="UTF-8" ?>
<NewDataSet>
  <Customers>
    <CustomerID>
      11d59cb7-bf61-4540-9317-4f154d717796
    </CustomerID>
    <FirstName>Greg</FirstName>
    <LastName>Maddux</LastName>
    <Address>53 Peachtree Center</Address>
    <City>Atlanta</City>
    <State>GA</State>
    <Zip>30342</Zip>
    <HomePhone>404-555-1234</HomePhone>
    <Stamp>AAAAAAAAH8=</Stamp>
    <CheckedOut>false</CheckedOut>
    <Invoices>
      <InvoiceID>
        463cdf10-2609-41f3-99a3-05f4cedf9fe2
      </InvoiceID>
      <InvoiceNumber>100</InvoiceNumber>
      <InvoiceDate>
        2002-03-21T00:00:00.0000000-05:00
      </InvoiceDate>
      <Terms>Net 10th</Terms>
      <PO>100042</PO>
      <CustomerID>
        11d59cb7-bf61-4540-9317-4f154d717796
      </CustomerID>
      <InvoiceItems>
        <InvoiceItemID>
          c7395127-891d-4ed4-8c37-d4e73bcfdf55
        </InvoiceItemID>
        <InvoiceID>
          463cdf10-2609-41f3-99a3-05f4cedf9fe2
        </InvoiceID>
```

```
            <ProductID>4</ProductID>
            <Quantity>2</Quantity>
            <Discount>4.25</Discount>
          </InvoiceItems>
          <InvoiceItems>
            <InvoiceItemID>
              b30b585f-5fe7-48fd-b97a-e7a31bad0d72
            </InvoiceItemID>
            <InvoiceID>
              463cdf10-2609-41f3-99a3-05f4cedf9fe2
            </InvoiceID>
            <ProductID>2</ProductID>
            <Quantity>3</Quantity>
            <Discount>0</Discount>
          </InvoiceItems>
        </Invoices>
      </Customers>
    </NewDataSet>
```

In this file, we have more of a notion of entity identification. The Customers element owns Invoices elements, which own InvoiceItems elements. To fill a DataSet with this XML file, follow Listing 9.10.

Listing 9.10: *Reading XML into a DataSet*

```
// Fill the DataSet with XML
DataSet dataSet = new DataSet();
dataSet.ReadXml(@"good.xml");

Console.WriteLine(dataSet.GetXml());
```

In the real world, I have only really found it useful to use ReadXml() when using XML that was serialized out of a DataSet, as shown in Listing 9.11.

Listing 9.11: *Reading XML into a DataSet*

```
...

// Create a StringWriter to stream into
StreamWriter writer = new StreamWriter("test.xml");

// Create an XmlTextWriter to use to format the XML
XmlTextWriter xmlWriter = new XmlTextWriter(writer);
```

```
// Write the XML file out
dataSet.WriteXml(xmlWriter);

// Close the writer
xmlWriter.Close();

// Fill the new DataSet with XML
DataSet newDataSet = new DataSet();
newDataSet.ReadXml(@"test.xml");

// Compare and report the result
bool areTheySame = dataSet.GetXml() == newDataSet.GetXml();

Console.WriteLine("Are they the same? {0}", areTheySame);
```

We can see in this sample that if you get XML from an unchanged DataSet and fill a new DataSet with that data, the DataSets would be equal to each other.

Just like the `DataSet.WriteXml()` method, the `DataSet.ReadXml()` method has a number of overloads that deal with the form of the XML when read. The most important part of these overloads is the use of the `XmlReadMode` enumeration to determine exactly how to read XML into the DataSet. These are the possible values for `XmlReadMode`:

- **Auto:** This is the default behavior. The DataSet will attempt to figure out the best method of reading the XML into itself. If you already know the mode of XML read, you will see a performance gain by specifying the mode.
- **DiffGram:** Reads the DiffGram and applies the changes to the DataSet. RowStates are preserved. This mode is similar to `DataSet.Merge()` behavior.
- **Fragment:** Reads XML documents. Any inline namespaces are read in as schema. This reads standard XML documents, like the documents generated by SQL Server's FOR XML syntax.
- **IgnoreSchema:** This is like `Fragment`, but if any inline schema is encountered, it ignores the inline schema and attempts to read the data into the existing DataSet schema. Any data that does not match the existing schema is discarded, including data that does not exist in the same namespaces. If the DataSet contains no schema, all the data will be discarded.

- **InferSchema:** Much like `IgnoreSchema`, any inline schema is ignored when reading in data, but the form of the XML is used to infer the actual schema that is added to the DataSet. If the DataSet already contains schema, the DataSet is expanded to include the additional schema.

- **ReadSchema:** Reads the inline schema information and data and attempts to add it to the DataSet schema. Unlike `Fragment`, if any of the schemas already exist in the DataSet, an exception will be thrown.

9.2.5 DiffGram Strategies

DiffGrams are a special beast in ADO.NET. As we have already found, DiffGrams contain all the information about the data in a DataSet—both the original and the current values of rows. You can do one of two things with this information: merge DataSets or transmit DataSets for database updating.

Merging allows you to get a DiffGram of the changes in a DataSet and to merge them with another DataSet. This functionality is identical to that of `DataSet.Merge()`. But why would you use a DiffGram instead of a `DataSet.Merge()`? Merging is great if you need to merge two local DataSets, but in the case where you want to use a Web service or Message Queuing to send the changes to the middle tier for updating, the DiffGram is much more efficient. There are some caveats, however, that Listing 9.12 should expose.

Listing 9.12: *Using DiffGrams to Exchange Changes between DataSets*

```
. . .

// Grab our tables for simplicity
DataTable customerTable    = dataSet.Tables["Customers"];
DataTable invoiceTable     = dataSet.Tables["Invoices"];
DataTable invoiceItemTable = dataSet.Tables["InvoiceItems"];

// Set up PrimaryKeys
customerTable.PrimaryKey = new DataColumn[]
  { customerTable.Columns["CustomerID"] };
invoiceTable.PrimaryKey = new DataColumn[]
  { invoiceTable.Columns["InvoiceID"] };
invoiceItemTable.PrimaryKey = new DataColumn[]
  { invoiceItemTable.Columns["InvoiceItemID"] };
```

```
// Create a StringWriter to stream into
StreamWriter writer = new StreamWriter("test.xml");

// Create an XmlTextWriter to use to format the XML
XmlTextWriter xmlWriter = new XmlTextWriter(writer);

// Write the XML file out
dataSet.WriteXml(xmlWriter, XmlWriteMode.WriteSchema);

// Close the writer
xmlWriter.Close();

// Fill the new DataSet with XML
// to make dataSet and newDataSet identical
DataSet newDataSet = new DataSet();
newDataSet.ReadXml(@"test.xml", XmlReadMode.ReadSchema);
newDataSet.AcceptChanges();

// Change both DataSets
dataSet.Tables["Customers"].Rows[0]["Zip"] = "98765";
newDataSet.Tables["Customers"].Rows[1]["State"] = "FL";


// Create writer and stream
Stream newStream = new MemoryStream() as Stream;
XmlTextWriter xmlNewWriter =
                        new XmlTextWriter(newStream, null);
xmlNewWriter.Formatting = Formatting.Indented;

// Get DiffGrams of DataSet
newDataSet.GetChanges().WriteXml(xmlNewWriter,
                                XmlWriteMode.DiffGram);

// Write the DiffGram to the console window
newStream.Position = 0;
StreamReader rdr = new StreamReader(newStream);
Console.WriteLine(rdr.ReadToEnd());

// Reset the stream
newStream.Position = 0;

// Apply changes to DataSet
dataSet.ReadXml(newStream, XmlReadMode.DiffGram);
```

The only way `DataSet.ReadXml()` will know to merge a row in the DiffGram is if you have the primary keys set up so that it can test against identity of a row. You will notice when we created a copy of our DataSet by reading in the whole XML document of the original DataSet, that we needed to call `DataSet.AcceptChanges()` to tell the new copy that all the rows were unchanged. We can alleviate this by making our DataSet copy using a DiffGram instead of a simple XML read. In addition, the `Diff-Gram`'s granularity is at the row level. If you have a row with a change in the DataSet and another change in the DiffGram, the DiffGram will over-write it. To make the merge as efficient as possible, we got the DiffGram from the changed DataSet by calling `WriteXml()` on the `GetChanges()` DataSet that was created. This will include only the items changed in the DataSet. If we were to get a DiffGram of the entire DataSet, the merge would need to attempt to merge each and every row. Pretty low cost in this simple example, but this can become a real performance drain if your DataSets become large.

9.2.6   DataSet Schema

We have seen in the preceding sections that we can add inline database schema to the XML output from a DataSet with little difficulty, but what about getting schema alone from a DataSet?

9.2.6.1   *Saving a DataSet's XSD*

You can create an .XSD file by simply calling one of the DataSet's `XmlSchema` methods. Much like reading or writing XML, there are `Get`, `Read`, and `Write` methods:

- **GetXmlSchema:** Returns a string containing the schema information (the XSD document) of the DataSet.
- **ReadXmlSchema:** Reads the schema information from a file path, `Xml-Reader` object, or `Stream` object.
- **WriteXmlSchema**: Writes the schema information to an `XmlWriter` object, `Stream` object, or file path.

To write an XSD and read it into another DataSet, follow Listing 9.13.

Listing 9.13: *Working with DataSet Schema as an XSD Document*

```
...

// Create a StringWriter to stream into
StreamWriter writer = new StreamWriter("test.xsd");

// Create an XmlTextWriter to use to format the XSD
XmlTextWriter xmlWriter = new XmlTextWriter(writer);

// Write the XSD file out
dataSet.WriteXmlSchema(xmlWriter);

// Close the writer
xmlWriter.Close();

// Make a new DataSet with the same
// schema as our existing DataSet
DataSet newDataSet = new DataSet();
newDataSet.ReadXmlSchema(@"test.xsd");
```

The XSD that is generated from the `WriteXmlSchema()` method is:

```
<?xml version="1.0" encoding="utf-8"?>
<xs:schema id="NewDataSet"
        xmlns=""
        xmlns:xs="http://www.w3.org/2001/XMLSchema"
        xmlns:msdata=
                "urn:schemas-microsoft-com:xml-msdata">
  <xs:element name="NewDataSet" msdata:IsDataSet="true">
    <xs:complexType>
      <xs:choice maxOccurs="unbounded">
        <xs:element name="Customers">
          <xs:complexType>
            <xs:sequence>
              <xs:element name="CustomerID"
                        msdata:DataType="System.Guid"
                        type="xs:string"
                        minOccurs="0" />
              <xs:element name="FirstName"
                        type="xs:string"
                        minOccurs="0" />
              <xs:element name="LastName"
                        type="xs:string"
                        minOccurs="0" />
```

```
                    <xs:element name="MiddleName"
                                type="xs:string"
                                minOccurs="0" />
                    <xs:element name="Address"
                                type="xs:string"
                                minOccurs="0" />
                    <xs:element name="Apartment"
                                type="xs:string"
                                minOccurs="0" />
                    <xs:element name="City"
                                type="xs:string"
                                minOccurs="0" />
                    <xs:element name="State"
                                type="xs:string"
                                minOccurs="0" />
                    <xs:element name="Zip"
                                type="xs:string"
                                minOccurs="0" />
                    <xs:element name="HomePhone"
                                type="xs:string"
                                minOccurs="0" />
                    <xs:element name="BusinessPhone"
                                type="xs:string"
                                minOccurs="0" />
                    <xs:element name="DOB"
                                type="xs:dateTime"
                                minOccurs="0" />
                    <xs:element name="Discount"
                                type="xs:double"
                                minOccurs="0" />
                    <xs:element name="Stamp"
                                type="xs:base64Binary"
                                minOccurs="0" />
                    <xs:element name="CheckedOut"
                                type="xs:boolean"
                                minOccurs="0" />
                </xs:sequence>
              </xs:complexType>
            </xs:element>
            <xs:element name="Invoices">
              <xs:complexType>
                <xs:sequence>
                    <xs:element name="InvoiceID"
                                msdata:DataType="System.Guid"
                                type="xs:string"
                                minOccurs="0" />
```

```
            <xs:element name="InvoiceNumber"
                        type="xs:int"
                        minOccurs="0" />
            <xs:element name="InvoiceDate"
                        type="xs:dateTime"
                        minOccurs="0" />
            <xs:element name="Terms"
                        type="xs:string"
                        minOccurs="0" />
            <xs:element name="FOB"
                        type="xs:string"
                        minOccurs="0" />
            <xs:element name="PO"
                        type="xs:string"
                        minOccurs="0" />
            <xs:element name="CustomerID"
                        msdata:DataType="System.Guid"
                        type="xs:string"
                        minOccurs="0" />
        </xs:sequence>
      </xs:complexType>
    </xs:element>
    <xs:element name="InvoiceItems">
      <xs:complexType>
        <xs:sequence>
          <xs:element name="InvoiceItemID"
                      msdata:DataType="System.Guid"
                      type="xs:string"
                      minOccurs="0" />
          <xs:element name="InvoiceID"
                      msdata:DataType="System.Guid"
                      type="xs:string"
                      minOccurs="0" />
          <xs:element name="ProductID"
                      type="xs:int"
                      minOccurs="0" />
          <xs:element name="Quantity"
                      type="xs:int"
                      minOccurs="0" />
          <xs:element name="Discount"
                      type="xs:double"
                      minOccurs="0" />
        </xs:sequence>
      </xs:complexType>
    </xs:element>
  </xs:choice>
```

```
      </xs:complexType>
    </xs:element>
  </xs:schema>
```

9.3 The XmlDataDocument Class

In the past sections of this chapter, we have seen how to get XML out of the DataSet. If you wanted to treat the DataSet data as XML (to support XPath queries, Extensible Stylesheet Language [XSL] transformations, and other operations), a natural notion would be to create the XML, put it in an Xml-Document object, and work on it from there. ADO.NET has an even better notion: the XmlDataDocument class. This class holds a reference to a DataSet and exposes all the data in the DataSet as an XML document. If you change a value in XmlDataDocument, the change can be seen in the DataSet, and vice versa.

XmlDataDocument derives directly from XmlDocument, so it has all the same functionality as a standard XmlDocument object. The major difference is that you need to set a DataSet as a property, either in the constructor or by setting the property. After you have created the XmlDataDocument, you can use it to navigate the nodes, search with XPath expressions, or transform the XML with XSLT, as shown in Listing 9.14.

Listing 9.14: *Using an XmlDataDocument*

```
// Create and open the connection
SqlConnection conn = new SqlConnection(
  "server=localhost;" +
  "database=ADONET;" +
  "Integrated Security=true;");
conn.Open();

// Create a DataAdapter for each of the tables we're filling
SqlDataAdapter daCustomers = new
  SqlDataAdapter("SELECT * FROM CUSTOMER;",
                 conn);
SqlDataAdapter daInvoices = new
  SqlDataAdapter("SELECT * FROM INVOICE;",
                 conn);
SqlDataAdapter daInvoiceItems = new
  SqlDataAdapter("SELECT * FROM INVOICEITEM;",
                 conn);
```

```
// Create your blank DataSet
DataSet dataSet = new DataSet();

// Fill the DataSet with each DataAdapter
daCustomers.Fill(dataSet, "Customers");
daInvoices.Fill(dataSet, "Invoices");
daInvoiceItems.Fill(dataSet, "InvoiceItems");

// Close the connection
conn.Close();

// Grab our tables for simplicity
DataTable customerTable    = dataSet.Tables["Customers"];
DataTable invoiceTable     = dataSet.Tables["Invoices"];
DataTable invoiceItemTable = dataSet.Tables["InvoiceItems"];

// Set up PrimaryKeys
customerTable.PrimaryKey = new DataColumn[]
  { customerTable.Columns["CustomerID"] };
invoiceTable.PrimaryKey = new DataColumn[]
  { invoiceTable.Columns["InvoiceID"] };
invoiceItemTable.PrimaryKey = new DataColumn[]
  { invoiceItemTable.Columns["InvoiceItemID"] };

// Set up relations
// Create the first relationship (between INVOICE
// and INVOICEITEM)  We tell the relation to set
// up a constraint to make sure the
// Relationship is created on a unique key
dataSet.Relations.Add( "Invoices_InvoiceItems",
  dataSet.Tables["Invoices"].Columns["InvoiceID"],
  dataSet.Tables["InvoiceItems"].Columns["InvoiceID"],
  true);

// Create the first relationship (between CUSTOMER
// and INVOICE) We tell the relation to set up a
// constraint to make sure the
// Relationship is created on a unique key
dataSet.Relations.Add( "Customers_Invoices",
  dataSet.Tables["Customers"].Columns["CustomerID"],
  dataSet.Tables["Invoices"].Columns["CustomerID"],
  true);

// Create an XmlDataDocument
XmlDataDocument dataDoc = new XmlDataDocument(dataSet);
```

```
// Do an XPath query
XmlNode node = dataDoc.SelectSingleNode("//Invoices");

// Show the XML of the first node found.
Console.WriteLine(node.OuterXml);
```

All we have done here is create a new `XmlDataDocument`, passing our DataSet in to the constructor. Once we are done, we query the XML to find the first descendant called `Invoices`. We can write out this node (and its children):

```
<Invoices>
  <InvoiceID>
    463cdf10-2609-41f3-99a3-05f4cedf9fe2
  </InvoiceID>
  <InvoiceNumber>100</InvoiceNumber>
  <InvoiceDate>
    2002-03-21T00:00:00.0000000-05:00
  </InvoiceDate>
  <Terms>Net 30</Terms>
  <PO>100042</PO>
  <CustomerID>
    11d59cb7-bf61-4540-9317-4f154d717796
  </CustomerID>
</Invoices>
```

9.3.1   Searching the DataSet with XPath Expressions

The DataSet lacks a real SQL engine, so we have had to use filters and searches in DataViews to search for data contained in the DataSet. DataViews work fine, but since we have the power of the `XmlDataDocument`, why not use XPath to search the DataSet? Building on our last example, we can use conventional XPath searching, as shown in Listing 9.15, to find the first customer with the first name of "Tom."

Listing 9.15: *Searching a DataSet with an XPath Expression*

. . .

```
// Create an XmlDataDocument
XmlDataDocument dataDoc = new XmlDataDocument(dataSet);
```

```
// Search it
string xpath = "//Customers[FirstName = \"Tom\"]";
XmlNode node = dataDoc.SelectSingleNode(xpath);
if (node != null)
{
  Console.WriteLine("Found:");
  Console.WriteLine(node.OuterXml);
}
else
{
  Console.WriteLine("No Nodes found");
}
```

This results in:

```
Found:
<Customers>
  <CustomerID>
    80fce1c0-176f-4367-aefa-66deb58e6bed
  </CustomerID>
  <FirstName>Tom</FirstName>
  <LastName>Glavine</LastName>
  <Address>100 Henry Aaron Way</Address>
  <City>Atlanta</City>
  <State>GA</State>
  <Zip>30307</Zip>
  <HomePhone>404-555-1235</HomePhone>
  <Stamp>AAAAAAAAGo=</Stamp>
  <CheckedOut>false</CheckedOut>
</Customers>
```

The `XmlDataDocument` is just an `XmlDocument`, so every XML operation is appropriate. The benefit is that we are saving time generating an XML document and reparsing it. The document inside the `XmlDataDocument` points at the data contained directly in the DataSet table data.

For more information on using XPath expressions, please see the MSDN documentation (msdn.microsoft.com/library/en-us/cpguide/html/cpconcompileselectevaluatematcheswithxpathxpathexpressions.asp).

9.3.1.1   *Namespaces and Searching DataSets*

The DataSet supports specifying a namespace for a DataSet. In day-to-day practice this is not often needed unless the DataSet is serialized to a known XSD schema. The most likely case where you will run into a namespace within a DataSet is in a Typed DataSet. Since the Typed DataSet is based on an .XSD document, they are more likely to have an XML namespace associated with the schema.

Though this is not specific to ADO.NET or DataSets, there is some confusion about how to search with XPath with an associated namespace. In most XSDs, there is a default namespace specified. Unfortunately XPath does not support searching within a default namespace. To perform a search on an XmlDataDocument that has a default namespace, you will need to use an XmlNamespaceManager object to specify the namespace and create an alias to the default namespace. Listing 9.16 shows how this is done.

Listing 9.16: *Executing an XPath Query with a Namespace Prefix*

```
. . .

// Create an XmlDataDocument
XmlDataDocument dataDoc = new XmlDataDocument(dataSet);

// Create the Namespace Manager
XmlNamespaceManager nsMgr;
nsMgr = new XmlNamespaceManager(dataDoc.NameTable);

// Add the namespace to the Manager
nsMgr.AddNamespace("x", dataSet.Namespace);

// Search it
string xpath = "//x:Customers";
XmlNode node = dataDoc.SelectSingleNode(xpath, nsMgr);

if (node != null)
{
  Console.WriteLine("Found:");
  Console.WriteLine(node.OuterXml);
}
else
{
  Console.WriteLine("No Nodes found");
}
```

In order to be able to search the `XmlDataDocument`, we create the `Xml-NamespaceManager` with the `NameTable` of the `XmlDataDocument`. We can now add our DataSet's namespace with the alias of x. When we actually construct the XPath query, we prefix the entity with the namespace alias (`//x:Customers`). And lastly, we need to send the `XmlNamespace-Manager` into the `SelectSingleNode` method along with the XPath query.

9.3.2 Transforming a DataSet with XSLT

Using XSLT to change the format of the DataSet's XML is really handy with `XmlDataDocument`. Much like the above example, we are saving performance by eliminating a couple of steps that are usually required (writing out the XML file and parsing the file). To perform an XSLT, you can simply follow Listing 9.17.

Listing 9.17: *Transforming an XmlDataDocument*

```
using System.Xml.Xsl;

. . .

// Create an XmlDataDocument
XmlDataDocument dataDoc = new XmlDataDocument(dataSet);

// Make a StringWriter to hold the results
StringWriter writer = new StringWriter();

// Transform it
XslTransform xslt = new XslTransform();
xslt.Load(@"XmlDataDocSample.xsl");
xslt.Transform(dataDoc, null, writer);

// Show the results
Console.WriteLine(writer.ToString());
```

Again, this code would be identical if you were transforming an `Xml-Document`. XSL transformations are a complex topic. Please refer to the MSDN documentation for more information (msdn.microsoft.com/library/en-us/cpguide/html/cpconxslttransformationswithxsltransformclass.asp).

9.4 Conclusion

The core of ADO.NET's integration with XML has to do with ADO.NET's relationship to the DataSet. By loading XML into a DataSet or using XML schema to define DataSets, we can use a common language to share data between our applications and the rest of the world. In addition, by utilizing `XmlDataDocument`, you can treat the DataSet like a live `XmlDocument` and perform whatever XML functions you are already familiar with.

▟ 10 ▪
Data Binding with ADO.NET

W E   H A V E   S P E N T   nine chapters helping you to retrieve data in a sensible format. Now what? Getting the data to the user is the next important step. You will need to tie your data to the interfaces that the user actually interacts with. That is where data binding comes in.

10.1   What Is Data Binding in .NET?

Microsoft knows that those of us who write database-driven applications spend most of our time writing data entry screens and reports. They also knew that it would save us time if there were a straightforward way to tie controls together with our database data. That is the ultimate goal of data binding in .NET, and in ADO.NET by extension.

In previous data binding frameworks, Microsoft made it fairly simple to tie the actual values held in controls to values in the database, which made our work easier. However, this facility was missing Web-enabled applications. In .NET, data binding not only is available to the web developer but is modeled to be remarkably similar to desktop application development.

Data binding in .NET needed to be more than just a way to get data to the user—it also needed to support data-driven applications, both desktop and Web-based. To that end, data binding allows us to bind any writable property on a control to a data source. If you want to have a database that has the color, size, and location of a control on a form, data binding will manage pushing the data into the control.

10.2   **Data Binding in Windows Forms**

Before .NET, most windowing frameworks (MFC, Visual Basic, and so on) had support for data binding of one sort or another. Windows Forms is no different—it is built to allow binding of any data to any property of controls.

Windows Forms supports two types of data binding. For controls that hold a single value (such as `TextBox`, `CheckBox`, and the like), Windows Forms supports simple data binding. For controls that hold multiple values (such as `ListBox`, `ComboBox`, `DataGrid`, and the like), they support complex data binding.

But before we throw ourselves headlong into how different types of data binding are done, we must have data to bind to. Listing 10.1 is the code that is filling in the data for all of the examples.

Listing 10.1: *Common Database Code*

```
private DataSet dataSet = new DataSet();
private DataTable customerTable;
private DataTable invoiceTable;
private DataTable invoiceItemTable;
private DataTable productTable;

private void InitializeData()
{
  // Create and open the connection
  SqlConnection conn = new SqlConnection(
    "server=localhost;" +
    "database=ADONET;" +
    "Integrated Security=true;");

  // Create a DataAdapter for each of the tables we're
  // filling
  SqlDataAdapter daCustomers =
      new SqlDataAdapter("SELECT * FROM CUSTOMER", conn);
  SqlDataAdapter daInvoices =
      new SqlDataAdapter("SELECT * FROM INVOICE", conn);
  SqlDataAdapter daInvoiceItems =
      new SqlDataAdapter("SELECT * FROM INVOICEITEM", conn);
  SqlDataAdapter daProducts =
      new SqlDataAdapter("SELECT * FROM PRODUCT", conn);
```

```
// Create your blank DataSet
DataSet dataSet = new DataSet();

// Fill the DataSet with each DataAdapter
daCustomers.Fill(dataSet, "Customers");
daInvoices.Fill(dataSet, "Invoices");
daInvoiceItems.Fill(dataSet, "InvoiceItems");
daProducts.Fill(dataSet, "Products");

// Grab our tables for simplicity
customerTable    = dataSet.Tables["Customers"];
invoiceTable     = dataSet.Tables["Invoices"];
invoiceItemTable = dataSet.Tables["InvoiceItems"];
productTable     = dataSet.Tables["Products"];

// Set up PrimaryKeys
customerTable.PrimaryKey = new DataColumn[]
            { customerTable.Columns["CustomerID"] };
invoiceTable.PrimaryKey = new DataColumn[]
            { invoiceTable.Columns["InvoiceID"] };
invoiceItemTable.PrimaryKey = new DataColumn[]
            { invoiceItemTable.Columns["InvoiceItemID"] };
productTable.PrimaryKey = new DataColumn[]
            { productTable.Columns["ProductID"] };

// Set up relations
// Create the first relationship (Between INVOICE
// and INVOICEITEM)
// We tell the relation to set up a constraint to make
// sure the Relationship is created on a unique key
dataSet.Relations.Add( "Invoices_InvoiceItems",
  invoiceTable.Columns["InvoiceID"],
  invoiceItemTable.Columns["InvoiceID"],
  true);

// Create the first relationship
// (Between CUSTOMER and INVOICE)
// We tell the relation to set up a constraint to make
// sure the Relationship is created on a unique key
dataSet.Relations.Add( "Customers_Invoices",
  customerTable.Columns["CustomerID"],
  invoiceTable.Columns["CustomerID"],
  true);
```

```
        // Create the second relationship
        // (Between CUSTOMER and INVOICE)
        // We tell the relation to set up a constraint to make
        // sure the Relationship is created on a unique key
        dataSet.Relations.Add( "InvoiceItems_Products",
          invoiceItemTable.Columns["ProductID"],
          productTable.Columns["ProductID"],
          false);

        // Add a few expression columns
        customerTable.Columns.Add("FullName", typeof(string),
                           "LastName + ', ' + FirstName");
        invoiceItemTable.Columns.Add("Price", typeof(string),
                           "Avg(Child.Price)");
        invoiceItemTable.Columns.Add("Total", typeof(string),
                           "Quantity * Avg(Child.Price)");
        invoiceItemTable.Columns.Add("Description",
                           typeof(string),
                           "MAX(Child.Description)");
        invoiceTable.Columns.Add("Description", typeof(string),
                           "InvoiceNumber + ': ' + InvoiceDate");
}
```

Most of this code should be familiar by now. The interesting part of this code is the new columns we are creating to bind to. These are expression (or calculated) columns, which are very useful to bind to because the columns do the formatting for us.

10.2.1 Simple Data Binding

In order to "wire-up" data binding with Windows Forms controls, you must add new `Binding` objects to the `DataBindings` property of the control. This member is defined in the base `Control` class, and all Windows Forms controls must inherit from it. The `DataBindings` property is a collection of `Binding` objects. This is a collection because we can bind to a number of different properties on a control. For example, we can add a binding to the `Text` property to set the text based on our data, and have a second binding to another table in our data that fills in the color of the text.

To create a binding, do the following:

- Specify the property you want to bind to.
- Specify the data source of the data you are going to bind from.
- Specify the data member (if any) of the data source to get at the particular data.

In ADO.NET applications, the `dataSource` is usually a DataTable or a DataView and the `dataMember` is the column you want to extract. It takes the form of:

```
{Control}.DataBindings.Add("{Property}",
                           {dataSource},
                           "{dataMember}");
```

For example, you may have a table that contains information about specific products that you have in inventory. If you want to bind the description to a textbox and availability status to a checkbox, you would follow Listing 10.2.

Listing 10.2: *Simple Windows Forms DataBinding*

```
// Bind the textbox to the product's description
txtDesc.DataBindings.Add("Text",
                         productTable,
                         "Description");

// Bind the value of the checkbox to the InStock column
chkInStock.DataBindings.Add("Checked",
                            productTable,
                            "InStock");
```

The resulting dialog box would look like that shown in Figure 10.1.
There needs to be a way of telling the bindings which record you should be on. Such a method does exist; we'll get to that in Section 10.2.5.

10.2.2 Complex Binding

Complex binding (as Microsoft refers to it) is not really all that complex. What Microsoft is really referring to is binding to a list or collection of elements.[1] This is great because we are dealing with database data. Let's

---

1. For a more complete discussion of Windows Forms, including data binding controls, please see Chris Sells' forthcoming book *Essential Windows Forms*.

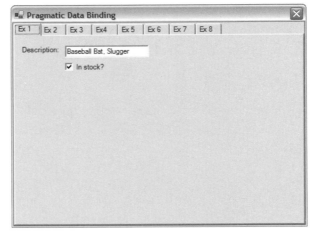

Figure 10.1: *Simple data binding*

continue to assume that we have a DataTable with product information. If we want to show all the products we ever carry, we might want to bind the table to a list box. To accomplish that binding, there are three pieces of information we need to provide to the list box:

- **DataSource**: An object that supports IList (like DataTables and most collection classes)
- **DisplayMember**: The property of the DataSource to show in the control
- **ValueMember**: An identifier to store within the control that may be used to determine which row of data you are referring to in the DataSource (for example, if DisplayMember is FullName and ValueMember is CustomerID)

In our example, we want to show the user the description of the product, but be able to retrieve the ProductID when the user selects something. To accomplish this, follow Listing 10.3.

Listing 10.3: *Complex Windows Forms DataBinding*

```
// Bind the products to the ListBox
listProducts.DataSource = productTable;
listProducts.DisplayMember = "Description";
listProducts.ValueMember = "ProductID";
```

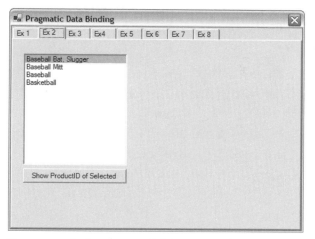

Figure 10.2: *A* `ListBox` *containing our products*

Once we do this, we will be displaying the `ListBox` with all of the descriptions, as shown in Figure 10.2.

Because we want to be sure that our `ProductID`s are tied to the specific `ListBox` item, let's show a dialog box with the `ProductID` when the button is pressed:

```
MessageBox.Show(string.Format( "Selected Product's ID: {0}",
                    listProducts.SelectedValue));
```

As it shows here, we can display the value of the item selected by simply asking the `ListBox` to tell us what the `SelectedValue` is. The value returned is the row element that was specified in the `ValueMember` property of the control. This is different than the `SelectedItem`, which returns the row value that was specified in the `DisplayMember` property.

10.2.3   DataGrid Binding

Compared to data binding of other Windows Forms controls, binding to a `DataGrid` is a special beast. Unlike in simple binding where you are binding an atomic value to a control, or complex binding where you are binding a list of values to a control that has multiple items, when you bind to a `DataGrid` you are binding a larger set of data. The `DataGrid` supports setting the DataSource property to the actual data source (such as DataTable,

DataSet, DataView, and so on). If you simply change the DataSource at runtime, the control does not take the change into effect until the control is reloaded. If you need to refresh the control immediately with a new DataSource, use the `DataGrid.SetDataBinding()` method. This method takes the DataSource and DataMember of the source to bind to. The DataMember is a named entity to bind to. You might want to bind directly to a DataSet if you have several tables. In this case you actually bind to the list of tables in the DataSet. If you are binding directly to a DataTable, there is no name necessary. You can also bind to a DataTable by binding to a DataSet and setting the DataMember to the name of the DataTable. For example, see Listing 10.4.

Listing 10.4: *Windows Forms DataGrid Binding*

```
// Bind the grid to the ProductTable
theGrid.SetDataBinding(productTable, "");

// Could have used the following:
theGrid.SetDataBinding(dataSet, "Products");

// Bind to a DataSet
theGrid.SetDataBinding(DataSet, "");
```

When you bind to a table, you get the predictable result shown in Figure 10.3.

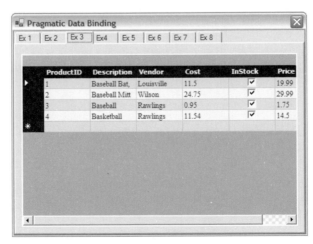

Figure 10.3: *Binding a DataGrid to a table*

You can bind directly to a DataView just as you can a table, as shown in Listing 10.5.

Listing 10.5: *Windows Forms DataGrid Binding Using a DataView*

```
// Create a DataView that is sorted by Price
DataView sortedView = new DataView(productTable,
                            "",
                            "Price",
                            DataViewRowState.CurrentRows);

// Set the DataBinding to the DataView
theDataViewGrid.SetDataBinding(sortedView, "");
```

Creating DataViews to bind to is convenient if you need to force a sorting or filtering on the underlying data. The data is now sorted in the `Data-Grid`, as shown in Figure 10.4.

The `DataGrid` supports the relational nature of DataSets. If we were to bind to the customer table, we could navigate through its relationships:

```
theGrid.SetDataBinding(customerTable, "");
```

Note that this is identical to the above `productTable` binding. The difference is that the `DataGrid` recognizes that the `customerTable` has

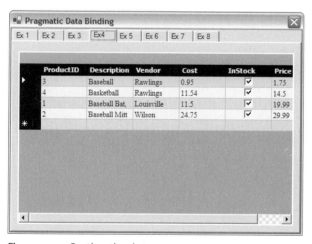

Figure 10.4: *Sorting the data*

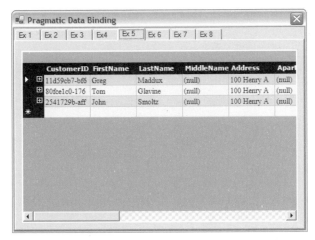

Figure 10.5: *DataGrid binding with a related DataTable*

relationships (whereas the `productTable` does not). After binding you would get a grid that looks like that shown in Figure 10.5.

This grid will let you navigate through the relationships to see which invoices belong to just this customer and continue down to the customer items that those invoices own. This is useful, but not as convenient as master detail binding.

10.2.4 Master Detail Binding

Master detail binding simply refers to tying some control binding to the parent table in a relationship within a DataSet, and another control to the child table in that relationship. Figure 10.6 shows how the top grid is the master binding and the bottom grid is the detail binding.

To do this, bind the parent table to the master grid by specifying the DataTable as the DataSource, and nothing in the DataMember. To attach the child table to the detail grid, you would specify the parent DataTable for the DataSource of the detail grid, and the name of the relationship as the DataSource, as shown in Listing 10.6.

Listing 10.6: *Master Detail Binding*

```
// Bind the master
masterGrid.SetDataBinding(customerTable, "");

// Bind the detail
detailGrid.SetDataBinding(customerTable,
                          "Customers_Invoices");
```

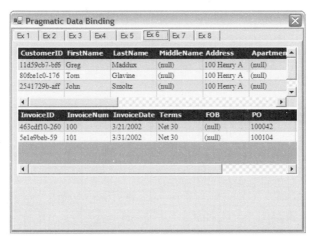

Figure 10.6: *Master detail binding*

When you bind them in this way, selecting different rows in the master grid will give you only the items in the detail grid that are part of the relationship of the parent item selected. Data binding can continue to support multiple layers of master detail. If we continue our example to set the first grid to the `customerTable` and the second grid to the `invoiceTable` (like we did in Listing 10.6), we can add another grid and bind it to `invoiceItemTable`, as shown in Listing 10.7.

Listing 10.7: *Multiple Levels of Master Detail Binding*

```
// Bind the master
masterGrid.SetDataBinding(customerTable, "");

// Bind the detail
detailGrid.SetDataBinding(customerTable,
                          "Customers_Invoices");

// Bind the detail
detail2Grid.SetDataBinding(customerTable,
                "Customers_Invoices.Invoices_InvoiceItems");
```

What is interesting here is that in order to do this binding, all the grids are bound to the `customerTable`, but the `InvoiceDetail` grid sets the DataMember to the invoice's relationship tree. In this case, the `Customer` table's `Customer_Invoices` relationship and the `Invoice` table's

`Invoice_Invoices_InvoiceItems` relationship. Again, the related nature of how the controls handle the synchronization is based on the fact that all the grids are using the `Customer` table as the data source. Our example dialog now looks like that shown in Figure 10.7.

10.2.5　Using the `CurrencyManager` Class

Let me introduce you to the most ill-named class in the framework: `CurrencyManager`. This class is used to determine and manipulate the cursor of the data source of a complex data binding. In our earlier example, we always changed the cursor of the data source by clicking on a different user in the master grid. By using `CurrencyManager`, you can manage this yourself.

Let's assume that we have a form with several controls bound to elements of our customer (name, address, and so on), a `ListBox` complexly bound to the invoices of our current customer, and a grid to show the detail items of the invoice when selected. Notice that we do not have a grid with all the customers. We want to use the VCR control panel–type control (like the `DataBinding` control from Visual Basic), which has four buttons: forward, reverse, first, and last. First, we bind the controls (again using the `customerTable` as the data source in all cases, as shown in Listing 10.8).

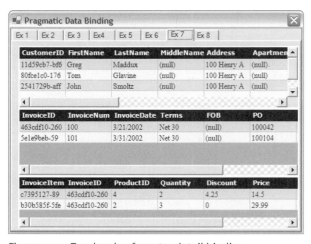

Figure 10.7: *Two levels of master detail binding*

Listing 10.8: *Using the CurrencyManager Class*

```
// Bind the master controls
txtCustName.DataBindings.Add(  "Text",
                               customerTable,
                               "FullName");
txtAddress.DataBindings.Add(   "Text",
                               customerTable,
                               "Address");
txtCity.DataBindings.Add(      "Text",
                               customerTable,
                               "City");
txtState.DataBindings.Add(     "Text",
                               customerTable,
                               "State");
txtZip.DataBindings.Add(       "Text",
                               customerTable,
                               "Zip");
txtHomePhone.DataBindings.Add("Text",
                               customerTable,
                               "HomePhone");
txtWorkPhone.DataBindings.Add("Text",
                               customerTable,
                               "BusinessPhone");

// Bind the invoices
listInvoices.DataSource = customerTable;
listInvoices.DisplayMember =
             "Customers_Invoices.Description";

// Bind the detail
Detail6.SetDataBinding(customerTable,
             "Customers_Invoices.Invoices_InvoiceItems");
```

Next we need to move `CurrencyManager` based on our button clicks. We implicitly created a `CurrencyManager` when we set up the bindings in Listing 10.8. We will need to use that `CurrencyManager`. We get at the `CurrencyManager` by navigating to the form's `BindingContext` property, which has an indexer that takes the DataSource to get the `CurrencyManager` for that DataSource. We can change the position of the `CurrencyManager` by changing its `Position` property. Listing 10.9 illustrates how this is done in the click events.

Listing 10.9: *Moving the Cursor with the CurrencyManager*

```
private void btnFirst_Click(object sender,
                             System.EventArgs e)
{
  BindingContext[customerTable].Position = 0;
}

private void btnPrev_Click(object sender,
                             System.EventArgs e)
{
  if (BindingContext[customerTable].Position != 0)
    BindingContext[customerTable].Position -= 1;
}

private void btnNext_Click(object sender,
                             System.EventArgs e)
{
  if (BindingContext[customerTable].Position <
            BindingContext[customerTable].Count - 1 )
    BindingContext[customerTable].Position += 1;
}

private void btnLast_Click(object sender,
                             System.EventArgs e)
{
  BindingContext[customerTable].Position =
                 BindingContext[customerTable].Count - 1;
}
```

When this is all put together, you get a dialog that looks something like the one shown in Figure 10.8.

10.3   Data Binding in ASP.NET

Web development (including ASP.NET) is all about dealing with the disconnected nature of the HTTP[2] protocol. Web Forms data binding is disconnected and read-only to reflect this disconnected nature. This is unlike Windows Forms data binding, in which the data that is bound is directly tied to the data sources. In other words, ASP.NET data binding is more of

---

2.   Hypertext Transport Protocol; see www.w3.org/protocols for more information.

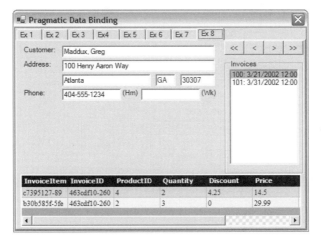

Figure 10.8: *CurrencyManager at work*

a convenience to get our data into the Web controls than it is a way to tie the control to our data. That makes data binding in ASP.NET somewhat simpler than in Windows Forms.

10.3.1   Simple Binding

In ASP.NET, simple binding of data to a control is done by using the `<%# %>` syntax in the ASP.NET page. The data that we are binding against is really any data attached to the page. For example:

```
<asp:TextBox id="theTextBox"
             text='<%# productTable.Rows[0]["Price"] %>'
             runat="server" />
```

This tells the page to call the `productTable` and get the first row's `Price` column value and place it in the text of the `TextBox`. You must call `DataBind()` on the `TextBox` to force the binding to actually occur. This is a critical difference between Windows Forms binding and Web Forms binding. In Windows Forms you are binding that actual data (changes in the control will affect the real data), whereas in Web Forms you are binding to a copy of the data. Listing 10.10 shows how to have data binding to happen on a Web control.

Listing 10.10: *Calling DataBind( ) in Web Forms*

```
// Force the binding to occur
// on the data binding that we created in the
// ASP.NET page
// Or you could call DataBind() on the page to
// force all controls to data bind.
theTextBox.DataBind();
```

Interestingly enough, what actually happens is that the ASP.NET engine generates code that creates the binding in code. The resulting data binding of the text attributes looks like this:

```
target.Text =
          Convert.ToString(productTable.Rows[0]["Price"]);
```

In this way, we needed to make the `productTable` a member of the code-behind page to make this binding work. Because we are not binding a list, this works just fine. But in most cases, the binding is more helpful with large pieces of data.

10.3.2 Complex Binding

Like in Windows Forms, the goal of complex binding is to bind a collection or list of items to a user interface (UI) element. In ASP.NET this is usually a `ListBox` control or `DropDownList` control. These controls (and others like them) support the following data binding properties:

• **DataSource**: The data object to bind to. Usually a DataTable or DataView.

• **DataTextField**: The column in the DataSource to get for the part of the control visible to the user.

• **DataTextFormatString**: An optional format string to help the Web control format the `DataTextField` into something more useful. For example, setting the `DataFormatTextString` to {0:d} on a date field will show the date in a shorter form.

• **DataValueField**: The column in the DataSource to store in the control for the value of the Web control.

For example, see Listing 10.11.

Listing 10.11: *Complex Web Forms Data Binding*

```
// Bind the ListBox
theListBox.DataSource = Session["customerTable"];
theListBox.DataTextField = "FullName";
theListBox.DataValueField = "CustomerID";
theListBox.DataTextFormatString = "Name: {0}";

// Bind the DropDown control
theDropDown.DataSource = Session["productTable"];
theDropDown.DataTextField = "Description";
theDropDown.DataValueField = "ProductID";

// Make the bind happen on all the controls
DataBind();
```

10.3.3   Data Control Binding

In ASP.NET there are several data controls that show more than one column in a table for us. These are the `DataGrid`, `DataList`, and `Data-Repeater` controls. These controls are bound like the `DataGrid` in Windows Forms—they simply take a DataSource and an optional Data-Member (see Listing 10.12).

Listing 10.12: *Binding to Data Controls in Web Forms*

```
// Bind the grid to the productTable
theGrid.DataSource = productTable;

// Alternatively
// theGrid.DataSource = dataSet;
// theGrid.DataMember = "Products";

// Cause the binding to happen
DataBind();
```

Once the control is bound, the specific controls can be made to bind specific columns or just let them automatically generate the columns or rows.

10.3.4 Binding with a DataReader

Because data binding in ASP.NET is read-only, you can bind to a DataReader object even though it is a forward-only view of the data. ASP.NET just walks through the DataReader and fills the particular object with each row of the DataReader as necessary. For example, see Listing 10.13:

Listing 10.13: *Data Binding to a DataReader*

```
// Create a connection
SqlConnection conn = new SqlConnection();
conn.ConnectionString = "Server=localhost;" +
                        "Database=ADONET;" +
                        "User ID=ADOGUY;" +
                        "Password=ADOGUY";
conn.Open();

// Create a command to read the product descriptions/IDs
SqlCommand cmd = conn.CreateCommand();
cmd.CommandText =
            "SELECT Description, ProductID FROM PRODUCT";

// Create a DataReader to use to bind to the ListBox
SqlDataReader rdr = cmd.ExecuteReader();

// Bind to the ListBox
theListBox.DataSource = rdr;
theListBox.DataTextField = "Description";
theListBox.DataValueField = "ProductID";
theListBox.DataBind();

// Close the connection
conn.Close();
```

In the case where the data is changing a lot (where caching would be more of a hindrance than a help), running a DataReader every time the page is hit is an appropriate use of the DataReader data binding.

10.3.5 Performance Considerations

Being able to bind to ASP.NET is useful, but how the data is saved behind the Web pages is an important consideration that will determine how your pages will perform. The common question is whether to cache or not, and if you do cache, where do you do it? In Chapter 11, I will be delving deeper into dealing with performance and scalability issues with ADO.NET solutions in general.

10.3.5.1   *DataReaders (Noncaching)*

Most ASP sites do not even try to cache. They assume that the database is high performance enough for every page to read the data directly from the database. This is surprisingly effective. If you are developing an intranet application or a small site that does not expect any real volume of traffic, using DataReaders to avoid ever caching is a perfectly acceptable solution.

10.3.5.2   *Server Caching*

When caching is required because of the scope or size of your site, server-side caching has usually been the solution. Whole systems have been designed to help keep certain information in memory and available to ASP pages to help performance. In ASP.NET, the options are a bit broader.

Unlike in ASP pages, in ASP.NET using the Session State Management System to hold data pertaining to a specific user works really well. ASP.NET supports local, Web farm, and SQL Server–based Session State, so there should be a Session State facility that works for your situation.

When there is data to be cached that is not specific to a user (such as a product list), you can cache the data either by using a static class (a class that has all static members and properties) or by storing information at the application level. Application-level caching is most appropriate when you have the same information available to all users. The downside is that when changes occur to the underlying data, it changes for all sessions at once.

10.3.5.3   *Client Caching*

In the old days when we needed to store state on the client, we would create hidden fields that contained the data we needed. When the user submitted our form, we would get the data in the hidden field posted back to us. In ASP.NET, there is native support for caching data in Web Forms, called View State. View State works just like our old hidden field solution, but it is more integrated into Web Forms. When View State is enabled for pages or controls, the View State is stored as a single hidden field that contains state information about the page and controls. The problem with View State is that it causes the size of most Web pages to balloon up to much larger sizes than you would ordinarily want. A simple form that contains a single control with View State disabled might be 1,384 bytes in size, whereas the same form with View State enabled would be 3,800 bytes. This is not necessarily a representative example, but it does illustrate the problem with view state: the size of the page. Depending on your ultimate customer, this bloat is either fine or a performance drain. If you expect users to get at your pages across the Internet on a 28.8Kbps modem, that extra 2,416 bytes can be significant. If you are developing for an intranet application, users will not even notice the difference.

10.4 Conclusion

Whether you are developing for Windows Forms or ASP.NET, data binding your data to controls is a powerful tool in your arsenal. The key to using this tool is to understand the differences among the various types of data binding. Knowing the differences between simple and complex binding and when to use master-detail binding will help you develop more intuitive user interfaces in less time.

■ 11 ■
Scalability and Performance

THIS CHAPTER IS really where the rubber meets the road. ADO.NET gives you the tools to help you make scalable, high-performance software, but you can take those tools and build software that does not scale well or that underperforms. The trick is in understanding how you can tell the difference. My goal is to teach you how to tell what the difference is and to help put a lot of arrows in your quiver so you have plenty of ammunition to hunt down solutions to your problems.

11.1 Should You Worry?

When developers design systems, much of their time is focused on making sure that a particular piece of functionality can be accomplished. If we finish our design at the point where we can get the functionality to work, however, we are doomed to fail. Let me tell you a story from my past where I was more worried about the functionality than the performance.

Some years back I was charged with writing some code to enable doctors using a pen computer to pick a medication for a prescription. I wanted the doctors to be able to pick from any drug so I thought, simple: create a list box with all the drugs. I wrote the database queries, the screens, and the reports that would shoot out prescriptions on a printer for the doctor. Everything worked end to end on my machine.

The day I released it to the testers I was excited to watch it work for them, so I camped myself in the QA lab for the day. I was expecting to be available to field questions about the application, but they got to my screen and it seemed like it froze up. The hourglass cursor just sat there, mocking me. We gave up after a few minutes. I was perplexed.

That night, QA forgot to reboot one of the pen systems and left it running overnight. Surprisingly, the next day they brought me one of the units and showed me that the screen was up. As I played with the screen, I noticed that all the drugs had names starting with the letter 'A'. When I tried to move the scrollbar, it froze up again. I asked the QA people how many drugs were in the database. They answered, "About twelve thousand, why?" "Oh," I replied. I had tested with 40.

I ended up changing the list box to a grid that could page and load only the drugs that could be shown on the screen at one time. What did I learn that day? I learned that understanding the capacity of a system is crucial to finding the right solution. So, should you worry? Of course you should.

11.1.1 Designing Scalable Systems

It is all a matter of design. When you design a component, application, or system, your design must balance the requirements of your project. You will need to understand how much performance, scalability, robustness, time to market, portability, and security your project requires. When you weigh all these requirements together, you will find out quickly how much scalability and performance you need in your project. You cannot design software that will be scalable and high performance in every possible situation.

What do I mean by scalability and high performance? These are subjective terms that have different meanings for different situations. When I talk of scalability, I mean the measure of how well a system performs as the size of the problem increases. In other words, as the demands of a system grow (for example, increased user demand, increased storage demand, or increased performance demands), the system must be able to grow with those demands to provide a level of performance similar to before the demand increase. For most systems today, there are clear-cut metrics for how much a particular system must scale. To steal a line from Tim Ewald, "An app is either scalable enough or it isn't."[1] At the end of the day, we still

---

1. *Transactional COM+: Building Scalable Applications*, Addison-Wesley Publishers, ISBN: 0201615940.

need to meet our system's requirements. If that means 1,000 simultaneous users, then we should know how to design it to be scalable enough to handle 100,000 simultaneous users. On the other hand, high performance is the measure of how responsive the system is for every request. Scalability and performance work hand in hand because the system needs to be high performing no matter how many simultaneous users are connected. Performance metrics should show that a system responsiveness does not vary much no matter what the load is.

Ultimately, scalability and performance must be dealt with together. Designing for scalability and performance is a matter of creating a system that can allow for further distributing the application as the size of the problem increases. For example, if you design a Web site and you have the performance requirement of a median response time per page of five seconds, unless you know the number of simultaneous users the Web site is expected to service, your five-second response time is useless. For a single user, it is easy to make a Web site that responds quickly. The hard part is designing a Web site that responds quickly, no matter how many users are accessing it.

11.1.2 Coupling Components in Systems

The days of designing monolithic systems are dead, right? Not quite. Just because you are designing your systems with components and object-oriented programming (OOP) techniques does not necessarily mean that they will scale well and are not monolithic. What do I mean by monolithic? I mean tightly coupled. When you design your system it is important to not assume where your code will eventually run or where your data will have to reside. If you tightly couple your components or other pieces of code and data, you are doomed to be constrained to only scale up (increasing size of a server's disk, memory, processors, and so on). If you design a system to scale out (distributing parts of the system onto discrete servers), you can make decisions about how much to distribute based on the current load of your system. As your system's load requirements grow, so can your system.

To me scaling up is a dead end. Scaling out is the magic. So if a system is one giant piece of code that must exist on a single server, it won't scale. The more pieces that can (optionally) be moved to a distributed environment, the easier it is to scale. I think of DB servers as monolithic (until recently with the advent of linked servers and cross-machine views), whereas Web sites can be more componentized because you have duplicate machines across a farm to serve identical site information, and move business tier stuff into another set of machines that are more easily scaled. These discrete, loosely coupled pieces of a system are easier to scale.

11.2   Before ADO.NET

Scalability is not a new issue. We should know how to scale database applications by now. Unfortunately, before ADO.NET scaling was difficult and time-consuming. In the beginning of a project we usually had the best intentions of how to make sure it was scalable, but when we met with schedule pressure and technical hurdles, scalability languished. The two areas that hit developers the hardest in recent history were scaling data-centric Web applications and scaling the database itself.

11.2.1   The Trouble with Connected Data

When Microsoft created Active Server Pages (ASP), it was intent on making it easier to create Web sites. For the most part, Microsoft succeeded. In those days, ADO was the one (and usually the only) way to get at database data. ADO's model made it easy to have long-running connections to the database. This was not a big problem for developing desktop applications or even smaller-scale client-server systems, but it was never designed to do Web site development.

Many companies wrote their first Web sites using ADO and ASP. These were plagued by the database servers running out of available connections. Their sites, which worked fine when they were getting a thousand hits a day, melted under any real load. Something had to give. Some developers attempted to mitigate the issue by reducing the time that they were actually connected to the database. Companies attempted to insist that their developers only use a connection within the scope of a single page. This was fine, unless the Web site needed to cache the data. Developers came up with many different solutions for handling this data caching, but most of these solutions relied on copying data from their database into their own data structures and saving them in some in-memory cache. These caches were very successful, until they had to scale past a single machine. In order to keep these caches in sync, they alerted the caches that the database had changed, which, in turn, caused all the caches to try to refresh themselves from the database. This worked reasonably well except under a large database load where a change at the database would cause a huge swell of database activity (caused by all the caches trying to query nearly at the same time). There were other solutions that many of these companies tried—some worked well and others did not.

The fact was that to make a data-centric Web site scalable to any extent developers had to write whole systems to help reduce the reliance on database connections. These caching layers needed to do all of the following:

- Manipulate database data
- Create data structures to hold the database data outside of ADO
- Create in-memory caches to hold the data structures of database data

Microsoft realized that this was becoming tedious and attempted to help by adding support for disconnected RecordSets in ADO. This did make things better, but assumed that developers knew about the capability and knew how to deal with disconnected data. When pressed for time, developers ended up writing connected data access with good intentions to go back later and change it to disconnected. Usually that never happened.

11.2.2 The Trouble with Scaling the Database Server

Eventually, reducing the need to keep connections to a database hits a wall where you cannot wring any more performance out of a system. Often the next tactic is to try to make the database server scale better. You can either scale up or out. Scaling up usually entails upgrading hardware, adding processors, increasing memory, or adding faster hard drives. This does help, but there is a limit to how much it can.

Another tactic is to scale out the database server. This usually involves segmentation (splitting up databases onto separate machines), duplication (making identical copies of the same data on separate machines), or clustering (joining two or more machines into a logical machine to share the load from clients).

Segmentation requires that some code somewhere have explicit knowledge of what data is where and be smart about how to formulate data access to get the right data from the right place. Sure this can be handled by switching database servers, but still some piece of code needs to be written in segmentation to do the lookup. In addition, when segmentation reaches its performance threshold, another round of segmentation is required. (An example of this is if you initially put the customer and vendor data on one machine and invoice and inventory data on another machine. Now that the servers are really busy, however, you need to put each table on its own machine.) Much of the code base needs to be revised to recognize this change, plus you'll need to do the database work required to actually move the data.

On the other hand, duplication is a good strategy if you are working with read-only data, because multiple copies of the same static data can be reported against with no real collisions. The problem still exists, however, that whenever new machines are added to the farm of duplicated database servers, someone needs to know how to tell the applications that they can use the new machine.

Building clusters of machines to host a database server is another popular option. In practice, though, clusters have a hard limit of two or four machines. This allows us to scale the servers out on a limited basis only.

None of these solutions are very satisfying, and continuing to scale out after the first iteration is time consuming and affects many systems.

11.3   How ADO.NET Can Help

ADO.NET can help, but it is not a panacea for bad development practices. You will still need to write the database access code. But with ADO.NET you should be able to write that code much faster, with less duplication. ADO.NET eliminates the possibility of using the database in a very connected way. The old ADO way of directly editing a record on the database server while locking the record simply does not exist in ADO.NET. In this way, ADO.NET is meant to help eliminate code that used to cause problems in ASP.

Because the connected nature of ADO is at the root of our scalability problems, we can leverage the ADO.NET disconnected architecture to avoid these pitfalls. But exactly how do we leverage ADO.NET? This depends on the nature of your application. You can leverage several strategies to gain scalability.

11.3.1   Data Caching on the Web Servers

In most public Web sites today, the Web servers are scaled out by creating identical machines and placing them in a farm of machines to handle incoming requests. We can leverage this scalability by reducing the dependencies on the database through caching on the Web servers. This is done by reading your database into a DataSet (or Typed DataSet) and storing it on the Web server. The level of caching really depends on your particular application. Common caching scenarios are shown in Table 11.1.

TABLE 11.1 Common Caching Scenarios

Scenario	Description	Drawbacks
Per User	A cached DataSet is stored in session state so that there is only one call to the database per session.	If users spend small amounts of time on your site, the caching benefits are minimal.
Per Application	A cached DataSet is either stored in application state or as a per-process singleton so that there is only one copy for an entire application or process.	If the data is volatile this can be problematic because the data is refreshed only occasionally. Also, there needs to be some automated process to push changes from the DataSet back to the database.
Per Server	A per-machine singleton is created (with remoting) to expose the DataSet to all applications.	This has the same drawbacks as per application.

Caching on Web servers is not very different than what we have in the ASP world, except that building DataSets and Typed DataSets makes the component development much simpler. In addition, with ASP.NET's session state, we have a session-based caching facility that is robust and scalable. The days of every company writing its own session caching system are gone.

11.3.2 Scaling Database Data

Another approach to getting scalability is to remove direct database interaction from Web servers entirely. As we discussed earlier, scaling a database server has its own problems. Again, ADO.NET gives us the tools to scale the database.

11.3.2.1 *Using DataSets Instead of Direct Database Access*

The DataSet is much like an in-memory database. We can store our tables and schema in a DataSet and make applications access only the DataSet. Unfortunately, many developers expect to be able to use SQL to access their database data. The lack of a true SQL engine can be a stumbling block if we maintain that expectation. Of course, it would be better to remove this expectation altogether. In a system with well-defined data, we ordinarily would want to isolate the Web developer from the SQL, whether it is through a business object layer or through stored procedures. In the ADO.NET paradigm this is done by exposing the DataSet or Typed DataSet as a Web site's object model. Remember, data might be in a database today, in XML tomorrow, or in a mixture of both. By using the `XmlData-Document`, we can expose our in-memory database as XML and get the developers used to using XPath to query the data.

Frankly, most of the access that developers need is not so they can do complicated analytical processing; usually it's just to find a particular entity that we are storing in the database. For example, when writing an e-commerce Web site, the developer may just want to find the user's entity. In that case, using XPath to search the DataSet is more than adequate to do the job. I suspect that when XQuery[2] becomes an approved standard, the DataSet and `XmlDataDocument` will support it.

---

2. See www.w3.org/XML/Query for more information on XQuery, and see xqueryservices.com for Microsoft's initial implementation of XQuery for the .NET Framework.

11.3.2.2   *Scaling Out a DataSet*

So at this point we have a DataSet that represents our database and we know how to query it. But how does this help us scale the database? It helps by allowing us to deploy our DataSet to middle tier machines. Whether we access that DataSet with remoting or through a Web service, we can create a farm of machines that will allow us to scale the database out. This is better than traditional caching systems because the DataSet machines can pass around DiffGrams to keep each of the machines in a consistent state instead of relying on database calls.

In addition, in .NET we can load balance these middle tier servers with the same techniques we already use to load balance Web server to spread the load of these remoted DataSets. If you look into .NET remoting, all object instantiation is done through a URL. Like Web applications, Web services can be load balanced easily. If you decide to use remoting, this still works because both HTTP remoting and TCP remoting instantiate objects from a well-known URL. Because it is just a URL, you can load balance it in the same way as a Web application or Web service.

11.3.2.3   *What Data to Store in Remoted DataSets*

The biggest question I had when I was creating these remoted DataSets was how to handle changes to the underlying data as well as changes in different instances of the DataSet itself. As I tried to understand the issues, I realized how much of the data in a particular system is actually fairly static. For example, in a typical e-commerce setting, using remoted DataSets to hold catalog data (which is usually fairly static) eliminates the need to handle concurrency with the remoted DataSets. In accounting systems or real-time monitoring systems, however, this simply does not work. How much of the data in your system is actually volatile? On the whole, the less volatile the data, the less work you need to do.

11.3.2.4   *Duplication or Segmentation?*

When deciding to remote the DataSets, you still must determine a strategy for storing the information. Do you want to create a duplicate of the entire database in a DataSet on each middle tier machine or would you rather segment the data into pieces?

Both solutions have problems to overcome. Duplication assumes that you will need to keep all copies in sync. Segmentation forces you to have a solution for finding the right remoted DataSet that contains the specific information you need. Segmentation does not work all that well if you need to merge or join data across segments. You could also opt for both solutions: Replicas of segments of the database stored in DataSets. Ultimately you will have to weigh these pros and cons and apply your domain-specific requirements to find the right solution.

11.3.2.5 *Synchronization*

If you allow for the DataSet data to be modified or added to, you will need to do the heavy lifting required to synchronize the different instances of your data. Luckily, that is not too difficult with ADO.NET. Keeping the different machines in sync is fairly easy. Simply applying DiffGrams (see Chapter 9) across the machines is a decent choice. Keeping machines in sync with the database is a little bit trickier. In the SQL Server space, you can always use Microsoft Message Queue (MSMQ) to deliver messages that the database has changed, but in other database engines it is a vendor-specific problem. My bias would be to attempt to have the middle tier be the only point of database changes, and to send off DiffGrams to the other servers every time a database update is done. Only the machine on which the change initially happened would need to be concerned with dealing with the database. The other servers would use the DiffGrams to keep consistency. This works better than older caching systems because we are removing the need for all the other servers to do database reads when a change takes place.

In actuality this will be less of a problem than it would seem on the surface. In many cases the data either is read-only (like the e-commerce catalog) or will only be edited one session at a time (like adding items to a shopping basket). Concurrency becomes less of an issue if you are using ASP.NET session state.

11.3.3 **In Practice**

You should opt for a hybrid solution of many of these techniques. You may decide to cache a particular customer in session state as an XML fragment,

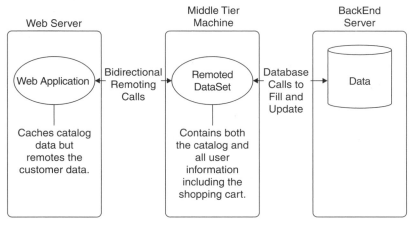

Figure 11.1: *DataSet scaling architecture*

while remoting the entire DataSet on middle tier machines to provide another layer of scalability. For example, in a run-of-the-mill e-commerce application you might arrange your system as shown in Figure 11.1.

In this example, we are using a remoted DataSet to get both customer and catalog information. We decide to cache the catalog information on every Web server, but to use the customer data directly from the remoted DataSet. The only piece that directly interacts with the database server is the middle tier software. As a side benefit, you can close any direct connection between the Web server and the database server.

This is not a cookie-cutter solution. You will still need to find out how this data caching fits into your system's design.

11.4   **Are DataReaders Scalable?**

In ADO.NET, you can make software that both fails to scale well and performs poorly. Again, ADO.NET is not a panacea that will do the right things for you. It simply tries to coax you in the right direction. In that light, DataReaders are no better or worse than DataSets. There is no flat rule that says that DataSets are better than DataReaders. They are completely different animals. The DataSet is in-memory storage for data (including, but not limited to, database data), whereas the DataReader is a vehicle from which you can read database data directly. Frankly, when you fill a DataSet with data, you are probably using DataReaders under the covers anyway. That fact gives us some clues about the right use for DataReaders.

So when should you use a DataReader? There are really two occasions when I can see using the DataReader in Web applications:

• **Volatile data:** The DataReader handles volatile data really well because it is interacting directly with the database and will have access to the freshest data possible. That does not mean that the DataReaders will scale well, but if the data is volatile, using a DataSet becomes very difficult.

• **Data warehouses**: The DataReader is the natural tool to deal with large warehouses of data. In that situation you probably do not want to cache terabytes of information (even if you could). Because DataReaders stream the database a handful of records at a time, you never need to try to have the entire set of data in memory at once. Again, this does not scale particularly well, but neither does a terabyte of data.

Of course by using ASP.NET's output caching you can mitigate any scalability issues with DataReaders. As we discussed earlier in the chapter, output caching can cache pages based on page criteria (e.g., query string, post data, etc.). For example, if we were using a DataReader to read information about a particular product we were selling, we could cache each version of the page based on the product ID. See Section 11.3.1 for more information on output caching.

If you decide to use DataReaders on a particular page, understand the scalability implications. There will need to be a connection to the database on every single request to that page. In the right circumstance this is the right thing to do, but rarely is that true.

11.5　**ADO.NET Performance**

ADO.NET is all about not letting the users' code interact directly with the database. With that in mind, it is a little more difficult to tune performance in ADO.NET. The upside of this is that when you are dealing with a cache of the data directly, the access is much faster than if you went to the database time and again.

In ADO.NET, performance can be measured in two different stages: interactions with the database (like filling or updating) and interactions between code and the DataSet.

11.5.1 Interactions with the Database

Aside from writing good queries and optimizing the way that we update the database (see Chapter 8), there is little you can do in ADO.NET to help or hurt performance. Database performance tuning is way beyond the scope of this book, but in the "Best Practices" section (Section 11.6) I do discuss the big killers of database performance and how to avoid them.

11.5.2 Interacting with the DataSet

In most cases, tuning the interaction you have with the DataSet comes down to shaving seconds off a marathon. Although this is a laudable goal, do not take too much of this to heart because it is saving milliseconds, not seconds.

Inside the DataSet, when you are referring to tables, columns, or values in rows, you have the option to specify the item by a human-readable string (for example, `myDataSet.Tables["Customers"]`). This comes at a small cost of a lookup. If you are really trying to save every possible millisecond, making these ordinal references or using a Typed DataSet will mitigate some of this lookup time because it is done only once during initialization, and all other references to items are strongly typed (and therefore early bound).

11.6 Best Practices

I have come to understand how ADO.NET can be used and in that process I have come up with a list of tips that I hope will help you avoid common pitfalls of ADO.NET. Following you will find a number of my opinions about how to do database development with ADO.NET, without pulling out all of your hair.

11.6.1 Use DataSet Schema

I hate roundtrips to the database. I especially hate roundtrips to the database when a failure is caused by a violation of the schema. DataSet schema is great at preventing this. By defining your schema in the DataSet, you will be alerted when the data is incorrect earlier in the process. For example, if I create a constraint in my DataSet to make sure that all social security numbers are unique, when I try to add a user twice, the DataSet will let me know (instead of waiting until I update the database and fail).

In addition, by using DataSet relationships, you can pass along object trees that are inter-related, thereby eliminating the need for a set of classes to map the relational data to a hierarchical model.

11.6.2 Use Typed DataSets to Create Business Rule Layers

As we saw in Chapter 6, we can create Typed DataSets to do all the hard work in handling the database and serialization. By inheriting from those Typed DataSets, we can write our business rules about our data without having to craft a whole mapping between our data and the database's data. By starting with a Typed DataSet, you are simply reducing the need to write a new interface into the data or any of the database code you would ordinarily use. As the schema of your data changes, you can regenerate the Typed DataSet and modify your code that inherits from the Typed DataSet. The important distinction is that you will need to write less code to start, and even less code as the schema changes. Stop working so hard and go home at six and see your family.

11.6.3 Reduce Roundtrips to the Database

Roundtrips are expensive. Repeat it with me please . . . roundtrips are expensive. Reducing the number of times you need to call the database will increase the performance of your client code dramatically. Reducing roundtrips will not reduce load on the server by a substantial amount, but the client (or Web site) code will benefit greatly. ADO.NET supports doing queries that return multiple resultsets (although not all managed providers support this), so fetching or updating data in a batch will increase performance.

11.6.4 Cache Data Early and Often

ADO.NET is, so to speak, an elaborate caching engine. In Web applications, caching of data is an enormous performance aid. Do not let the database become the bottleneck that slows your application. By caching all reusable information either in a middle tier or on Web servers, your applications will not only scale but also perform well.

Caching is very useful in desktop applications as well. Usually the payoff for caching in a desktop application is not very noticeable until you reach a huge number of users, but the benefits of using Windows Forms' data binding outweighs any additional work required to cache in desktop applications.

11.6.5 Get and Use a DBA

I really like database administrators (DBAs). If you have the luxury of having one on your project, please use him or her to help review your database designs, including stored procedures and schema.

Typically DBAs are experts on one or a small handful of database engines. Let them be the expert in that domain. I have been at too many companies where developers were reluctant to use their DBA because of silly turf wars or other political reasons. Believe me, they are usually your best ally as far as getting the database engine to purr.

Lastly, if they know your database code, they can help mitigate problems in a delivered environment by tuning the database code to eke out performance gains at runtime. They want to be used for more than backing up the database every night. And they are usually much too qualified to be doing only that sort of work.

11.6.6 Isolate Developers from the Database

Yes, we can create a business logic layer to isolate some developers from the database, but I would like to go a step farther. Use stored procedure for absolutely everything possible. Why? This further isolates the business logic layer from the database.

We have known for years that creating APIs that hide the implementation details from the day-to-day developer has tremendous benefits. Unfortunately, we have not taken that same leap with the database. Yes, there are times when you have to know about the database to do very sophisticated querying, but in a majority of cases, calling a named stored procedure and getting back a well-known table format is all you really need to know. The particulars of whether you are joining to get that table or going directly at a table is well beyond the knowledge you need as a day-to-day developer. In addition, this lets the DBA tune, scale, or even reorganize the database without having to consult you or ask you to change any of your code. As long as the stored procedure returns what you need, you should never need to know what is happening under the covers. In addition, stored procedures provide a higher level of performance than dynamic queries.

The downside to using stored procedures, though, is that you will make it more difficult to write systems that can use multiple database engines. I think this cost is worth it, though. Instead of dummying down the system to have mediocre performance on all database engines, taking the extra time to write the stored procedures for every platform will increase the performance on all engines. However, this does take more time.

11.6.7　Use the DataReader Sparingly in ASP.NET

There is a need for DataReaders in some situations in ASP.NET, but be very careful—this is a common place for scalability and performance to degrade. If an ASP.NET page uses a DataReader, each and every hit to that page will require a connection to the database. There is no smart caching. You may get lucky and get some caching of the query compilation on the database server, but you will incur the performance penalty of the roundtrip to the database.

11.6.8　Use Connection Factories

There are several key reasons I recommend using factory classes to generate database connections:

• **Eases connection pooling**: No matter the methodology of connection pooling (it is different in each managed provider), by having a single point of connection string creation, you can maximize the availability of pooled connections.

- **Isolates developers**: By having a factory to generate connections, most developers will never need to know what a connection string for your organization looks like. In fact, the factory should be retrieving connection strings from outside code.
- **Isolates changes**: Because there is one (and hopefully only one) place to create connections, any changes to the way connections are created are isolated to a single point of change.

11.6.9   Do Not Hard Code Connection Strings

Please do not use my examples in the book as a model of how to store connection strings. For clarity I have tried to make examples that are easy to read, but it is a very bad idea to have connection strings anywhere in code. The best idea is to keep connection strings outside the code. By embedding connection strings, anyone who can get their hands on your assembly will have a door through which they can access your database directly. Similarly, putting that same information in a web.config or a similar file on the Web server is likely to be a security risk as well. I usually default to putting them in machine.config or in a central repository that can be managed by nondevelopers (Active Directory is a good choice).

11.6.10   Keep Your Users Out of Your Database

I would suggest that you never add end users to your database just so they can use your application (be it Web or desktop). If they can get to your database through the application, they will also be able to get there outside the application. In that same light, please do not give the SYSTEM account, the IUSR_XXX account, or the ASPNET user direct access to your database. In each of these cases, a simple security failure will give a hacker direct access to your database. I suggest creating application-specific accounts on the database server that applications use to access the database. For example, I have created an ADONET user for my samples who has direct access to just the ADONET database. By using the database server's security, I could decide to have the ADONET user have just read-only access, or access to only stored procedures (not direct table access).

11.7 **Conclusion**

It should be clear by now that ADO.NET has some powerful tools for helping you develop scalable database solutions. Because our goal is to reduce the number of database calls that are required, we can create DataSets to be our caches of database information. Because we are using the DataSet as our cache, we can create caching systems in a much shorter development cycle by letting ADO.NET handle the database manipulation, the relational-to-hierarchical mapping, and the definition of data structures. We are left to simply write our business logic as part of a Typed DataSet. In addition, by utilizing ASP.NET's output caching, we can reduce the number of times we need to access even the data cache.

We have also learned that to make ADO.NET perform we have to realize it is just a database access layer. In order to make our interactions with the database perform well, we need to use the same SQL optimizations that worked well in the days before ADO.NET. We can make our interactions with ADO.NET quicker if we choose to use strongly typed ADO.NET code, though these savings are minimal in the bigger picture.

Lastly, we have some rules of thumb to follow to help us write better ADO.NET code. Most of these involve using ADO.NET to its fullest potential without sacrificing security or performance.

Appendix—ADO Migration Strategies

WHEN MICROSOFT RELEASED .NET, it did not have a magic tool to switch all legacy systems to .NET. Therefore, we will need to migrate our own ADO code to .NET. In order to accomplish this we need to understand the fundamental differences between ADO and ADO.NET.

A.1 Planning for Migration to ADO.NET

The hard part about migrating ADO code to ADO.NET is not the syntactical differences, but the fundamental differences in the way that the technologies are architected. By default, ADO is inherently connected, whereas ADO.NET is disconnected. Bridging these differences is the biggest challenge in migrating your ADO code to .NET.

A.1.1 Rearchitecting ADO Applications

When you want to migrate a particular piece of code to ADO.NET, you must redesign the code to deal with disconnection. Along the way you should gain performance and scalability, but changing the fundamental flow of older ADO code will not be easy.

You can divide any ADO code into two logical groups to determine how to rearchitect it. If you have ADO code that is simply reporting or dealing with the database in a read-only fashion, migration is easier. On the other hand, if you have ADO code that is changing the database in any way, migration will be more difficult.

A.1.1.1 *Migration of Database Reporting Code*

A large portion of the ADO code sitting out there is used to simply query the database and report on some data. Whether this is a simple query to fill in a list box for a desktop application or a complex query to show the historical financial information on a Web page, the ADO code is fairly trivial to migrate. Here is an example of VBScript code that queries the database and adds all the entries to a SELECT control on an ASP page:

```
...

<SELECT>
<%
Dim cmd, conn, rs

' Our connection string
const DBDSN = "Provider=SQLOLEDB;" & _
              "Server=localhost;" & _
              "Database=ADONET;" & _
              "UID=ADOGUY;" & _
              "Password=ADOGUY;"

' Set the connection
set conn = CreateObject("ADODB.Connection")
conn.Open DBDSN

' Set our command
set cmd = CreateObject("ADODB.Command")
cmd.ActiveConnection = conn
cmd.CommandText = "SELECT LastName FROM CUSTOMER"

' Get the results
set rs = cmd.Execute()

' Iterate through the results
while rs.EOF <> true

%>
  <OPTION><%= rs("LastName") %></OPTION>
<%
  rs.MoveNext
wend

' Close the connection
conn.Close
```

```
set conn = nothing
%>
</SELECT>
```

. . .

Converting this code to ADO.NET will be fairly trivial. In fact, setting up the ASP.NET page will probably be more work than the ADO.NET code. We could convert it by doing an object-by-object replacement:

1. Replace the `Connection` object with an `OleDbConnection` object.
2. Replace the `Command` object with an `OleDbCommand` object.
3. Replace the `RecordSet` (the object returned by the `Command.Execute` call) with a DataReader.

In my examples I am also converting the code to C#. The resulting ASP.NET code looks pretty similar:

```
. . .

<select>
<%
// Our connection string
const string DBDSN = "Provider=SQLOLEDB;" +
                     "Server=localhost;" +
                     "Database=ADONET;" +
                     "UID=ADOGUY;" +
                     "Password=ADOGUY;";

// Set the connection
OleDbConnection conn = new OleDbConnection();
conn.ConnectionString = DBDSN;
conn.Open();

// Set our command
OleDbCommand cmd = new OleDbCommand();
cmd.Connection = conn;
cmd.CommandText = "SELECT LastName FROM CUSTOMER";

// Get the results
OleDbDataReader rdr = cmd.ExecuteReader();
```

```
// Iterate through the results
while (rdr.Read())
{
%>
  <option><%= rdr["LastName"].ToString() %></option>
<%
}

%>
</select>

...
```

The flow of this code is the same as the ADO code, but it will also have
the same limitations, in that we are executing an ADO query every time the
page is executed. We are not gaining any of the benefits of ADO.NET. Let's
change this code to cache the results in session state:

```
...

<select>
<%
// Our connection string
const string DBDSN = "Provider=SQLOLEDB;" +
                     "Server=localhost;" +
                     "Database=ADONET;" +
                     "UID=ADOGUY;" +
                     "Password=ADOGUY;";

// Get this is a new session, create the
// cache of our data
if (Session.IsNewSession)
{
  DataSet dataSet = new DataSet();

  // Set the connection
  OleDbConnection conn = new OleDbConnection();
  conn.ConnectionString = DBDSN;

  // We no longer need to open the connection
  // because we're going to use a DataAdapter
  //conn.Open();
```

```
   // Set our command
   OleDbCommand cmd = new OleDbCommand();
   cmd.Connection = conn;
   cmd.CommandText = "SELECT LastName FROM CUSTOMER";

   // Create a DataAdapter
   OleDbDataAdapter dataAdapter = new OleDbDataAdapter(cmd);

   // Fill the DataSet
   dataAdapter.Fill(dataSet, "Customer");

   // Add the cached DataSet
   Session.Add("CustomerDataSet", dataSet);
}

// Get the results
DataSet custDataSet = (DataSet) Session["CustomerDataSet"];

// Iterate through the results
foreach (DataRow row in custDataSet.Tables[0].Rows)
{
%>
  <option><%= row["LastName"].ToString() %></option>
<%
}

%>
</select>
```

Writing the code to cache the result in a DataSet is similar to our original ADO code. We use a session state to cache the data at the page level. The important aspect of this is that when we convert this code, we change our philosophy to try to become more disconnected.

A.1.1.2 *Migration of Database Manipulation Code*

Converting ADO code where you have changed the database is more complex than our previous example. The reason for this is that ADO.NET has no support for editing a table directly, which is a typical use of ADO. Here is an example of editing a row and adding a new one:

```
Dim conn, rs

' Our connection string
const DBDSN = "Provider=SQLOLEDB;" & _
              "Server=localhost;" & _
              "Database=ADONET;" & _
              "UID=ADOGUY;" & _
              "Password=ADOGUY;"

' ADO enumerations
const adModeReadWrite  = 3
const adOpenKeyset = 1
const adLockBatchOptimistic = 4

' Set the connection
set conn = CreateObject("ADODB.Connection")
conn.Mode = adModeReadWrite
conn.Open DBDSN

' Get the results
set rs = CreateObject("ADODB.RecordSet")
rs.Open "CUSTOMER", conn, adOpenKeyset, _
        adLockBatchOptimistic

' Change the database
if rs.EOF <> true then

  ' Edit the current record
  rs("Zip") = "12345"

  ' Add a new record
  rs.AddNew
  rs("FirstName") = "Bob"
  rs("LastName") = "Smith"

  ' Update it
  rs.UpdateBatch

end if

rs.Close
conn.Close
```

ADO.NET does not support updating in this way, but we can get something very similar by using a DataSet and updating disconnectedly:

```
// Our connection string
const string DBDSN = "Provider=SQLOLEDB;" +
                     "Server=localhost;" +
                     "Database=ADONET;" +
                     "UID=ADOGUY;" +
                     "Password=ADOGUY;";

// Set the connection
OleDbConnection conn = new OleDbConnection();
conn.ConnectionString = DBDSN;

// Set our command
OleDbCommand cmd = new OleDbCommand();
cmd.Connection = conn;
cmd.CommandText = "SELECT * FROM CUSTOMER";

// Create a DataAdapter
OleDbDataAdapter dataAdapter = new OleDbDataAdapter(cmd);

// Get the results
DataSet dataSet = new DataSet();
dataAdapter.Fill(dataSet, "Customer");

// Get the table we want to change
DataTable custTbl = dataSet.Tables["Customer"];

// Change the first row
custTbl.Rows[0]["Zip"] = "12345";

// Add a new row
DataRow newRow = custTbl.NewRow();
newRow["FirstName"] = "Bob";
newRow["LastName"] = "Smith";
custTbl.Rows.Add(newRow);

// Create a CommandBuilder to help us update the database
OleDbCommandBuilder bld = new
                          OleDbCommandBuilder(dataAdapter);

// Update the database
dataAdapter.Update(dataSet, "Customer");
```

We have the identical functionality, but we are now updating the database in a disconnected way. Of particular interest is that we never have any code to open the connection. The DataAdapter's job is to keep the connections as short-lived as possible; therefore, it automatically opens the connection during the fill and closes it as soon as it is done. Likewise, this is done in the `Update` call. We also needed to use a CommandBuilder object to generate the commands to update and insert into the database for us. This class does for us what ADO does behind the scenes for us: It generates the SQL commands to do all the hard work of commanding the database with the changes we want.

A.1.2   What Is Missing from ADO.NET?

When evaluating what needs to be changed when you migrate your code to ADO.NET, some very specific pieces of ADO functionality simply do not have equivalents in ADO.NET:

- **`Cursors`**: In ADO, you could specify what kind of cursor you would use while navigating the database. In ADO.NET, you retrieve the data from the database, and iterate through it on the client side only. The DataReader acts like a forward-only cursor.
- **`In-place editing`**: Manipulation of the database in ADO.NET is completely disconnected. Updating records and adding records with the whole add . . . edit . . . update philosophy has no equivalent in ADO.NET.
- **`Database locks`**: There is no way to lock the database with ADO.NET. ADO.NET uses concurrency to handle changes to the database. Locks are expensive and a detriment to scalability and therefore are missing from ADO.NET. In other words, you cannot lock a row while you edit it. You must either write disconnected concurrency code (see Chapter 8) or use the CommandBuilder to get optimistic concurrency when you are updating the database.

A.2   ADO.NET Equivalents for ADO Objects

As you analyze your ADO code for migration, you will want to attempt to map your ADO code line for line with ADO.NET. Although this is not always possible (as we have seen in the previous section), there are some specific strategies for migrating ADO data and objects.

A.2.1   **Mapping ADO to .NET Data Types**

Not every datatype in ADO has a direct equivalent in .NET, but most do. When you are working with ADO data in the .NET environment (whether through Interop or custom components that return data directly from ADO), you will need to understand how to map the ADO datatypes to the .NET Framework datatypes. ADO Recordsets have late bound types. This is fairly equivalent to the way that DataTable and DataColumn types work. In order to map between what ADO knows the type to be and what the corresponding .NET Framework type is, we need to have mapping between ADO and ADO.NET. Table A.1 shows that mapping.[1]

A.2.2   **Providers and Managed Providers**

For most ADO to ADO.NET migrations, you can simply use the OLE DB Managed Provider to access the database. With the OLE DB Managed Provider, you can use the identical connection strings and OLE DB Providers that you used before with one sizable exception: ODBC. In the OLE DB Managed Provider, the ODBC Provider is specifically not supported. To use ODBC, you would use the ODBC Managed Provider. This provider does not ship with Visual Studio .NET or the Framework. Microsoft does, however, provide it as a download from its Web site (msdn.microsoft.com/downloads/sample.asp?url=/msdn-files/027/001/668/msdncompositedoc.xml). When working with the ODBC Managed Provider, you can still use the same connection strings, except you would remove the `Provider` attribute. For example, the following code

```
Provider=MSDASQL.1;DSN=ADONET;UID=ADONET;PWD=ADONET;
```

would become:

```
DSN=ADONET;UID=ADONET;PWD=ADONET;
```

---

1.   This table is taken directly from MSDN. It can be found at msdn.microsoft.com/library/en-us/cpguide/html/cpconadotypemappingtonetframeworktype.asp.

TABLE A.1 Type Mappings between ADO Type and .NET Type

ADO Type (DataTypeEnum)	.NET Framework Type	ADO Type (DataTypeEnum)	.NET Framework Type
adEmpty	Null	adDBTime	DateTime
adBoolean	Int16	adDBTimeStamp	DateTime
adTinyInt	SByte	adFileTime	DateTime
adSmallInt	Int16	adGUID	Guid
adInteger	Int32	adError	ExternalException
adBigInt	Int64	adIUnknown	Object
adUnsignedTinyInt	Promoted to Int16	adIDispatch	Object
adUnsignedSmallInt	Promoted to Int32	adVariant	Object
adUnsignedInt	Promoted to Int64	adPropVariant	Object
adUnsignedBigInt	Promoted to Decimal	adBinary	byte[]
adSingle	Single	adChar	String
adDouble	Double	adWChar	String
adCurrency	Decimal	adBSTR	String
adDecimal	Decimal	adChapter	Not supported
adNumeric	Decimal	adUserDefined	Not supported
adDate	DateTime	adVarNumeric	Not supported
adDBDate	DateTime		

A.2.3   Migrating Connections

ADO supports a number of different connection types and modes that provide quite a lot of server-side functionality. Because ADO.NET is disconnected, there is no support for cursors, which means that creating connections with ADO.NET is easier than with ADO. For example, this is ADO code to open a read/write connection:

```
' Our connection string
const DBDSN = "Provider=SQLOLEDB;" & _
              "Server=localhost;" & _
              "Database=ADONET;" & _
              "UID=ADOGUY;" & _
              "Password=ADOGUY;"

' ADO enumerations
const adModeReadWrite  = 3

' Set the connection
set conn = CreateObject("ADODB.Connection")
conn.Mode = adModeReadWrite
conn.Open DBDSN
```

We cannot do a direct conversion because there is no notion of read/write permissions on a connection in ADO.NET. We can convert the ADO code to look like this:

```
// Our connection string
const string DBDSN = "Provider=SQLOLEDB;" +
                     "Server=localhost;" +
                     "Database=ADONET;" +
                     "UID=ADOGUY;" +
                     "Password=ADOGUY;";

// Set the connection
OleDbConnection conn = new OleDbConnection();
conn.ConnectionString = DBDSN;
conn.Open();
```

ADO and ADO.NET differ in how connections are closed if they are not explicitly closed. They would be identical if we all remembered to always close our connections, but sometimes we do not. Both ADO and ADO.NET close the connection (if it was not closed earlier) upon the destruction of the object. ADO is COM-based, so it uses reference counts to handle destruction of objects. .NET uses garbage collection. Therein lies the problem: When the ADO connection gets released, the reference counting will destroy it if no one is holding the object any longer, which in turn causes a connection to close. In ADO.NET it works differently.

The Garbage Collector only collects unreferenced objects when it runs out of memory, so we do not know how long it takes after our ADO.NET connection object goes out of scope for it to actually be destroyed. In fact, on Web pages or other long-lived processes, it could be days before it gets collected. To mitigate this, .NET has the `IDisposable` interface that supports a single method, `Dispose()`. `IDisposable` allows for deterministic destruction of objects. I have two suggestions when migrating ADO connection code. First, always explicitly call `Connection.Close()` when you are done with the connection. Second, `Dispose()` connections as well. For example, here is how I would defensively code the use of a connection object:

```
// Our connection string
const string DBDSN = "Provider=SQLOLEDB;" +
                     "Server=localhost;" +
                     "Database=ADONET;" +
                     "UID=ADOGUY;" +
                     "Password=ADOGUY;";

// Set the connection
OleDbConnection conn = new OleDbConnection();
conn.ConnectionString = DBDSN;
conn.Open();

...

// Close and Dispose the connection
conn.Close();
conn.Dispose();
```

A.2.4 Migrating Command Objects

Much like connection objects, ADO commands are exceptionally similar to their ADO.NET counterparts. The conversion between them becomes somewhat trivial:

```
' Set our command
set cmd = CreateObject("ADODB.Command")
cmd.ActiveConnection = conn
cmd.CommandText = "SELECT LastName FROM CUSTOMER"
```

becomes:

```
// Set our command
OleDbCommand cmd = new OleDbCommand();
cmd.Connection = conn;
cmd.CommandText = "SELECT LastName FROM CUSTOMER";
```

A.2.5 Migrating Recordsets

ADO's Recordsets do not have a single equivalent in ADO.NET; they actually have two. DataReaders are much like forward-only Recordsets. In many cases you can do a one-to-one replacement:

```
' Get the results
set rs = cmd.Execute()
```

becomes:

```
// Get the results
OleDbDataReader rdr = cmd.ExecuteReader();
```

The caveat to this approach is that, unlike Recordsets, DataReaders are forward-only firehouses of data from the database. You can only navigate forward and cannot edit the data in the DataReaders.

In addition, there is no support for creating a DataReader without Connection and Command objects. In ADO we could create a Recordset and send it the same information we would put into the Connection and Command, and it would shortcut the work for us. Therefore, this ADO code has to be converted differently:

```
' Our connection string
const DBDSN = "Provider=SQLOLEDB;" & _
              "Server=localhost;" & _
              "Database=ADONET;" & _
              "UID=ADOGUY;" & _
              "Password=ADOGUY;"

' Get the results
set rs = CreateObject("ADODB.RecordSet")
rs.Open "CUSTOMER", DBDSN
```

becomes:

```
// Our connection string
const string DBDSN = "Provider=SQLOLEDB;" +
                     "Server=localhost;" +
                     "Database=ADONET;" +
                     "UID=ADOGUY;" +
                     "Password=ADOGUY;";

// Set the connection
OleDbConnection conn = new OleDbConnection();
conn.ConnectionString = DBDSN;

// Set our command
OleDbCommand cmd = new OleDbCommand();
cmd.Connection = conn;
cmd.CommandText = "SELECT * FROM CUSTOMER";

// Get the results
OleDbDataReader rdr = cmd.ExecuteReader();
```

The other equivalent to the Recordset in ADO.NET is the DataTable. DataTables are tables of data that are always contained within a DataSet. We can convert that same code to the following code to get a DataTable:

```
// Our connection string
const string DBDSN = "Provider=SQLOLEDB;" +
                     "Server=localhost;" +
                     "Database=ADONET;" +
                     "UID=ADOGUY;" +
                     "Password=ADOGUY;";

// Set the connection
OleDbConnection conn = new OleDbConnection();
conn.ConnectionString = DBDSN;

// Set our command
OleDbCommand cmd = new OleDbCommand();
cmd.Connection = conn;
cmd.CommandText = "SELECT * FROM CUSTOMER";

// Create a DataAdapter
OleDbDataAdapter dataAdapter = new OleDbDataAdapter(cmd);
```

```
// Create a DataSet (which will contain our DataTable)
DataSet dataSet = new DataSet();

// Get the results
dataAdapter.Fill(DataSet, "Customer");

// Grab the DataTable
DataTable customerTable = DataSet.Tables["Customer"];
```

A.2.6 Accepting ADO RecordSets in ADO.NET

A common strategy in ADO was to create components that would pass around connected or disconnected RecordSets. These RecordSets would be used as a container for data that could even be passed between tiers in a distributed environment. Because you may not have the luxury of rewriting your entire system, end to end, you can use ADO.NET's ability to accept RecordSets as input. To accomplish this, you will need to add references to ADO and your component that is passing around RecordSets. In the release in Visual Studio .NET, Microsoft added ADODB as a standard interop assembly, so all you need to do is add a reference to the `adodb` assembly. Once that is complete, you can accept the RecordSet as input into your DataSet. For example:

```
...

// Get the RecordSet
ADODB._RecordSet rs = YourComponent.GetARecordSet();

// Build a DataAdapter, no need to specify
// CommandText or a Connection
// We're going to get the data from the Recordset
OleDbDataAdapter dataAdapter = new OleDbDataAdapter();
DataSet dataSet = new DataSet();

// Fill the DataSet table named MyRS with the RecordSet
dataAdapter.Fill(dataSet, rs, "MyRS");
```

This will fill the DataSet, but it is a one-way street. There is no built-in support for updating the `RecordSet` from the changes in a DataSet or DataTable.

A.3 Conclusion

If you can change your perspective about how database access works, you can migrate your ADO code to ADO.NET with few headaches. ADO.NET was designed to mitigate some of the problems that ADO has in a Web development or high-load system. If you do blind conversions of your ADO code to ADO.NET, you will have the same performance and scalability problems you had before. Migration requires a new perspective on how to write disconnected data access.

Index